CULTURE CRASH

Yale UNIVERSITY PRESS | NEW HAVEN AND LONDON

CULTURE
CRASH

THE
KILLING
OF THE
CREATIVE
CLASS

SCOTT TIMBERG

Yale University Press books may be purchased in quantity for educational,
business, or promotional use. For information, please e-mail
sales.press@yale.edu (U.S. office) or sales@yaleup.co.uk (U.K. office).

Printed in the United States of America.

Library of Congress Cataloging-in-Publication Data
Timberg, Scott.
Culture crash : the killing of the creative class / Scott Timberg.
pages   cm
Includes bibliographical references and index.
ISBN 978-0-300-19588-0 (hardback)
1. Creative ability—United States—History—21st century.   2. Social
classes—United States—History—21st century.   3. Social change—United
States—History—21st century.   4. Popular culture—United States—
History—21st century.   I. Title.
BF408.T55 2015
305.5'50973—dc23   2014015252

A catalogue record for this book is available from the British Library.

This paper meets the requirements of ANSI/NISO Z39.48-1992
(Permanence of Paper).

10 9 8 7 6 5 4 3 2 1

To Sara, for helping us survive
this wave of creative destruction;
and to Ian, who may live to see
how the story ends

The present is only faced, in any generation, by the artist. . . . The absolute indispensability of the artist is that he alone, in the encounter with the present, can give the pattern recognition. He alone has the sensory awareness to tell us what our world is made of. He is more important than the scientist.
—Marshall McLuhan, 1968

He won't hear the thing come in. It travels faster than the speed of sound. The first news you get of it is the blast. Then, if you're still around, you hear the sound of it coming in.
—Thomas Pynchon, *Gravity's Rainbow*

CONTENTS

CONTENTS

INTRODUCTION

DOWN WE GO TOGETHER

AFTER A WHILE, I GOT accustomed to walking in circles. Most days I told myself things would be okay, but then I'd get news so unpleasant and disorienting—or have to pass something grim over to someone I cared about—that all I could do was slowly orbit, phone in hand, whatever room I was in, either trying to understand what was going on or working to make the person on the other end feel better. It's hard for me to do this while standing still.

This time, I was in Portland, Oregon, in the basement of the home of an old college friend, just waking up and getting ready for a day trip into the countryside. Then my cell phone rang, the face of my wife back home in Los Angeles showing up on its small screen. She didn't waste time. "The bank," she said, "is suing us." She'd woken up to a courier posting a note on our front door. "I'm sorry," was all he said before taking off. Pulling the photocopied forms off our door—in triplicate—she saw that one of the largest banks in the world had initiated legal action to take our little house from us. While offering various reassurances, trying to keep my wife from despair, I think I paced fast enough to wear a groove in my friend's stone floors.

The bank's action was not entirely unexpected. There had been bad news, dire warnings, and false alarms—as well as form letters sent to our address offering, in both English and Spanish, to "help"—for some time. In 2008, a risk-taking real-estate mogul had bought the newspaper I wrote for. In the months immediately before and after he drove the company into bankruptcy, the paper laid off hundreds of us—more than a third of its staff. We should have seen it coming. Various owners and regimes had come and gone, but we mostly ignored them, telling ourselves we were laboring for "the reader"—someone we'd never met, but whose idealized interests and curiosities we hoped to engage. The reader was of little help, as a combination of market forces, new technologies, and clueless corporate overlords tore our business apart.

As my family limped through the next few years—I kept writing, but for less and less money—I found myself telling my five-year-old son over dinner one night that we'd be leaving the house he'd been raised in but we didn't know when, we didn't know where we would go, and we couldn't really explain to him why. "But then," he said, looking up from a Scandinavian high chair purchased in better times, "we'll come back, right?" Within a year or so, it was done, and I couldn't help but notice that the locksmith who arrived to lock me out of my first house drove a fancier and substantially newer car than my seventeen-year-old Honda.

Of course, I had plenty of company. The collapse of

several of the best-known banks and trading firms on Wall Street in the same season as my layoff meant that not only journalists were suffering. I'd spent my two decades in the business writing about culture of various kinds—rock bands, graphic artists, piano tuners, classical composers, underground cartoonists—so I knew a lot of people who'd been hammered. Architects I knew watched their practices implode. Some of my favorite bookstores sold off their stock in a hurry as they closed their doors. A talented and energetic friend—a photographer who'd become a photo editor as a means to stability—lost his job, twice. A cousin in Oregon who'd started a small graphic design firm closed the company and moved into his brother's basement. A sweet, gifted couple, both of whom worked in art galleries, left for a midwestern family farm. For those who stayed, marriages and friendships often became collateral damage. An animator neighbor whose cheerful little daughter played with my son lost his job and, eventually, his health and his marriage. A close friend—a landscape painter who'd seen his income cut in half with the market crash—came over one night with a mandolin and we started an acoustic duo dedicated to slow, sad country songs, some of them from the Great Depression. (The band was intended more as fun than therapy, but the gallows humor may have been lost on our wives, who wondered how long we'd be able to keep our hold on the middle class.) Before long, my friend and his family sold their house and left the country. I worried that we too might have to go into exile.

My path into the creative class—as an observing reporter —was pretty typical. Growing up a middle-class kid, I had no illusion that I'd ever become wealthy, but I had a sense that I could get really good at something if I worked as hard as I could and surrounded myself with what someone once called—in a phrase that now sounds antique—the best that had been thought and said. Mine was a pragmatic, find-a-summer-job, get-Triple-A-and-change-your-oil-regularly kind of family. But there was also a respect for culture. Reading James Joyce's *Dubliners* showed me a new way to see: there was a world behind the world that you could discern if you squinted just right. People around me would often tell me they were not religious, they were *spiritual,* but I was neither: art and literature did all that religions were supposed to, without Crusades or cults or scented candles.

Whether it was endlessly spinning the Beatles' *Revolver* in elementary school—until I knew every detail of George Martin's production—or obsessively rereading Kurt Vonnegut in high school or sinking into the work of Thomas Pynchon and Billie Holiday in college, or Elizabeth Bishop's and Luis Buñuel's in the apprentice years that followed, I wanted to bathe in the work of great artists, even if I had no expectations of becoming a jazz singer or a surrealist filmmaker. I saw myself in the third generation of people who had worked in culture without either striking it rich or going broke. My grandfather had played piano on the vaudeville circuit and wrote songs for black-and-white cartoons, my grandmother was a dancer in Ziegfeld's shows, and my dad—their son—wrote about politics for a living. My mother and many of the women on her side of the family taught school; some were English teachers who passed on their love of literature. My aunt and uncle were RISD-trained graphic artists.

Stanford University Hospital had welcomed me into the world; my father studied in the school's journalism program while recovering from serious wounds he sustained in Vietnam, so going into that field made a kind of symbolic sense. Despite my teenage dream of becoming a "writer"—I'd had some minor success penning short stories in high school— working as a journalist seemed like the right compromise for a risk-averse child of the suburbs like me. So I did everything I could—writing for the college paper, working at a record shop and bookstores for something like minimum wage, moving six times over two years as I chased graduate journalism school and unpaid internships, running up enormous student loan debt—with the goal of devoting my adulthood to chronicling the makers and making of culture. I wrote for free often enough that I won the dubious honor of becoming a staff writer at a publication that did not pay. But for a while, it was going pretty well. In my first real job, I filed deadlined copy by day; by night, I got lost in smoky rock clubs, or chased Bach down what James Merrill called his "eternal boxwood mazes."

By my early thirties I was writing for one of the nation's Big Four newspapers, one emerging from complacency with a new energy, and a few years later I had what seemed like a dream job: working for the best editor I'd ever had, interviewing novelists and writing about authors and intellectual trends in the literary world. The work was around the clock, but that's the way fulfillment sometimes works. Like most new parents, my wife and I were woken up at least once a night, and I was able to put myself to sleep by reading one of the numerous books I was responsible for knowing about. The abrupt end in the fall of 2008, a few weeks after a modest raise and some praise for how "productive" I'd been, came when a woman in Sarah Palin glasses and a clipboard told me I had until five o'clock to clean out my desk and exit the building. And in spite of a White House that spoke about the importance of protecting people who worked hard and played by the rules, no significant relief came for those who struggled to hold on to their houses after job losses. (Simultaneously, the enormous bank that owned our mortgage—a bank that had been saved from collapse by our tax dollars—refused to negotiate with us to save the place.) An entire political movement, inspired by the writings of Ayn Rand and a hatred of those who hoped the government could do something to help them during difficult times, would swing elections and become strong enough to shut down the nation's government five years later. They would denounce people like me as "losers" and sometimes worse.

But I'm telling this story not because of what happened to me, or what happened to my friends. As I took a broader look at where our culture was going, I saw that the predicament we found ourselves in was about more than the Great Recession. And while the Internet and other digital innovations had taken a huge bite out of some professions—disemboweling the music industry, for instance, through both piracy and entirely legal means—this was about more than just technology. Some of the causes were as new as file sharing; others were older than the nation. Some were cyclical, and would pass in a few years; others were structural and would get worse with time. There was a larger nexus at work—factors, in some cases unrelated ones, that had come together in the first decades of the twenty-first century to eviscerate the creative class.

These changes have undermined the way culture has been

created for the past two centuries, crippling the economic prospects of not only artists but also the many people who supported and spread their work, and nothing yet has taken its place. The price we ultimately pay is in the decline of art itself, diminishing understanding of ourselves, one another, and the eternal human spirit.

Though highlighted and exacerbated by the Great Recession, these shifts started earlier and almost certainly will extend for years into the future, even as other elements of the economy recover. The arrival of the Internet and the iPhone, while crucial, are not the only forces at work here. And for all the current complaints about Miley Cyrus and YouTube videos of cats playing the piano, we appear to be at the beginning—not the middle and certainly not the end—of historic shifts that threaten the creative class.

While the fading fortunes of the creators of culture is alarming, it's equally disturbing that their often-mocked supporting casts—record store clerks, roadies, critics, publicists, and supposedly exploitative record label folk—are being forced out of the culture industry. This broader cultural middle class has long played an underappreciated role in connecting artists to their audiences. Without them, too much quality art becomes a tree falling in empty woods, and each artist, regardless of temperament, must become his or her own producer, promoter, and publicist.

Several important strands have tangled together and become hard to separate. They add up to a cheapening of the culture and to the fraying of the middle-class middle ground that allows the creative class to thrive. They reinforce existing notions that the only thing that matters is money and winning. In the long run, people who have to earn a living will find something else to do. "Do you really think people are going to keep putting time and effort into this," David Byrne asked, "if no one is making any money?" The only people who will be able to work in culture will be those who don't need to be compensated—celebrities, the very rich, and tenured academics.

How did we get here? Some of the roots are historical, others are economic, yet others are technological. Still others involve shifting social norms.

Since the Renaissance, we've associated the arts and culture with the wealthy and powerful. Michelangelo, Titian, and others like them became cultural gods; popes and emperors bowed to them. That was fun while it lasted, but the relationship created deep long-term problems. More recently, two centuries of Horatio Alger stories have built to a blockbuster culture that venerates celebrity above all else, overlooking the forces of history and ignoring material conditions. On the other side, artists' discomfort with the market economy, which dates at least back to the time of Charles Baudelaire, has led to a bohemian self-deception that has created another dead end. (Historical research on nineteenth-century Paris, for what it's worth, makes clear that the day's bohemians and bourgeoisie—classes that defined themselves in opposition to each other—had far more in common than either side let on.)

Simply put: Since the birth of the modern era, we've been kidding ourselves. We've become accustomed to seeing creative beings as either soaring deities or accursed gutter-dwellers. Certainly, some were, and some are. But these two associations have obscured the fact that culture, as we understand the term, tends to originate in the middle class, depends on a middle-class audience for its dissemination and vitality, and leads most of its practitioners, if they are lucky, to a middle-class existence. There are plenty of exceptions. But Virginia Woolf and the rest of the upper-mid Blooms-bury circle were not anomalous; much of Anglo-American culture has roots among the burghers as well. The Beatles were essentially middle-class for their time and place, despite American associations of them with Liverpool's proletariat; it's even more true of the Rolling Stones, in spite of their self-mythologizing as raw, dangerous bohemians. Much of British rock music since the 1960s, including glam-rock and politically radical post-punk, sprang from the middle-class world of art schools. Most American jazz artists, black and white, square or hip, have begun middle class, and hoped to end up that way; many were able to establish themselves because of programs like the G.I. Bill. Most literary writers, and visual artists, and architects, and journalists, and cura-tors, and publicists, start in the middle and end up there if they can. But these tales are rarely told, and the economic roots of the many thousands of the creative class who do not appear in magazine profiles are even more obscure.

There is, then, an invisible class of artists and artisans whose fortunes are worth taking seriously. We rarely hear about them, and we don't have a stable context in which to consider them, because of centuries of myths and misper-ceptions. We need to understand the situation, and its vari-ous layers, as clearly as possible if we're going to work to repair the current fracture.

CREATIVITY FASCINATES PEOPLE BOTH INSIDE and out-side of the creative class. Malcolm Gladwell and his disciples write with verve and insight about the way product designers and computer engineers approach the creative process, discussing them alongside genuine, unimpeachable artists—W. H. Auden, Bob Dylan, the Beatles—in a way that emphasizes what these figures have in common. Pundits like David Brooks write about the way bourgeois bohemians have adopted the tastes of creative people—casual wardrobe, fancy coffee, laptops, an interest in aesthetics—no matter what they do for a living. These authors are right in a lot of ways. But it's important to note that the actual artists these corporate mavericks and hip lawyers are emulating are not, for the most part, doing quite as well. Nor has the fashionableness of the artistic lifestyle—late hours, black clothes—created more opportunities, or even a broader audience, for people who work in the arts or who pursue creative impulses outside a corporate structure.

What is this thing called the creative class? Richard Florida, the urban theorist who has done the most to describe it, defines this group as effectively anyone who works with their mind at a high level—so research scientists, medical professionals, and software designers are thrown in with jazz trumpeters and lyric poets. This may make sense in some contexts, but a more useful understanding of the creative class would include anyone who helps create or disseminate culture. So along with sculptors and architects, I mean deejays, bookstore clerks, theater set designers, people who edit books in publishing houses and so on. At least since the Renaissance, a supporting class has been crucial. Our image of the lone creative genius is mostly a relic from the romantic age. Without these other figures, culture does not reach the audience. It's one hand clapping.

Any "class," by nature, includes a wide range. The middle class, for instance—a term we've been using, despite its ambiguity and elasticity, for many decades now—contains everything from auto workers to elementary school teachers to aerospace engineers, with many possible gradations along the way. (George Orwell once described himself as coming from the "upper lower middle class.") But the usefulness of any such sociological term does not depend on its contents being homogenous.

A novelist I admire has argued that people like him—independent artists, motivated by the irrational, romantic urge to write, paint, whatever, with an assumption that material rewards will never come—have little in common with those, however creative, who work in a guild or a profession, whether architects or journalists or publishers. I acknowledge these differences, but I think all of us in the creative arts, at whatever level, have a lot in common. The sciences divide themselves into "pure" and "applied" categories, and numerous subfields, but they're all, at their essence, up to the same thing. The late poet Donald Justice wrote about the compulsion to create, and I think it fits most of us in the creative class, regardless of what niche we occupy. My novelist friend is right in one major respect: This kind of life usually means giving up the comforts and certainties of a more conventional path.

"At a certain point in life, usually during adolescence, the artist dedicates himself or herself to art," Justice has observed. "The vows may not be codified and published, but they are secretly known and one does take them. I am perfectly serious about this. Years later the significance, the great emotion involved in this commitment, may prove difficult to recall, and especially hard to keep in mind during the excitations and fluctuations of a career, the temporary successes and, if one is lucky, the only temporary failures. . . . It may be that we become like the priests in the stories of J. F. Powers, so much taken up with affairs in the parish that the high moment of original dedication seems a contradiction. But for some of us it is always there, if only as a nagging whisper or the twinge and throb of guilt." Social critic Lee Siegel points to "the sense that something is missing, that doesn't satisfy you in everyday life—so you turn to these invisible things."

For all of Justice's romanticism about an aesthetic calling, he titled his essay "Oblivion: Variations on a Theme," because it's oblivion, not fame, where many of even the most talented figures typically end up. And all of us—once we've moved beyond school or our parents' couches—depend not just on that original inspiration, but on an infrastructure that moves creations into the larger culture and somehow provides material support for those who make, distribute, and assess them. Today, that indispensable infrastructure is at risk, imperiling an entire creative class.

Creativity, in the end, is not about self-fulfillment, but about work, focus, and rigor. The short-story master Tobias Wolff sees this all in pragmatic terms. "The literature that makes life possible for me and others is not a given," he writes. "It has to be made, day after day, by those who are willing to take on the solitude and uncertainty of work. Writing affords pleasure too, but mostly it's hard work."

Whether we work as a songwriter with a penthouse in what Leonard Cohen calls the Tower of Song—the place where the best lyrics and melodies live forever—or as a bookstore employee passing on a passion for Ursula Le Guin, we're all in this together.

The group I'm describing, then, is broad. But I'll concentrate on a few specific patches of the larger map. I'm not particularly interested in James Cameron, for instance, or Kanye West: Celebrity and corporate entertainment—good and bad—hardly needs defenders. And the luckiest and best financed figures within a structure like movie studios or major labels will, if they can keep from self-destructing, earn enormous riches and convince the rest of us that everything is fine. Although figures like these are undeniably creative, they're so far out on the edge of the reality of the creative class as to be anomalous. Similarly, when Apple or Facebook or Warner Bros. experience a big quarter, it doesn't mean that the creative class is thriving, any more than record profits for Big Oil translate into prosperity for the middle class. What's left, when you remove the wealthiest and most overexposed entertainers and their flacks and stylists, is an enormous group that encompasses film, novels and poems, music, journalism, theater, and much else.

In the end, the challenge to the creative class is broader than it may seem. My main concern with this set of issues is seeing not simply that creativity survives—that aspect of human experience will never entirely die—but that its exercise remains open to any talented, hard-working person. The stakes here are bigger than the employment prospects of video store clerks or architects. It comes down to something not merely aesthetic, but something that speaks to American identity and even our founding national myth and folklore: the idea of meritocracy. Is a life in the world of culture, whether producing it or distributing it or writing about it, something available to only the very lucky or well born? Furthermore, if working in culture becomes something only for the wealthy, or those supported by corporate patronage, we lose the independent perspective that artistry is necessarily built on. This goes double for the journalist.

If we're not careful, culture work will become a luxury, like a vacation home. Just as a democratic nation benefits from a large, secure, and informed middle class, so too we need a robust creative class. Painting a landscape or playing a jazz solo does not guarantee that an individual will become nobler or more virtuous. But a broad-based class making its living in culture ensures a better society. This book is about why they're worth saving.

SOMEDAY THERE WILL BE A snappy moniker for the period we're living through, but right now—years after the crash of 2008—American life is still a blurry, scratched-out page that's hard to read. Some Americans have recovered, or at least stabilized, from the Great Recession. Corporate profits are at record levels, and it's not just oil companies that are flush. Technology corporations have become as big as nation-states: Apple's market cap is as big as the GDP of Taiwan or Saudi Arabia.

For many computer programmers, corporate executives who oversee social media, and some others who fit Florida's definition of the "creative class," things are good. The creativity of video games is subsidized by government research grants; high tech is booming. This creative class was supposed to be the new engine of the United States economy, post-industrial age, and as the educated, laptop-wielding cohort grew, America was going to grow with it.

But for those who deal with ideas, culture, and creativity at street level—the working or middle classes within the creative class—things are less cheery. Book editors, journalists, video store clerks, all kinds of musicians, novelists without tenure—they're among the many groups struggling through the dreary combination of economic slump and Internet reset. From their vantage point, the creative class is melting.

That implosion is happening at all levels, small and large. Record shops and independent bookstores close at a steady clip; newspapers and magazines announce repeated waves of layoffs. Tower Records crashed in 2006, costing 3,000 jobs. The bankruptcy of Borders Books in 2011—almost 700 stores closed, putting roughly 11,000 people out of work—is the most tangible and recent example. One of the last video rental shops in Los Angeles—Rocket Video—closed soon after. On a grand scale, some 260,000 jobs were lost in traditional publishing and journalism in the three years after 2007, according to *U.S. News and World Report*. In newspapers alone, the website Paper Cuts tracked more than 40,000 job cuts in the three years after 2008.

Some of these employees are young people killing time behind a desk or a counter; it's hard for them, but they will live to fight again. Having education, talent, and experience, however—criteria that help define Florida's creative class, making these supposedly valued workers the equivalent of testosterone injections for cities—does not guarantee that a "knowledge worker" can make a real living these days. "It's sort of like job growth in Texas," said Joe Donnelly, a former deputy editor at *L.A. Weekly,* who was laid off in 2008 and poured savings and the money he made from selling his house into a literary magazine. "Governor [Rick] Perry created thousands of jobs, but they're all at McDonald's. Now everyone has a chance to make 15 cents. People are just pecking, hunting, scratching the dirt for freelance work. Living week to week, month to month." The British-born singer-songwriter Richard Thompson likens the current situation to the brutal Highland Clearances of the eighteenth and nineteenth centuries, in which the commons were enclosed, at the expense of peasant farmers, as aristocratic families seized the northern part of Scotland. Aristocrats "preferred the idea of sporting estates to having people actually working the land," he said. "So people were forced out to Canada and Australia."

In today's Britain, the situation has become dire even for accomplished novelists: forget about those toiling to break in. Hanif Kureishi, celebrated for the novels and screenplays *My Beautiful Laundrette* and *The Buddha of Suburbia,* is now struggling. The veteran award-winning novelist Rupert Thomson—perhaps appropriately for a writer influenced by Franz Kafka—has given up his office to construct an attic space in which he cannot entirely stand up. "All I want is enough money to carry on writing full time," Thomson said. "And it's not a huge amount of money." Writer and journalist Robert McCrum calls the changes since 2008 a revolution. "To writers of my generation, who grew up in the age of Penguin books, vinyl records, and the BBC, it's as if a cultural ecology has been wiped out." It wasn't just what the British call the post-2008 credit crunch, or the shredded safety net, or Amazon, "but the IT revolution was wrecking the livelihoods of those creative classes—filmmakers, musicians, and writers of all sorts—who had previously lived on their copyrights." He calls copyright "the bone-marrow of the Western intellectual tradition. Until the book world, like the music world, can reconcile the extraordinary opportunities provided by the Web with the need for a well-regulated copyright system, artists of all kinds will struggle."

Past groups punctured by economic and technological change have been woven into myth. Charles Dickens wrote sympathetically about Londoners struggling through the upheavals of nineteenth-century England; British folk songs valorized a rural village culture destroyed by the Industrial Revolution. John Steinbeck brought Dust Bowl refugees to life; Woody Guthrie wrote songs about these and others with no home in this world anymore. One of his inheritors, Bruce Springsteen, did the same for America's declining industrial economy.

But the human cost of this latest economic and technological shift on the prospects of our creative class has been largely ignored. Many of us, said Jaime O'Neill, a writer in northern California, are living in a depression. "It's hard to make the word stick, however, because we haven't developed the iconography yet," he wrote in an essay that asked, "Where's today's Dorothea Lange?"

Perhaps a fading creative class—experiencing real pain but less likely to end up in homeless shelters, at least so far, than the very poor—may not offer sufficient drama for novelists, songwriters, or photographers to document.

But journalists themselves also have downplayed the story. In fact, the media—businesses that have been decimated by the Internet and corporate consolidation, as surely as the music industry—have been mostly reluctant to tell the tale of this erosion. Some newspapers, of course, have offered responsible coverage of the mortgage meltdown and the political wars over taxes and the deficit. But it's harder to find in the pages of our daily newspapers stories about people who lose their livelihoods, their homes, their marriages, their children's schooling because of the hollowing-out of the creative class and the shredded social safety net. Meanwhile, coverage of luxury homes, fashions, watches, cigars, and sports cars continues to be a big part of magazines and newspaper feature sections.

Optimists like Florida may be right that America doesn't make industrial goods anymore and perhaps never will again, because what the United States produces now is culture and ideas. Unfortunately, making a living doing this has never been harder. It wasn't supposed to be this way. The Internet, it was widely thought, would democratize culture while boosting the prospects of those who make it. Allison Glock, a magazine journalist and writer, recently returned to her native South because she and her novelist husband could no longer afford to live in New York. "Wasn't the Internet supposed to bring this class into being?"

Much of the writing about the new economy of the twenty-first century, and the Internet in particular, has had a tone somewhere between cheerleading and utopian. One of the Net's consummate optimists is Chris Anderson, whose book *The Long Tail: Why the Future of Business Is Selling More,* championed the Internet's "unlimited and unfiltered access to culture and contents of all sort, from the mainstream to the farthest fringe of the underground." With our cell phones, MP3s and TiVos, we're not stuck watching *Gilligan's Island* over and over again, he suggested. Now we can groove to manga and "connect" through multiplayer video games.

In 2009, Anderson came out with a second book, the intelligently argued *Free: The Future of a Radical Price,* which suggested that new revenue streams and the low cost of computer bits meant that both businesses and consumers would benefit as the Internet drove down prices. It's nice to contemplate, but the human cost of "free" becomes clear every day a publisher lays off staff, a record store closes, or a documentarian finds her film uploaded to YouTube without her permission.

Of course, the meltdown of the creative class can't be blamed entirely on the Internet. David Brooks's influential *Bobos in Paradise: The New Upper Class and How They Got There* traced a multi-ethnic, meritocratic elite and a fantasia of latte shops, retro-hip consumers, and artisanal cheese stores. The cheese stores are, in some cases, still there, but much of what Brooks predicted has fallen through. He wrote—in 2000—that we were living "just after an age of transition," with the culture wars dead, a "peaceful middle ground" politically and a nation improved by the efforts of a class that had reconciled the bourgeois ethos with bohemianism. This was easier to accept when things seemed to be humming along. But even after the 2008 crash—where unemployment hit 12 percent and above in California, which, thanks to Hollywood and Silicon Valley, is also the state most driven by the creative class—blind optimism persists.

Florida argued that the creative class would make cities rich in "technology, talent, and tolerance" and jolt them back to life. His 2010 book, *The Great Reset: How New Ways of Living and Working Drive Post-Crash Prosperity,* wrestled with the difficulty of the past few years. But he continued to put faith in knowledge workers to bounce back stronger than ever.

Others were more suspicious. The new economy "is good for whoever owns the computer server," said Jaron Lanier, a computer scientist who has done pioneering work with virtual reality. "So there's a new class of elites close to the master server. Sometimes they're social network sites, other times they're hedge funds, or insurance companies—other times they're a store like the Apple Store." Lanier debunked a lot of Internet hype in his first book, *You Are Not a Gadget,* and he goes even further in *Who Owns the Future?* which argues that the Internet has destroyed the livelihoods of the creative class's middle tier—musicians, photographers, and journalists—but that it will move on to undercut other middle-class jobs. We're just getting started.

Andrew Keen is another Silicon Valley insider who's seen the dangers of the Net. "Certainly it's made a small group of technologists very wealthy," he said. "Especially people who've learned how to manipulate data. Google, YouTube, a few of the bloggers connected to big brands. And the social media aristocracy—LinkedIn, Facebook." In his first book, *The Cult of the Amateur,* Keen looked at the way the supposedly democratizing force of the Net and its unpaid enthusiasts has put actual professionals out of work. It's not just the Web, he said, or its open-content phase, but a larger cultural and economic shift. "We live in an age where more and more people think they have a book in them," he observed. "Or a film in them, or a song in them. But it's harder and harder to make a living at these things."

When Google is used as an excuse to fire the librarian, or "free" access to information causes circulation to drop and newspapers to lay off staff, the culture pays a very real price. Will the result be a neutron bomb culture? Lots of art and information left standing, but no people making it?

AS CULTURAL WORKERS LOSE THEIR jobs, where will they go? Not only is the person who works in the book/record/video store a kind of low-paid curator, but these jobs have long served as an apprenticeship for artists, including Patti Smith, Quentin Tarantino, R.E.M.'s Peter Buck, and Jonathan Lethem.

Joe Donnelly, who co-edited the Los Angeles literary magazine *Slake,* has watched numerous friends leave writing, art, and acting. "I've seen a lot of people go into marketing —or help companies who want to be 'cool.' What artists do now is help brands build an identity. They end up styling or set decorating. That's where we're at now."

The hard times and frustration are not confined to actors and writers. Eric Levin is a kind of entrepreneur of the creative class: he owns Aurora Coffee, two cafes in Atlanta that employ artists and musicians as baristas, and Criminal Records in the Little Five Points neighborhood, a record shop that thrived for twenty years and then was saved by a community effort after going on economic life support. One of his coffee shops closed in 2013. When asked if he knows anyone who's hurting, he replied, "Everybody I know." And he emphasized that independent businesspeople are in the same boat with writers and musicians. "Main Street U.S.A. is suffering. If you like big-box retailers—they're winning. Corporations are winning."

CULTURE CRASH

The arts—and indeed, narratives of all kinds—can capture a time, a place, and a culture, and reflect something of the inner and outer lives of its people. "But the tale of our times," Jaime O'Neill wrote in his piece on the silence of the new depression, "is mostly being told by our unwillingness to tell it."

In trying to understand how we came to this place—a place that hollows out the middle class and destroys those who would give it something resembling a democratic culture —I've pieced together the stories that follow. This is not a work of scholarship. I am neither a historian nor a professor. I am a longtime cultural journalist who has labored as a reporter—speaking especially to people upended by these changes—and as a reader of roughly a century's worth of social criticism and cultural history. It's helped clarify things for me to see today's crisis in context with the emergence of the mass audience and the tensions between a triumphant middle class and a dejected artistic bohemian in the nineteenth century. My reporting and research have also convinced me that reporters, editors, graphic designers, and photojournalists—who have seen the business model that supported them disrupted as severely as musicians and bookstore workers have—fit squarely into this class, and I consider the plight of journalists in a chapter along the way.

I have tried to gather together a number of diverse strands which, when seen whole, tell a story—a story too little remarked upon but one that is all around us. We have not seen it clearly because we have seen it only in fragments.

1

WHEN CULTURE WORKS

I'm referring to that special moment when a creative flowering
seems to issue forth from a social nexus—a clump of galleries, a
neighborhood, or a bar that doubles as a music club. I've often
asked myself why such efflorescence happens when and where it
does, rather than in some other time, in some other place.

—David Byrne, *How Music Works*

BEFORE GRAPPLING WITH WHAT HAS gone awry in our
culture, it will be helpful to look at what has worked in the
past.

What does it take to make great art or music or literature
happen? Here's one overlooked element: a car so old and
broken down it has to be parked facing downhill so you
can get it going again. It's something we hear about in
both the Los Angeles art scene of the 1960s and the outlaw
country subculture of Austin in the '70s. "I was driving a
1937 Pontiac Phaeton with a blown clutch and no starter,"

the L.A. artist Billy Al Bengston recalled. "I couldn't afford a battery so I parked on a hill. It didn't have a top. The upholstery was tuck and torn. But it was wheels." Early in his career, selling vacuum cleaners and Bibles, Willie Nelson did the same thing. In both California and Texas, the topography allowed the car's respective drivers to get their vehicles started without spending the money to fix them. It may be only because of the prevalence of public transportation in Boston that we don't hear about this kind of thing happening there.

In previous eras, artistic production was often a top-down affair: the Catholic church assembled a chorale group, a Florentine merchant prince commissioned a painting. Later, Romanticism and nineteenth-century bohemia insisted on the artist's distance from society—whether dwelling in an exalted, hyper-aware state or an absinthe-soaked demimonde —and modernism took this character even further into the realm of alienation. The twentieth-century creative personality had its own defiant, individualistic ethos, but artists did much of their best work laboring together, in cities and the subcultures they made possible. There were brilliant fiddlers in the mountain hollows, skilled painters laboring in the deserts, but the creative class and its institutions had become heavily urbanized. We got what economists call *agglomerations.*

It's tempting to say that something inevitably, organically happens when great artists are assembled. But sometimes, even when talent exists, something remains stillborn. In the 1950s, for instance, Indianapolis had not only substantial jazz artists—Wes Montgomery, Freddie Hubbard, Leroy Vinnegar, pianist Carl Perkins—but its players offered a distinct relaxed, gently swinging sound that Gunther Schuller praised as "a caliber of jazz quite superior to the often blasé big-name jazz of the metropolitan centers." And the city had nearly half a million residents during the '50s—more than twice as large as London during Shakespeare's heyday and significantly larger than Austin during its '70s flowering. But after Wes Montgomery was discovered at the after-hours club the Missile Room, he left town. The others did too. Partly, it was because a supporting and thriving creative class—record labels, music journalists, club owners—didn't exist in sufficient numbers.

Encounters between artists—including figures in different genres—can also have lasting transformative effects. *A Chance Meeting,* Rachel Cohen's book (subtitled "Intertwined Lives of American Writers and Artists"), gets at how this can occur: "A careful arrangement after long admiration, a friend's casual introduction, or because they just happened to be standing near the drinks." In some cases, nothing takes place except a fleeting conversation or a brief friendship. In other cases, "strong and altering loyalties emerged, permanent conditions of influence were established, and acts of rebellion were set in motion." A whole new body of work can be brought into being.

Some of what makes an urban arts scene cohere has little to do with the artists involved, but instead relies on existing structures. Jane Jacobs, the great writer on the history of urbanism, argued that for cities to thrive and innovate, they need short blocks (leading to frequent streets and pedestrian traffic) and aged edifices. As she wrote in *The Death and Life of American Cities:* "For really new ideas of any kind—no matter how ultimately profitable or otherwise successful some of them might prove to be—there is no lee-way for such chancy trial, error and experimentation in the high-overhead economy of new construction. Old ideas can sometimes use new buildings. New ideas must use old buildings."

Recently, David Byrne has boiled down what kind of chemical reaction made the New York punk scene around CBGB possible. "Our days (and even nights) were often routine, boring," he wrote in *How Music Works.* "It wasn't like a movie, where everyone's constantly hopping from one inspirational moment or exciting place to the next and con-sciously making a revolution." But the quality of the great bands that developed around that little world—Patti Smith, Television, Blondie, the Ramones, Byrne's Talking Heads—makes it clear that something seismic was taking place. He argues that this sort of thing comes very much from institu-tions, in the case of rock music, a venue of the right size in the right place to offer new music, since "not every space works for every kind of music." The musicians who perform there should be allowed in free on off nights (and, ideally, given beer), they should be allowed to play their own songs, and they should also be a bit estranged from the musical mainstream. ("A successful scene," he writes, "presents an alternative.") Last, and not least: "Cheap rent allows artists, musicians, and writers to live without much income during their formative years. It gives them time to develop, and it gives creative communities that nurture and support their members time to form." Variations on Byrne's model apply to virtually every artistic genre.

By taking a close look at several distinct cultural scenes from the past, we can tease out several key factors that are critical for a flourishing larger culture. Throughout this chapter, my abiding questions are: What do these heydays of the creative class tell us about the most fruitful relations between commerce, the state, the academy, and the artists themselves? And what is the role of a bohemian fringe that tries to keep its distance from all centers of power and influence?

IT'S EASY TO FORGET THAT once upon a time, not all that long ago, poetry engaged a sizable general audience, and poets wrestled with the larger issues in American culture. A sense of excitement surged around the writing of verse, as the genre sought to free itself from one era and remake itself for another. The new poetry—dubbed Confessionalism —drew its energy not from debates in academia, but largely from adapting Freud, Jung, and feminist ideas that had seeped into the groundwater of educated American life in the years after World War II.

In the 1950s, a new generation of poets, among them Sylvia Plath and Robert Lowell, assembled among the red-brick townhouses and grassy courtyards of Boston and Cambridge, chain-smoking, falling in and out of bed, and quarreling among themselves about who would take up the literary torch from the aged but still imposing Robert Frost. They would embody some of the changes in midcentury America, and—in between trips to the sanitarium— transform their art into a darker, more personal means of expression. This group would also galvanize the press and media. Several of these poets became stars, and many of them continue to fascinate readers and writers six decades later.

Talented people, of course, can gradually come together in any reasonably large city in any decade. For these poets, the universities—and in some cases, public funding—were important magnets. The courtly Richard Wilbur returned from World War II, where he had begun to write verse as a way of ordering thoughts and feelings the war threatened to shatter. Thanks to the G.I. Bill, he studied at Harvard. Others maintained a distance from the academy: the elusive, faunlike W. S. Merwin arrived in 1956, a year later than Wilbur, after years working across Europe as a translator of poems and plays for radio broadcast. In other cases, dormant talents were awakened by the civil society around literature. In the aftermath of a mental breakdown, the suburban housewife Anne Sexton watched a public television program about how to write a sonnet, and she began to channel some of her swirling anxiety into verse.

Even more than Robert Frost, then in his eighties and based part of the year at Amherst College, the figure who connected nearly all of the poets was Robert Lowell, who was teaching at Boston University. As Peter Davison wrote in his memoir of the period, *The Fading Smile:* "Robert Lowell's unmistakable voice—weary, nasal, hesitant, whining, a curious hybrid blend of Yankee and Confederate intonations that descended from both family and literary sources—seems in retrospect to dominate the poetic harmony of the late 1950s in Boston. He was audible everywhere: reading, writing, teaching, socializing, translating— and dramatizing his own suffering in semi-public agony."

It was Lowell's move from a formal, T. S. Eliot–influenced voice to Confessional poetry with his book *Life Studies* in 1959 that drew the literary world's attention, and helped give a direction to the larger shift of the dozen or so major poets around him. This "flawed titan," as Davison called him, with his roots in one of America's most distinguished literary families, attracted an enormous amount of attention—including from the New York press—to the Boston-Cambridge scene. But Lowell had a role that may have been more important than his literary achievements, which have faded a bit without the force of his personality: he helped engage not only the larger American literary world, he connected these poets and writers to each other. Some were friends, others students, others rivals. (His role resembled that of a very different poet—Lawrence Ferlinghetti—in the Beat subculture of San Francisco.)

But the health of American postwar culture wasn't all about Lowell, or the older, wounded Stanley Kunitz—who was alienated from the Ivy Leagues early on because of anti-Semitism—or the awakening feminist pioneer Adrienne Rich, or the lyrical ad man L. E. Sissman, or any of the other writers then coming into their own, but about a fortuitous kind of ecology, what the poet and critic Dana Gioia called "those rare moments when academic, bourgeois, and Bohemian culture promisingly intermingle." Although many of the poets were in Boston or Cambridge because of their universities, this story wasn't just about Harvard—or BU, or Brandeis, or Tufts, all of which employed some of the key players at least briefly. At any given moment, at least half the poets Davison chronicles were *not* teaching. Plath, Sexton, and Rich were young mothers, Sissman sold vacuum cleaners door to door and later worked as a copywriter for Prentice-Hall. Wilbur, whose luminous stanzas may be the most enduring work from this period, spent some of his time teaching at Harvard and Wellesley, but an equal measure went to writing, translating, or adapting Leonard Bernstein's *Candide* for theatrical appearance in New York.

The first decade or so after World War II—with students and writers returning from the front—was a rich and symbiotic time for authors in the academy. University employment helped a lot of poets and novelists move comfortably into midcareer after an initial burst of youthful publication. "You'd get drunk, get fired, and then go down the street and get hired again," said Gioia. "Because they were hiring you not for good behavior but for at least the presumption of literary excellence." Most of the jobs were temporary or part-time freelance positions, so the poets and writers would drop in and out of the academy and the marketplace, as best suited their work.

"It's meant a lot to me as a human being, I think," Lowell said of his teaching, in an interview published in the *Paris Review*. "But my teaching is part-time and has neither the merits nor the burdens of real teaching. . . . Now, I don't know what it has to do with writing."

Other institutions were as important as the universities —the Boston Center for Adult Education (where some taught and some studied), WGBH-TV (which sometimes put poets on the air), numerous churches that held panels about the writing and reading of verse, and especially the Poets' Theatre in Cambridge. Davison himself worked as an editor at Harvard University Press and as the poetry editor for the *Atlantic Monthly*. The Poets' Theatre was perhaps the most pivotal of these non-academic institutions. It hit its stride around 1955, the year it moved to a forty-nine-seat space on Palmer Street and put on Wilbur's translation of Molière's *The Misanthrope*. The theater, and grant money provided by the Rockefeller Foundation, brought Merwin to Boston after seven years of living in Portugal, Spain, and the south of France, to try his hand at writing a verse play. During Donald Hall's year as a junior fellow at Harvard, where he also served as poetry editor for the *Paris Review* and co-edited an important anthology, he booked the theater's poetry readings.

Humble though it was—actors typically changed costume in nearby shops because of the lack of space—the theater not only put on poetry readings but offered the Boston poets employment and a hangout, and it brought the work of poets from outside the Lowell circle into town. By the time it burned down in the '60s, the theater had staged work not only by important modernists but by young writers including John Ashbery and Frank O'Hara. The theater's motivator was Bunny Lang, a former debutante who became, in Davison's phrase, a "voluptuous, husky-voiced, purple-eyed, seductive" Mae West–like figure who acted, stage-managed, and painted sets before an early death.

Frost, teaching indifferently at Amherst College, was holding court during about half the year in a house on Brewer Street in Cambridge. "It is difficult to describe the comforting tones of his monologue," Davison recalled, "drawling on for hours at a time, with his open palm gesturing in the air like a conductor beating time to his own rhythm," as he leaped from topic to topic. Davison was one of a handful of younger poets in charge of "Getting Frost Home Before Midnight," since the older poet was so amplified after readings that he needed to walk and talk off his nervous energy.

This was all decades before Boston's conquest by bankers and hedge-fund managers, and a life of genteel poverty was still possible. Sissman lived in a then-cheap part of Cambridge; Sylvia Plath and Ted Hughes pledged to work as poets outside the university and managed to live in Beacon Hill for $115 a month.

It's also striking, looking back, to see the number of outlets there were for poetry in the '50s. These writers were published in the *Atlantic,* the *New Yorker,* and the *Nation*— all of which offered vastly more space for verse than they do today—as well as now defunct publications like *Partisan Review.* Maxine Kumin, who met Sexton at the Center for Adult Education and helped keep her alive and productive over the next few years, began by publishing light verse in the *Christian Science Monitor, Saturday Evening Post,* and *Good Housekeeping.* "That generation got the best of both worlds," said Adam Kirsch, a poet-critic who is the author of *Why Trilling Matters.* "They were the first generation of writers who went into the university. But that wasn't how they thought of themselves. These days, poets go into an MFA program, and then become a university teacher. They have no idea of a public, or of a poetry infrastructure outside academia."

What comes across when recalling the circumstances of the scene that led to "For the Union Dead," "Advice to a Prophet," and "Snapshots of a Daughter-in-Law" is not that it was an idyllic golden age—though an extraordinary amount of good writing emerged—but rather how much it resembled any engaged group of smart, talented people. These years involved cooperation and collaboration, but also competition and moments of bad blood. Such a group might emerge from almost anywhere, whether an energized, ambitious newsroom or a fertile, rivalry-rich music scene.

Admittedly, it's hard to imagine Emily Dickinson or Philip Larkin thriving in this sort of hothouse. But for many of these writers, the human energy in Boston and Cambridge was a tonic. Lowell, who had come to Harvard after a dry spell—what he called "five messy poems in five years"—came alive in Boston, just as the scene around him did. He dropped in and out of mental institutions—as did Plath and Sexton—but when he was productive, he was on fire. "He plays a dinner party at the pitch at which he plays tennis," the poet Philip Booth said of Lowell. "Given an audience of more than one, Cal turns conversation into his best competitive sport. . . . He has many appetites but the surest of these is for talk. Cal serves with high wit; his wild intelligence never misses an opportunity to score. The dinner table is, for him, center court at Longwood. As if in total relief from writing, or from shop talk, Cal tries every shot in the book: drop-shot, lob, slam." Anyone who's ever played music, or basketball, with someone better than they are knows the effect this kind of thing can have.

IN LOS ANGELES, A CITY far newer and less self-consciously cultivated than Boston, a prankish gang of surfers, Dust Bowl refugees, and macho bikers came together to make Southern California's first important visual arts scene. Throughout the 1960s, a group formed that included Ed Ruscha, Robert Irwin, Ed Kienholz and—standing at a slight distance in his canyon retreat—David Hockney. These and others opened up new artistic possibilities, came up with their own dry, sun-glinted take on pop art, and energized a class of artistic patrons and art dealers that had never existed south of San Francisco Bay. Artists, underground filmmakers, and architectural innovators in Los Angeles fed off each other's energy. And despite the white-boy machismo of the core group, the city's art world expanded enough that a strong feminist subculture could develop, as well as an important black arts scene, focused on jazz and assemblage, centered around Watts.

These years saw Wallace Berman's show of assemblages, which concluded abruptly when the police took the artist away in handcuffs over an erotic drawing, Irwin's serene minimalist sculptures, Kienholz's scandalous installations of a bordello and a lynching, Ruscha's paintings of the Hollywood sign, movie logos, and other pop iconography, and the obsessive visually austere pencil drawings of Vija Celmins. (Hunter Drohojowska-Philp's *Rebels in Paradise: The Los Angeles Art Scene and the 1960s* has belatedly brought some mainstream attention to this artistic generation.)

L.A.'s artistic '6os started early, with the founding of Ferus Gallery in 1957. Originally a modest space established by the burly, Idaho-bred farm boy Kienholz and the visionary, consistently unreliable curator Walter Hopps, it was the first of several pivotal galleries. Others, such as the Westwood gallery run by 3M heiress Virginia Dwan, helped demonstrate the importance of the non-artist creative class. Any business depends on buying and selling, and similar hard-headed priorities, but the best of the dealers found a way to promote commerce and provoke art at the same time.

That wasn't always the case with Ferus, run by the diffuse Hopps, early on, in a way best described as unpragmatic. The heyday of Ferus began when two very different sensibilities came together. In 1958, the New York artist Adolph Gottlieb, teaching a term at UCLA, drifted into Ferus's new space on La Cienega Boulevard with his wife one day. "All of a sudden this guy comes in whom I'd seen several times before but never met," Hopps recalled.

> He had a booming, bogus Cary Grant accent, a very special style. Anyway, he walks in, flings his arms wide and says, "Adolph! Esther! It's Irving Blum. How are you?" At this point, he throws me a wink. "Isn't this an extraordinary place?" He says, "Best gallery in Los Angeles! Let me introduce you to the proprietor." And he walks over and says, "Walter, I'd like you to meet Adolph and Esther Gottlieb." Well, I say to myself, "This guy is something else." The Gottliebs leave eventually, and I say, "Irving Blum, I think you and I should go across the street and have a drink. We may have some business to discuss." And Irving, in that accent, says, "I think we do have business to discuss. I hear you're looking for someone."

Later that year, Blum bought Kienholz out. The artists, of course, made the work Ferus sold, but the sensibility of the place came from its owners. Though the complementary Lennon-and-McCartney-style leadership of Hopps and Blum lasted only a few years, they laid down the scene's DNA, and it continued to replicate.

The Los Angeles scene was also shaped by its geography, at the far edge of the American West. Many of the artists who came to L.A. during this period did not come from urban or intellectual backgrounds; they were hot rod–

loving Okies, or movie-mad surfers, who did not care much about a New York scene dominated by abstract expressionism, despite its influence in the rest of the world. "The New York artists had angst and ambition," Blum says now. "The West Coast people had neither." In a city with billboards, freeways, and Hollywood movies instead of a museum-based art scene, pop art was almost a folk art: pop was the imagery of daily life.

Within a few weeks of each other, two arrivals landed in the city's art life like a pair of grenades. In 1963, Blum brought Andy Warhol—whose first exhibit anywhere had been a show of Campbell's soup cans at Ferus the year before—to the gallery for a show of celebrity silkscreens. The city's art world was electrified. Ruscha felt "a great kinship. . . . It was like a logical departure from the kind of painting that was happening at the time." A week later, and a few miles to the east, the Pasadena Museum of Art—where Hopps was curator—brought Marcel Duchamp to town for his first-ever retrospective. The two shows, and the appearance of two major artists in sleepy, conservative Southern California, helped orient artists, collectors, and dealers alike toward Warhol's pop art and the Dada style Duchamp had originated in the despairing years around World War I.

For "second cities," this kind of galvanizing event is not unusual. It happened in 1945, when Charlie Parker and Dizzy Gillespie arrived from New York to play at Billy Berg's, a jazz club in Hollywood. Even more rare than a venue in L.A. with integrated audiences was a place to see bebop, a harmonically complex, small-group style of jazz. The traditional, swing-oriented Southern California jazz scene was never the same, and was a source of constant innovation for the next fifteen years. Similarly, when punk avatars the Sex Pistols put on a ragged, defiant show in front of a few dozen people at Manchester's Lesser Free Trade Hall in 1976, they inspired not only the future musicians assembled—eventual members of the Buzzcocks, the Smiths, Joy Division, New Order, the Fall—but the indie rock scene in Britain for the next generation. In all these cases, the physical presence of the artists or musicians was decisive.

After the Warhol and Duchamp shows, Los Angeles began to percolate. A group of collectors was coalescing, in part by a roaming lecture-and-slideshow series run by Hopps and his wife Shirley. Some became genuine patrons, commissioning new works of art or pieces of contemporary music. "Collectors like Stanley Grinstein left accounts open at hardware stores so artists could buy paints and canvas," the art critic Dave Hickey recalled. Galleries opened on La Cienega Boulevard, which began to have a Monday-night art walk. In 1964 alone, Hockney visited L.A. from England and made the first of his swimming pool paintings, artist Noah Purifoy helped found the Watts Towers Art Center, and the city's civic leaders came together to open the Music Center downtown—as a growing Los Angeles became the nation's second largest city. Styles that drew from California's sunshine and the materials of its car-customizing and surfing culture— "hard-edge," "finish fetish," Light and Space—gave L.A. art a distinctive stamp.

In 1965, *ArtForum* magazine moved from San Francisco to a space above Ferus, giving a scene that just a few years before had been isolated and provincial a sense of its consequence and connection to a larger conversation. (The magazine also employed Ruscha as its art director.) By contrast, the opening that year of the Los Angeles County Museum of Art had little initial impact on the region's art scene, largely because of conservative leadership and a lack of interest in local work.

The continuous growth of California's vigorous postwar economy—much of it driven by public spending on the burgeoning defense industry—provided some of the larger momentum. (The G.I. Bill, which helped educate many players in L.A.'s postwar jazz scene, helped keep the schools full and gave the artists occasional employment.) These were days when wealth got passed around in a nation with a swelling middle class. The macho Bengston supported his art in part by winning motorcycle races, the cerebral Irwin through betting on horses at Hollywood Park and triumphing at dance contests, where he typically danced the Lindy. It was possible to live as a struggling artist in Venice Beach—where many of the Ferus crowd and some of the architects were centered—and the hills around greater Silver Lake.

Two other industries helped provide oxygen for the art scene. The early sprouting of New Hollywood amid the ruins of the decaying studio system meant a few like-minded figures—Dennis Hopper most prominently—were curious about contemporary culture and served as creative instigators as well as patrons. At the same time, the ferment of modernist architecture—powered by space, money, population growth, and car culture—intersected with the art world. In some cases this led to a major architect like Frank Gehry being tangled up socially and intellectually with the artists; other times, the sprawling metropolis provided artistic inspiration, as the gas stations, dingbat apartment buildings, and Sunset Strip storefronts did for Ruscha.

But in the late '60s—as European interest in the L.A. art world peaked—something began to drop out of the city's art life. By 1966, Hopps had left the West Coast and Ferus closed. *ArtForum* left for New York the following year. Dwan followed in 1968, and Blum departed as well a few years later. "We pretended that this was an art center," Dwan says now, "with a lot of collectors. But that wasn't really true."

For all the artistic heat, the scene stalled out. The recession of the 1970s slowed sales—and art making—as well. "L.A. didn't really burgeon until the '90s," says Peter Plagens, an artist and critic who wrote the first book on this era, *Sunshine Muse: Contemporary Art on the West Coast*, from 1974, "because there was only a handful of big-time collectors. L.A. finally got them when show business people started collecting."

After *ArtForum*'s departure, the city lacked the kind of serious critical discourse that could have pushed the art scene to the next level of maturity. "It was only there for a brief period of time, but it was crucial," said Plagens, who also left town, eventually ending up in New York. "You need criticism. You need some polemic—a negative commentary in a magazine here, a positive article there." Contentious criticism brings heat to the artists' subculture, as well as corralling the public into the conversation, in a way that a-good-time-was-had-by-all cheerleading doesn't. "Art criticism has gone hand in glove with modern art since the beginning," Plagens says. "There were critics writing about Manet, poets writing about Manet. And so it went, through Cézanne, Picasso, Pollock, and more recent modern artists such as Helen Frankenthaler and Louise Bourgeois. In fact, what would modern art be without its accompanying criticism?"

Compared with poetry, which ended up being inhaled into academia and lost its connection to the literary and intellectual mainstream, art from Los Angeles went a bit fallow, but then sprouted up again. By the 1990s, a substantial collector class developed, and a constellation of museums— the Museum of Contemporary Art, the Hammer, the Getty —and art schools grew up. Visionary curators such as Paul Schimmel gave the city's art a context and a narrative. In the twenty-first century, the Ferus artists' work came to sell for millions at auction, the Pompidou Center in Paris celebrated postwar art from Los Angeles, Ruscha became a de facto international cultural ambassador, and L.A. turned into a major art capital, and remained one.

AUSTIN, TEXAS, OFFERS another example of how an artistic —in this case, musical—scene comes together. For more than a decade, country and rock music—and their audiences—were estranged, and things got far worse when long-haired Brits and the introspective urban folk of Bob Dylan began to dominate. When the Byrds tried to bridge the gap with *Sweetheart of the Rodeo* in 1968, their show at the Ryman Auditorium in Nashville drew boos and heckling; a country deejay brought the band into the studio and mocked the music to their faces on the air. ("I remember seeing the *Sweetheart of the Rodeo* cover on a bulletin board at a country radio station in Los Angeles," the band's singer Roger McGuinn has said. "I was overjoyed . . . until I got closer and saw written in red DO NOT PLAY—THIS IS NOT COUNTRY.") *Sweetheart* was the band's first commercial failure as well. Meanwhile, Dylan's rustic *John Wesley Harding* album provoked bafflement in the rock world. Nashville was dominated by the country establishment, California by the counterculture. This marriage, in a culturally polarized nation, with assassinations and riots and a president railing against seditious young people, was not going to be easy.

But a few years later, a city settled by pioneers and buffalo hunters would attract musicians hoping to forge a style more soulful than the product churned out by Nashville's song factories. The artists in '70s Austin cobbled together a rough blend of country, folk, blues, and gospel that—in the decades that followed—made the place into a legendary live-music city, giving birth to "outlaw country" and what came to be called the alt-country movement. Some of them, such as Willie Nelson, became international stars. Others remained important cult figures. The best of them exerted an influence over several successive generations of musicians.

Texas, with its mix of racial and ethnic groups—German yodelers, Cajun accordion players, Mexican Tejano singers, and so on—had always had music, and musical hybrids, to spare. "Austin was the most bohemian city in a very conservative state," Jan Reid noted in *The Improbable Rise of Redneck Rock,* explaining that "artists of all stripes were naturally inclined to think they could find an amiable climate and perhaps a receptive audience there. But the state capital was often shunned by major touring performers, for the chances of handsome gates were greater in the larger cities like Dallas, Houston, and San Antonio. In between those concerts, Austinites contented themselves with what was available locally. Folk singers strummed their guitars for nickels and dimes in the university area. Rock and rollers lived communally, tried to imitate their heroes' best licks in free concerts in the park, and paid their bills by playing rubber-stamp dance music for fraternities and sororities." It was, in other words, like a lot of mid-sized cities across America, if hotter, more racially segregated, and with better Mexican food.

What happened? As with Boston and Los Angeles, Austin's transformation was prompted by strong personalities. Willie Nelson had seen a profitable but frustrating stretch as a Nashville songwriter, and when he moved to Austin in 1972 he not only attracted other out-of-town musicians, he found a way to break down the resistance between left-leaning longhairs and conservative country fans. "Willie had some kind of force around him," said Ed Ward, a first-generation *Rolling Stone* writer who was based in Austin in the '70s and '80s. He once saw Nelson defuse, with a smile and a few words as he walked to the stage, what promised to be a lethal bar fight between Hell's Angels jumped up on crystal meth. "He has this incredible ability to navigate social structures." It didn't hurt that Austin's cultural tone had long been more tolerant and easygoing than most other towns in Texas.

Nelson came along at a cultural hinge point. Much of the energy of the outlaw-country scene came from frustration with Nashville, where the "Countrypolitan" movement was diluting country records with orchestration and middle-of-the-road ambitions. (An earlier war on Nashville convention had been waged from Bakersfield, California.) The Music Row establishment also made no pretense that its output had anything to do with art. When the Nashville guitarist and record executive Chet Atkins was asked

what the Nashville sound was, he shook the loose change
in his pocket. "That's what it is," he said. "It's the sound of
money." Even in laid-back Austin, hardly a Marxist hotbed,
such unabashed commercialism rankled. But it gave the
Austin musicians—for all their stylistic differences—a sense
of mission, a desire to carve out a place of their own.

Geography was crucial. Austin was not large enough to
attract all the major bands from Britain, New York, or California. But it had something else, besides many thousands
of college students: it was at the approximate geographi-
cal center of a state with a large number of cities—and a
fierce cultural defensiveness. Within three hours or so from
Austin—a distance that makes touring easy for a young
band—are Houston, San Antonio, Dallas, Fort Worth, and
Arlington. In under four hours, you are in Laredo, Galves-
ton, Corpus Christi, or Denton, the site of the nation's first
university jazz program. Even distant Lubbock—home of
Buddy Holly and the seminal band the Flatlanders—would
exert itself. These were all cities with a university, a large
population, or a fledgling music scene, or all three, but
mostly lacking the array of clubs, larger halls, or music publications necessary to launch an artist. Texas had no shortage of musicians, fans, and musical possibilities, but it did
not—through the '50s and '60s—have a single great music
scene. "You could compare Austin to Denver," said David
Menconi, a music critic who has lived in both Colorado
and Texas, "which always had a certain amount of stuff
going on, but never quite cohered," since mountains and
distances cut its musical life off from other currents. "It's a
place you'd go to get away from everything, to isolate yourself."

There was also a pressure coming from the larger Texas culture. Young people and urbanites were liberalized by the late '60s and early '70s, but much of the state, like the country in general, changed far more slowly. So while the outlaw country and cosmic cowboy movement sparked in various parts of Texas, its exemplars were not equally comfortable. Austin acted as a magnet in a way it would not have had it been in, say, Massachusetts. "If you are in Texas and you're the least bit freaky—if you have long hair—you come to Austin as an oasis," said Menconi. "It is not the reddest of the red states, but it is the most aggressive in its redness. In Austin you are behind enemy lines." Austin had a less imposing police presence, and also offered what may have been the lowest cost of living of any city its size around 1970, when its population was about 250,000 people.

Institutions were also as vital as they had been in Los Angeles. The role of Ferus Gallery or the Poets' Theater was played by two clubs, Armadillo World Headquarters, founded by a group of hippies in 1970, and Threadgill's, a longtime folk den run by a bootlegger turned country singer, originally in a filling station, that took off during these years. The Armadillo sat in a former armory in a neglected corner of South Austin; when it opened in the year of a particularly hot, unpleasant summer, it was not expected to last long. "The place was huge, had an industrial kitchen, a big beer garden, with food," recalled Ed Ward. "The whole thing was economically structured so they didn't have to make money every night of the week." When the owner Eddie Wilson, a former philosophy student, sold an unprecedented amount of beer during a packed Willie Nelson show, he approached Lone Star Brewing about marketing long necks to long hairs. "They did these posters of an Armadillo walking out of the desert," said Ward. "And it *worked*." The emcee Jim Franklin, who created the posters and introduced the acts while wearing enormous cowboy hats and bizarre suits, slept on a mattress in the club's attic.

Once the scene started to develop, the rivalry with Nashville acquired a focus. Recalled Ward: "Because Willie was in Austin, other songwriters who'd been in Nashville and struck out said, 'If Willie can do it, I can do it.' And these people attracted other people, and pretty soon there were all these songwriters in town who were onstage in Armadillo's." It wasn't just lonely men with acoustic guitars, either. Nelson persuaded the Western swing band Asleep at the Wheel to leave the Bay Area and come to Austin.

Threadgill's had a smaller, tighter crowd of folk and blues fans. "They had an audience who'd go there every night, no matter who was playing," said Menconi. "And it tended to be participatory—hootenannies or open mikes. That's how Janis Joplin got started. They were all like regulars at a bar. It fostered an eclecticism you wouldn't have had otherwise."

Soon, smaller venues opened, and their modest size allowed for unexpected things to happen. Surrounding it all, by the 1970s, was a local culture that—in part because of the lack of major cultural outlets at the time—was about going out and seeing live music. In 1974, the live television program *Austin City Limits* began; the South by Southwest music festival was founded in 1987. "I get asked all the time," said Menconi, now based in Raleigh, North Carolina, "how do we make something like South by Southwest happen here. I say, 'Go back in time seventy-five years, and start up a dozen live music venues—and somehow keep them going.'"

Even without a traditional music-industry structure— labels, recording studios, radio stations—the growing numbers of venues and musicians built a critical mass. Musicians from out of town—Guy Clark and Townes Van Zandt from Houston's folk scene, Kris Kristofferson from Nashville, Freddie King from the touring circuit—came through, sometimes staying for extended periods. The volatile and eclectic Doug Sahm moved back to town after spending the late '60s in San Francisco. He and the mellower Nelson played the Robert Frost role, mentoring younger musicians.

In Austin, the non-artist creative class—especially the club owners and a few sympathetic politicians—proved crucial. Radio had been slow to respond to the regional heat, but KOKE radio began a Progressive Country format when a deejay pulled records "from a stack of albums set aside by KOKE jocks because the artists on the covers had long hair," as Jan Reid puts it. The programming, originally played only on weekends, proved crucial for the fledgling scene because both rock and country radio outside Austin almost completely ignored what was happening there. In most of the nation, Led Zeppelin and prog rock ruled the airwaves in the mid-'70s; "country rock" meant the cocaine cool of the Eagles or the Doobie Brothers.

By the time the '70s ended, Austin's outlaw-country movement hadn't really caught fire outside Austin itself, with the exception of a few Willie Nelson records. "Texas music," said Ward, "has sometimes been too damn Texan to sell to the rest of the country." Austin certainly didn't dethrone Nashville, where the music would get more reactionary and blandly corporate with every passing year. But over the next few decades, something important happened. The ethos of spending time—and money—going to shows numerous nights of the week persisted. A blues scene centered on Antone's and the Continental Club helped lead to the emergence of the Fabulous Thunderbirds and the guitarist Stevie Ray Vaughan. A punk scene even developed and took hold. The music coverage in a free newspaper, the *Austin Chronicle,* became so influential that in the 1980s parts of the city would nearly shut down around the time it came out. Austin became such a legend among musicians—with so many places to play—that residence there became a rite of passage for such musicians as Lucinda Williams, who spent important early years there, and a permanent home for an artist as stylistically restless as Alejandro Escovedo. By the '90s, Lyle Lovett, Jimmie Dale Gilmore, Patty Griffin, Robert Earl Keen, Joe Ely, and others would set up shop, as well as—in the years after—twang-free artists like Spoon and Gary Clark, Jr. Without the music-industry capitals of New York, L.A., or Nashville ever quite knowing what to do with it, the alt-country movement became, alongside indie rock, the most important rock genre since punk. And Austin would sustain a reputation as one of the world's great cities for nurturing live music.

FOR ALL THE DIFFERENCES BETWEEN Boston, Los Angeles, Austin, decades and genres, a few common denominators stand out. We can view them in a kind of X-ray that ignores the coincidences of talent and personality and exposes their respective common skeletons.

First is what we might call the day-job principle. "It helps to have a business—L.A. has the movie business, and Las Vegas has the casino business—that is vaguely related to art making," said Hickey, who has lived in Las Vegas for decades. During L.A.'s art explosion, movies and print shops and architecture provided temporary or full-time employment; it was true in the city's 1950s "cool jazz" scene, when many of the musicians toiled by day for studio orchestras, but followed their own muse at night. These associated businesses also generate an audience and potential patrons.

Austin's music scene operated similarly. The University of Texas and the statehouse drew people to the city, and provided employment—some of the city's songwriters and first-wave punk-rockers made their living proofreading bills in the legislature. Many musicians and audience members were students or former students. For all its protests of its maverick status, outlaw country was made possible by public funding.

Boston, of course, is an archipelago of academia. Universities played a strong role in all three of these scenes. "The perfect combination," said UCLA musicologist Robert Fink, who studies cultural life through the ages, "is a slightly decaying urban core, and a university that gives you an interested public. And a reasonably convenient way to move between them, at least at night. The key thing a university brings is a constantly changing cast of eighteen- to twenty-two-year-olds: A few drop out or stick around to become artists themselves, but the rest can provide the audience for whatever weird, cheap stuff is happening 'downtown.'"

And it's not just true for music. Sixties L.A. was the least academic art scene imaginable—at times it was resolutely anti-intellectual—but art schools brought students and teachers to the city. The Chouinard Art Institute attracted figures as different as Ed Ruscha, from Oklahoma, and the dealer Riko Mizuno, from Tokyo. UCLA drew Vija Celmins to town from New Haven. This process became even more pronounced in the decades that followed.

"Usually the people in college-town scenes are not formally associated with the colleges," said David Blake, a young scholar who has done significant work on universities and their non-academic impact. But a university shapes the culture produced nearby. It fosters institutions—record stores, art galleries, bars with bandstands, coffee shops with readings or music series, and so on—that would not exist in the same density otherwise. And a concentration of colleges does something to the local sensibility: its ethos sees culture as an exploration rather than a purely moneymaking activity, encourages journalistic criticism, and works out a crucial paradox. "The liberal arts idea is about being disinterested—you pursue the best thinking, the best art, whatever, without any considerations of utilitarian or careerist advantage," Blake noted. "But you go to college so you can get a job. So there are pressures underneath the disinterestedness. One of the things a college town scene does is focus them." The artists who best negotiate that contradiction—a band that sticks to its principles but also makes a living, for instance—typically become heroes to the scene, becoming part of the city's canon, its sense of itself. Canons, of course, reinforce the culture that grows up around them.

Second, such creative scenes contain discernible stylistic movements. "One thing you need to have is young people of the same generation," said Adam Kirsch. "It helps if they are rejecting old ideas. They start feeding off each other, and pretty soon you have a 'school.' Sometimes that's just a way of saying, 'Pay attention to me.'" The artists sometimes drift away from the restrictions of an aesthetic school as they get older, but it's often essential in establishing them. "Look at London in the 1910s, where you had Pound and Eliot; Frost was there for a while." No one at the time would have taken them for the most prominent writers in town. "They were thought of as pretty obscure—but they became the modernists." A corollary is the interplay of progressive and conservative, of artistic centers and "backwaters," and of rival establishments—Nashville, New York City—which encourage the churn of culture. If everything is flat and even, the winds don't blow.

Third, and most important: the first phase of artistic flowering can often come from disparate, anarchic sources, but it fades out—no matter how brightly it burns—without institutions. We saw this with L.A. in the '60s—the flame sputtered, but didn't entirely go out. (Portland, Oregon, followed a similar path—a large density of artists in a wide range of fields, but, until recent decades, few organizations to bring them together.) Sometimes the process happens the other way around: the institutions come first, but then independent artists need to show up. This is how it worked in Minneapolis, where civic leaders bet on the arts. "Minneapolis decided that art and culture was going to be part of its strategy," said Kristy Edmunds, who has run performing arts festivals or programs in Portland, New York, Melbourne, Australia, and Los Angeles, and collaborated with institutions in numerous cities. "So it attracted a number of Fortune 500 corporations because of the quality of life

in the '70s, and included in that definition were the arts."
But initially, even as foundations and *kunsthalles* like the
Guthrie Theater and the Walker Art Center rose from the
ground, the artists did not initially materialize. "You got an
institutional infrastructure. But after that, you have to find
a way to attract, engage, and support independent artists.
Otherwise, you'll start importing Broadway; your city is a
roadhouse." England found itself in a similar predicament
for much of the nineteenth century, when it had perhaps
the most highly developed classical music audience in the
world, beautiful concert halls, and almost no composers
and players. The Germans began to refer to it as "the land
without music."

In Boston, Los Angeles, and Austin, we see these principles at work in stark relief. All three cities drew and—for at
least a while—maintained a group of formidable artists. Los
Angeles saw its gallery scene flag for a few difficult years,
but other institutions—art schools, museums, and an art
press—filled in the art world eventually. Similarly, Austin
caught fire around 1970 because of clubs, and even while
the city and the surrounding music industry changed—and
clubs opened and closed—the institutions held steady and
the ecology of venues and festivals grew denser and more
complex. It was only in Boston that the institutions faded
out. When the Poets' Theatre burned down, no replacement grew up around it. The magazines that poets published in gave less and less space to verse; some of them
folded. When churches and television stations stopped in-
viting poets in, there was only one outlet for them: universities became the only game in town. The academy was a
necessary but insufficient condition.

Neither talent nor structures are quite enough—they need to come together in the right way. One useful way of looking at cultural scenes is actor-network theory, developed by the French sociologist Bruno Latour and typically applied to the history of science and technology. "There are a number of crashed-out cities where art can happen," said Fink, an admirer of Latour's work. "But not every one of them is going to have the right network of actors. An actor without a network can't do much—but a network is not a system you can just plug anybody into. If the right actors aren't there, nothing happens."

2

DISAPPEARING CLERKS AND
THE LOST SENSE OF PLACE

So the two birds had to sing together, but it wasn't a success, because the real nightingale sang in her own way, whereas the artificial bird went by clockwork. "It can't be blamed for that," said the Master of the Emperor's Music. "It keeps perfect time and follows my own methods exactly." After that, the artificial bird had to sing by itself. It was just as popular as the real one, and of course it was also much prettier to look at, glittering there like a cluster of brooches and bracelets.

—Hans Christian Andersen, "The Nightingale"

HE MAY NOT LOOK MUCH like Justin Timberlake, but Jeff Miller is something of a Hollywood player. Or, rather, he was—until he got a call on Labor Day, 2011, from his employers, the owners of the best and most important movie rental store in the orbit of Hollywood. For a decade the bearded, teddy-bear-like Miller helped run Rocket Video, a place frequented by directors, actors, and aspirants, and staffed by obsessive savants. But thanks to Netflix, streaming video, and the damage done to the store's rental revenue, it was all over for this onetime destination—in a hurry.

A few weeks later, the inevitable closing party arrived on its stretch of La Brea Avenue. "There was shock," recalled Miller, a native of steel-belt Pennsylvania originally drawn to movies by old horror films and Abbott & Costello. "There were women who came in crying. There were people who wanted to take photos of their family with me because they'd grown up with Rocket." Some of the store's patrons were regular film-lovers in the neighborhood; others were better known. Miller recalled William H. Macy renting '70s porn to prepare for his role in *Boogie Nights,* Courtney Love coming by until she got angry about the store stocking the unsympathetic documentary *Kurt and Courtney* and blew up at the staff, Frank Darabont renting zombie films while he was conceiving the TV series *The Walking Dead.*

The shop's most loyal celebrity customer was Faye Dunaway, who regularly came in to ask him for advice about foreign directors. "She said, 'I was gonna take a film course but I figured I could just come in here and talk to you guys.'" She paid back the debt by doing numerous events at the store.

Rocket's story—a strong reputation and longstanding community love, followed by sudden collapse—is not unique: thousands of bookstores, record stores, and video shops have gone under in the last few years. And with them, people like Miller have lost their jobs during the worst job market since the Great Depression. The years following the 2008 market crash have been hard on many people. But due to other transitions in the economy and culture—the continued trickling-up of wealth to the very top, the "storm of innovation" unleashed by the Internet, a growing faux-populist disregard for expertise—certain sectors have been hit harder than others. Shop clerks, however erudite, don't fit into the most influential definition of "the creative class"—Richard Florida considers these folks members of the service class, about which he is not optimistic. But they've been, over the decades, important conduits between consumers and culture —and their workplaces a training ground and meeting spot for some of our best writers, filmmakers, and bands.

OK, OK—we also know they're figures of fun. Kevin Smith made them into foul-mouthed suburban stoners in *Clerks,* and Nick Hornby and Stephen Frears made the *High Fidelity* gang into smug, retro-obsessed elitist losers. And some clerks, it's fair to say, are just killing time.

But for decades, bright, hard-working creative types— sometimes, though not always, lacking college degrees or professional connections—have been drawn to working in shops that allow them to filter the flow of culture, one customer at a time. One of these self-made savants was Jonathan Lethem, who worked at bookstores in New York and the Bay Area before, during, and after an aborted college degree, long before he became an internationally respected novelist.

"I think of bookstore jobs as my university," said Lethem. (His nonfiction collection, *The Ecstasy of Influence,* emphasized the catholic nature of his taste and his provocative way of discussing work he loves—qualities embodied by the best store clerks.) "The physical trade of books was a hallowed way to become a writer in the pre-MFA era.

It was the only work I wanted to do, and the only work I was qualified to do." Those years profoundly shaped his taste as a reader. "With bookstores, you go in and you find the things you weren't looking for. The clerk is doing that 24/7—my reading was shaped by what was left behind. And you develop a loathing for the false canon—the two books each year that everybody is supposed to read." It also shaped the writer he would become, known for a mongrel, genre-blending style. "You can't hang on to those sacred quarantines," he told me, "when you see the mad diversity around you."

Lethem, of course, is not alone: the writer Mary Gaitskill and the Decemberists singer Colin Meloy (now an author himself) started out in bookstores; punk heroine Patti Smith worked at the sprawling Strand bookstore in New York as well as Scribner's on Fifth Avenue. Jim James of My Morning Jacket and Peter Buck of R.E.M. worked at record stores in Louisville, Kentucky, and Athens, Georgia, respectively. Punk rock, especially, was driven by former bookstore workers. When they moved to New York in the early '70s, the musicians who later became Richard Hell and Tom Verlaine of Television labored in the film-noir-centric Greenwich Village bookshop Cinemabilia. Quentin Tarantino—who could almost be a character from Kevin Smith's *Clerks*—developed his distinctive blend of junk culture, Asian film, and European cinephile obsession while laboring at a video store in Manhattan Beach, California, Video Archives. The store was his film school.

These places speak to people other than urban bohemians, too. The poet and critic Dana Gioia, the former chairman of the National Endowment for the Arts, grew up in the

'50s in the rough Southern California town of Hawthorne, with parents who lacked college diplomas. "When I was a little kid, there was a used bookstore every ten blocks," he recalled. "There would be some grumpy old man running it: If you came in a couple of times he'd comment on your books—not in a charming way that you'd put in a movie. But it showed you that other people read and had opinions; it was a socialization. So much of culture is chance encounters between human beings."

As a curious fan seeking cultural artifacts that might have gotten lost, and as a journalist temperamentally drawn to the overlooked and obscure, I've spent a lot of time around clerks since I was a teenager. A little more than a decade ago, I realized that they were an endangered species and began to seek out the best of them. I got to know a guy named Charles Hauther, a science-fiction enthusiast at Skylight Books in Los Angeles whose tireless passion for David Foster Wallace's *Infinite Jest* helped make this unwieldy tome, for a while, the store's bestseller. I developed a fondness for several used bookstores right before they closed.

And I spent a lot of time in record stores. At a large one—like the Tower Records in Annapolis, where I worked through the early-'90s recession—the range of employees can resemble an old World War II movie in which the macho Texan, the Brooklyn Jew, and the simple boy from the plains all pull together for the defense of the U.S. of A. In record stores, it's the alt-country buyer with the Buddy Holly glasses, the skinny indie rocker who could belong to the Decemberists, the goth in her Joy Division T-shirt, and the dreamy, abstract jazzhead—all in service to the music.

I was not alone. The better clerks, Los Angeles music

journalist Steven Mirkin said, make finding music a pleasure. "It's almost like certain restaurants have professional waiters, like at Musso & Frank or Spago. When you sit down you feel comfortable being in their hands. It's not just connoisseurship—it's a desire to serve."

Take Karen Pearson, a philosophically minded Berkeley native who oversaw the hiring at Amoeba Music in Hollywood and who considers record store people "a tribe" who guard the culture's memories. "There's a particular type of character, the ones who don't stay in the lines, who I think is disappearing from indie stores in general, whether record stores or bookstores, because retail is becoming so homogenized as the big boxes take over. A lot of my job is to guard against that." Some of the personality Pearson was talking about was clearest at stores that sold classical music—people who had opted out of the pop-industrial complex to become an endangered species selling an embattled form of music. At Tower's classical annex on Sunset Boulevard in Hollywood, I met a clerk named Eric Warwick who quoted Nietzsche and Wilhelm Furtwängler in casual conversation, and described recordings with swooning praise or corrosive disdain. He'd clutch his heart over one piece of music, shake his head in weary resignation over another. He had theories—miles and miles—on why British sound engineers were the most sonorous, on the ruthlessness of mobile society, on why conductors get more action than the rest of us. What started out as an innocent question sometimes left me intellectually worn out. The lanky, shorts-wearing Warwick, an early-music and chamber-group enthusiast, had features so Germanic he seemed better suited for lederhosen. In his

heart, he was a rebel and an idealist, but he was also someone in humble service to the music.

Gary Calamar remembers moving to Los Angeles in the
late '70s, fresh from New York. He dropped in to a record
store in the Licorice Pizza chain and a punk-rock girl helped
turn him on to some new songs. "She would recommend
things and run back and play them for me over the in-store
system," he says now. "I remember walking out of the store
with singles from the Police, B-52's, Devo, the Knack. I was
in love with L.A."

Now indoctrinated, Calamar soon had a record store job
of his own, moving a career that would lead him to become
a deejay for KCRW in Santa Monica and music consultant
for TV shows like *Six Feet Under* and *Dexter*. Calamar is
also the author, with Phil Gallo, of *Record Store Days: From
Vinyl to Digital and Back Again,* which looks at places like
Waterloo Records in Austin, Texas, and Newbury Comics
in Boston—as well as many shops that have since closed and
taken their staffs with them. For someone like him today,
moving to a big city in the twenty-first century, that ladder
into the industry no longer exists.

Such people have shaped my experience of culture as decidedly as any critic, curator, or culture-industry executive.
("They're important acolytes to the artistic muse," Michael
Ward, an L.A. collector of CDs and 78s, said of music sellers, after dropping two hundred dollars on a Wagner box
set and other recordings at Tower.) Especially as music
education recedes from public schools, many people learn
about the classical tradition in informal ways—from older
relatives who saw a famous performer, or from a relentless

salesman like Warwick. "Take them away, and it's gone," Ward said of this door into music. "All it takes is a generation. So I'm not being sentimental when I say that record stores are important."

As he raced around the store, Warwick was especially excited about a disc that took a Beethoven piano concerto and arranged it for a chamber group. "To reawaken a masterpiece," he wrote in a staff-pick box, "is what music making is about." In general, he aimed to make people who ask his advice "less market-driven," less reliant on the same heavily promoted names. He's like a walking radio show. The 1950s and '60s, he said, were a golden age for classical music—a period when the players and conductors hit new peaks, and recording technology blossomed. He prefers labels like Mercury Living Presence and Decca that thrived in the early stereo years. "This is what good engineering is about," Warwick insisted. "It's not spectacular. It's very lucid and transparent to the back wall without drawing attention to itself, or hyping the upper midrange and being bright. It doesn't need kick-ass bass." In contrast, the German label Deutsche Grammophon is, to him, "Deutsche Grunge-a-phone."

There may be as many ways to sell music, though, as there are to make it. If Warwick was a kind of classical Catholic, whose connection to the spirit is mediated through a network of saints (serious collectors) and sinners (bad engineers), the sad-eyed Hammurabi Kabbabe—whom I met while he stocked the CD bins at Dutton's Brentwood Books—was a classical-music Puritan, or mystic. He was fed directly by the source, and tried to bring the fire straight to those who come to him. "I don't let anyone leave without giving them a barrage of my words, of the history," said Kabbabe, then a recent graduate of the University of Redlands in a faded maroon Taco Bell T-shirt and a young bohemian's beard. "The story makes a piece accessible." He also showed me a knack for outlandish but strangely effective metaphors: "If a score is something you feel, he touches it with burnt hands," he said of the conductor Herbert von Karajan's treatment of Sibelius. Of Sviatoslav Richter, the protean Russian pianist: "He plays from his jaw. When you see him play, you see he has that Russian jaw—big, it's got weight, it almost ricochets when he hits the keys."

Unlike the outgoing, almost hyper Warwick, who grew up surrounded by classical music, Kabbabe was self-contained, internal, and saw music like a secret—built of "forbidden knowledge"—passed from one believer to another. When customers asked him for suggestions, whether for themselves or a friend, Kabbabe would present a battery of questions, some quite personal: What do they read? Are they early risers or night owls? Where do they live? Do they have conservative or progressive tastes? What's going on in their lives? What other music, classical or otherwise, do they like? "I wait for something—it's almost like free-associating—until they come up with the answer themselves." As sensitive as he is to his customers' tastes, he also felt a "moral commitment" to contemporary music and unjustly overlooked composers from all eras.

For some people, clerking was a bridge to something else. David Mermelstein started working on the classical floor of Tower Records in Westwood in the mid-'80s as a college student who enjoyed music but felt no special commitment to it. "Not someone," he recalled, "who had strong opinions, even." But as he and his fellow employees blasted different recordings of the same concerto three, four times a night—Tower was open until midnight and later back then—his understanding deepened. "It raised the idea of interpretation, that a piece could be played in different ways," he said. "It was a way of thinking more like theater—that you could see *Hamlet* done seven different ways even if it's the same play. So you can have on your shelf ten different versions of Beethoven's Ninth Symphony, each with something personal." The other clerks were an important part of his education. "They tended to be older: grad students, men in middle age who'd given up something else to do this out of love for the music." Mermelstein would go on to write about music and film for the *New York Times* and the *Wall Street Journal*.

"In music school, they don't teach anything like that," said Timothy Mangan, who also learned about interpretation while toiling behind the counter at Tower Westwood, where he worked with an organ freak who played "air organ," a Liszt maniac and a diehard fan of the conductor Otto Klemperer. "I never had any courses about interpretation or performers," said Mangan, who earned a graduate degree in music at the Peabody Conservatory in Baltimore and is now the classical-music critic at the *Orange County Register*. "It was all music history and theory, classes on composers, training your ear to recognize intervals and chords. I've known a lot of music students, and none of them were trained this way. But the guys who weren't going to music school, who were working in record stores, were," he says. "They were like monsters of the gramophone."

A decade later, Amoeba Music is still going strong. But

the Tower Records chain is gone, as is Dutton's Books. The people who worked at these places—like their equivalents across the country—have found other things to do. But the culture lost an important component; it was hit hard.

What happened?

EACH INDUSTRY HAS ITS OWN story, but the common denominator seems to be the Internet.

Bookstores have had an especially hard time. Competing with Amazon and other online sources that discount books heavily and don't require bricks-and-mortar spaces in dense, urban areas has been a losing battle. In the past few years, Boston has lost Wordsworth, Los Angeles has lost Dutton's Brentwood Books, Metropolis Books, Village Books, and the Mystery Bookstore, and you can make a similar list for any city in the country. The Borders chain is history. Used bookstores continue to disappear so quickly it's hard to keep track. Even Portland's mighty Powell's Books, which not only takes up an entire block in a city of readers and was ahead of the curve in selling books over the Internet, laid off some of its expert staff and may not be done making cuts.

The collapse of record stores is part of a larger implosion of the music industry, said Steve Knopper, a *Rolling Stone* correspondent and the author of the industry chronicle *Appetite for Self-Destruction*. As his title implies, the record labels should have seen the threat of Internet piracy coming, but it dealt them a fatal blow. The new, Internet-inspired business model—replacing the sale of fifteen-dollar CDs by selling individual songs at ninety-nine cents a pop and sharing that with Apple—shrunk things further. "Apple had basically taken over the entire music business," wrote Knopper, who still misses the Tower Records in Denver and a shop called Hegewisch in Indiana that made his first newspaper job a lot less lonely. You can love the convenience of iTunes or music streaming and still recognize that they've made it much harder for stores to compete.

The loss of the people who labor to put books and music and movies into our hands is bad enough, but their departure doesn't just cut into the number of people who can make a living from working in culture. Every time a shop selling books or records, or renting movies, closes, we lose the kinds of gathering places that allow people oriented to culture to meet and connect; we lose our context, and the urban fabric frays.

Americans have long worried about big cities and the endemic poverty that seemed to take root in them. These days, plenty of cities—Detroit, Baltimore, some parts of even the richest burg—remain devastated. But it's excessive wealth, not poverty, that's making some cities unlivable. Culture merchants close their doors for a mixture of reasons, but next to disruptive technology, it's skyrocketing rents that are pushing these places out. The most recent economic recession has led to tenacious unemployment and a severe wounding of the American middle class—the median family has recovered only 45 percent of the wealth it lost since 2007, according to the Center of Household Financial Stability. But even in the face of these hard times, real estate prices are rising and in some cases spiking. The stock market surge, record corporate profits, and a plutocrat class thriving in an age of tax cuts and offshoring mean that the very rich can move into cities and force others out.

In New York City, the prices for luxury condos from up-town to downtown are pushing the creative class deeper into Brooklyn and Queens. Even outlying Hoboken, New Jersey, has seen its creative class pushed out by junior bankers who can pay $4,200 a month for a one-bedroom condo. The indie-rock club Maxwell's, a longtime watering hole for musicians and writers there, closed in 2013. In the Bay Area, real estate prices have begun to wage the economic equivalent of ethnic cleansing on the middle class. Rents in San Francisco increased by about 30 percent between June 2011 and two years later, with an accompanying surge in evictions. Cities such as Oakland, Denver, Miami, and Boston have seen annual increases above 10 percent since the recession. For objects with fixed prices—books and CDs, for instance—such enormous increases in overhead are hard for a small retailer, no matter how diligent or innovative, to keep pace with. And this sort of climb makes it nearly impossible for writers and musicians—not to mention bookstore workers—without trust funds to live in the kind of urban setting that allows for a critical mass and cultural friction. The resulting churn also makes it impossible for a city to maintain any urban context, any sense of itself. If you don't know where you are, the poet Wendell Berry has said, you don't know who you are.

There's an extensive literature about what makes neighborhoods function, including much by the New Urbanists, with Jane Jacobs as the most eloquent of the city's mid-century chroniclers. (Alfred Kazin's *A Walker in the City* and the essays of Walter Benjamin would be her Proustian antecedents.) Jacobs argued against inaccessible block-long urban acropolises and destructive central planning, and in favor of small shops that encourage pedestrian traffic and serendipity, along with mixed-use districts and buildings that can be accessed at street level—all things fostered by an interplay of independent culture merchants with other sorts of places.

Strolling, in particular, is something that these shops encourage, and when they close, they often make neighborhoods less walkable. "Walking, ideally, is a state of mind in which the mind, the body, and the world are aligned, as though they were three characters finally in conversation together, three notes suddenly making a chord," Rebecca Solnit, the great, eccentric author of place, wrote in *Wanderlust: A History of Walking*. "Walking allows us to be in our bodies and in the world without being made busy by them. It leaves us free to think without being wholly lost in our thoughts." Browsing through books, records, and movies resembles this motion—it's a kind of ambling of the mind.

One of the roles these places fill is that of the "third place." The term was coined by the urban theorist Ray Oldenburg, who refers to informal spots for gathering that are neither home nor work, but in their way as crucial to our well-being. "Third places exist on neutral ground and serve to level their guests to a condition of social equality," he observed in his 1989 book *The Great Good Place*. "Within these places, conversation is the primary activity and the major vehicle for the display and appreciation of human personality and individuality. Third places are taken for granted and most have a low profile. Since the formal institutions of society make stronger claims upon the individual, third places are normally open in the off hours, as well as at other times. The character of a third place is determined most of all by its regular clientele and is marked by a playful mood, which contrasts with people's more serious involvement in other spheres. Though a radically different kind of setting for a home, the third place is remarkably similar to a good home in the psychological comfort and support that it extends. . . . They are the heart of a community's social vitality, the grassroots of democracy, but sadly, they constitute a diminishing aspect of the American social landscape."

Certainly, bars and coffee shops and other spots can serve as this sort of oasis from work and home. But everyone who loves music, film, or literature has a shop that matters to them—or at least one that used to. In *Telegraph Avenue,* the novelist Michael Chabon created an emporium of used vinyl—Brokeland Records—whose crates of soul, jazz, and funk albums serve to bring together a group of music-loving misfits across generational and racial divides in Berkeley and Oakland. Writers, of course, love bookstores. Like libraries, the novelist Richard Russo writes in the introduction to *My Bookstore,* a recent collection of essays by authors on their favorite shops, bookstores "are the physical manifestation of the wide world's longest, best, most thrilling conversation. The people who work in them will tell you who's saying what."

That conversation, though, can go dead. Dutton's, which had an extensive outdoor courtyard perfect for readings and discussions, is gone. Rhino Records, which birthed an important reissue label in the late '70s and served as a rare oasis in L.A.'s Westwood, shut down as well. Until a few years ago, when Greenwich Village and environs became one enormous shopping mall, lower Manhattan supported numerous indie record stores, in addition to its Tower and Virgin, from Bleecker Bob's—now inhabited by a frozen yogurt chain—to Second Coming in the West Village, Etherea on Avenue A, and SoHo's Rocks in Your Head, which employed members of the city's indie-rock community and the poet Priscilla Becker. Now its storefront on Prince Street is a real-estate agency that fits hedge-fund managers into luxury lofts. (A similar list could be made of art-house cinemas, including Bleecker Street Cinema, Eighth Street Playhouse, the Thalia, and others.) And it's not just the big cities: When the Louisville record store Ear X-Tacy closed, a Panera Bread took over its spot. In 2013, Jackson, Mississippi, lost the small, hip BeBop record store; Plano, Texas, saw the 24,000-square-foot Legacy Books, with 100,000 titles, tank in 2010. Each of these places employed people, in some cases lots of people.

The novelist and travel writer Pico Iyer spends time in bookstores all over the world. But he's most loyal to Chaucer's, an independent store in an unfashionable mall in a fashionable city—Santa Barbara—that has survived not only economic ups and downs but the arrival (and departure) of several Borders and Barnes and Nobles. He haunts the place in part for a twenty-four-year-old clerk who turned him on to the Austrian novelist Thomas Bernhard and who dug up an obscure book on the director Werner Herzog that he hadn't known existed. A shop like that, which offers the human touch, offers an element of surprise. "It frees me from my habits as a website seldom does," he said.

"I was giving a talk to the World Monument Fund last year," Iyer went on to tell me, "and was reminded there that once you take a single wooden building out of a traditional, all-wooden neighborhood, you disrupt, perhaps even destroy the rhythm and integrity of the entire neighborhood. It's like knocking out Angelina Jolie's front tooth (I thought); a tiny blow, perhaps, but instantly the whole woman and her character and appeal are shattered. So our thoughts about local shops and our sense of connection to them are not just lazy sentiment or nostalgia; they spring from our instinctive awareness that the smallest changes can have the largest consequences. Take out a 'not' from a sentence and the whole text is transformed. Remove one record-shop from a neighborhood, and it's not just records or personal history or memories and friends that are knocked out (you can find all those elsewhere); it's everything around it that is subtly changed."

Enough subtle changes, and a town or neighborhood is transformed. "Places matter," Solnit writes in *Storming the Gates of Paradise*. "Their rules, their scale, their design include or exclude civil society, pedestrianism, equality, diversity (economic and otherwise), understanding of where water comes from and garbage goes, consumption or conservation. They map our lives." But what happens when we fall off the map, and we could be anywhere?

THE LOSS OF CLERKS—AND THE spaces where they work— is a loss for the culture as a whole. It's intangible, though. "So much of it is happenstance and chance," said Doug Dutton, who ran Dutton's Brentwood Books, probably the finest bookstore in Los Angeles, until it closed in 2008. One of his most beloved booksellers was a poet and crime-fiction junkie named Scott Wannberg. "All you had to do was say something about noir mysteries, and it would open a stream. Conversation can lead to all kinds of things—to mutual distaste, to romance, or profound meetings of the minds. These pathways of connections are very important, and disappearing." (Wannberg died in 2011, and was mourned by the city's literary world.)

There's a bigger, more tangible dimension: the vanishing of the clerk as cultural curator is part of a larger shift, as computers are putting educated "knowledge workers" out of jobs. It's not just the guy on the assembly line now—it's the autodidact at the bookstore. Next they're coming for librarians—many of whom are dreaded "public employees" that many Web utopians and school boards think have been made obsolete by Google. Other white-collar jobs could start to disappear as computers become more ruthlessly efficient and human beings find it harder and harder to keep up. Humans are now so sophisticated and technologically advanced as a species that we've begun to disregard actual human beings, and maybe humanistic values as well.

Science fiction novels often sketch future worlds in which computers have replaced—or tried to subvert—human beings. Frank Herbert's *Dune,* for example, opens well after wars between "thinking machines" and mankind. (Humans won, forbidding the construction of computers or robots; super-intelligent "mentats" perform the more intricate mental functions.) In Philip K. Dick's work, almost everything is uncannily automated—including pets. (Check out *Do Androids Dream of Electric Sheep?* the novel *Blade Runner* was based on.) Closer to home, the damage automation has done to blue-collar employment—assembly lines, bank tellers, customer-service types—is now a well-documented aspect of life in the developed world. When a character in Don DeLillo's *White Noise* encountered an ATM in 1985, he brooded over the machine's eerie inhumanity. These days we take such things for granted.

And technology—which began by replacing unskilled labor—has begun working its way up to fields that require real expertise. For now, doctors, lawyers, and hedge-fund managers are safe. But people whose connection to culture involves putting books, records, and films in the hands of paying customers are an endangered species. Employers don't have to pay medical benefits to algorithms that offer glib, simplified, if-you-like-this recommendations.

The actual work of creativity—making a short story or a film—is not yet something computers can replicate, says Andrew McAfee, the author, with fellow MIT economist Erik Brynjolfsson, of *Race Against the Machine: How the Digital Revolution Is Accelerating Innovation, Driving Productivity, and Irreversibly Transforming Employment and the Economy.* "But that doesn't mean that automation and technology isn't a threat to the creative class. Members of the creative class need day jobs, and some of those classic day jobs—Quentin Tarantino working in a video store—are endangered." Same with writers, he said, as the Web exerts a downward pressure on the price on their labor.

Artificial intelligence that replicates human abilities—websites that recommend books or CDs, for instance—have surged in the past few years. "I'm blown away by the power of some of these algorithms," McAfee says. "We now have digital alternatives to store clerks. Amazon has all the money and all the will in the world to get it right."

McAfee, a research scientist at the MIT Sloan School of

Management, says he breaks with his peers who see today's difficulties as similar to transitions like the Industrial Revolution that ultimately created more jobs than they destroyed. "We're talking about a new reality," he says. "When you don't need people for their muscle power, or for their communication abilities, or for their pattern recognition, an entrepreneur, someone wanting to start a company, looks around and says, 'Remind me what I need human labor for?' The pool of things that's uniquely human is shrinking."

McAfee recommends that aspiring members of the creative class return to one of their classic berths—waiting tables. That's harder to replace than a lot of the other options, he said, because people go to restaurants in part to interact with others, and because motion technology has not advanced enough for robot servers to become a reality. But MIT engineers came up with a device called the Presto that allows customers to order and pay at their table from a console that also lets them play games on it while waiting for their food to arrive. A Silicon Valley company, E La Carte, has begun moving these gadgets into restaurants, and motion technology is advancing. That cab-driving job is looking pretty good now—at least, until the driverless cabs arrive.

"I have a feeling we better start reading that science fiction," McAfee says. "That reality is coming to us, and coming to us sooner than we expect."

3

OF PERMATEMPS AND CONTENT SERFS

We have trouble grasping that something that empowers
the individual might also wreck the structures that have
protected the individual for decades.

—Thomas Frank, "Bright Frenetic Mills," *Harper's*

LISTEN TO THE OPTIMISTS AND the Great Recession and its
aftermath sounds like a great opportunity. This is the time
for the creative class to brand itself! A day job, they say, is so
twentieth century—as quaint and outdated as tail fins and
manual sewing machines. Thanks to laptops, cheap Internet connections, and structural changes in the world economy, we're living in a world of "free agents"—"soloists"
who are "self-branding" and empowered to live flexible and
self-determining lives full of meaning. We are all citizens of
Freelance Nation—heirs not to the old-school stodgy, gray-
flannel-suit Organization Man but to the coonskin-capped
pioneers and rugged, self-made types who built this coun-

try. "We are all CEOs of our own company," as business guru Tom Peters put it. "Me Inc."

But for those who must actually scrape together paying work in this new "gig economy"—architects, filmmakers, writers, musicians, bookstore managers, graphic designers, and other downsized members of the creative class, folks made obsolete by the Internet and the current predatory style of corporate power—Freelance Nation is a place where they fight to keep a home, a livelihood, or medical coverage.

Some are losing their houses. Others are watching marriages go up in smoke, or falling into heavy drinking. Still others are couch-jumping for months or years at a time. Or they're veering close to bankruptcy because of the risk of living without medical insurance.

Daniel Pink, a former speechwriter for Vice President Al Gore, wrote the witty and engaging bible of the freelance life, *Free Agent Nation.* "Today," he wrote in 2002, in a book still cited approvingly by followers, "in good times and bad, at the peak of the boom or the trough of the bust—the dice are loaded in favor of the individual. That's why I feel good about the future—a future in which more people can assert their independence and guide their economic and personal destiny." Sure, it might be rough at times, Pink conceded. But a wide range of people "will be able to throw off conformity, escape subservience, and live out their true potential." (Much of the rhetoric of this movement resembles the books from the 1970s that told Americans that marriage or monogamy was for squares and that they should enter the free-spirited world of swinging.)

"Democrats are as deep into it as Republicans are," said Thomas Frank, author of *What's the Matter with Kansas?*

"This whole idea of the 'free agent society' has gone so far; I don't know how you reverse that. And they didn't just sell it to management—they sold it to workers. They think it's *cool* to not have health insurance or benefits!"

But life on the ground shows that the free agent life isn't always so exhilarating—especially as incomes have fallen by roughly 10 percent since the latest recession began. "Everyone I know who's a graphic designer has had to take a pay cut of at least 40 percent over the last ten years," said Suzanne Rush, a former print designer for Warner Bros. who now freelances for movie studios and magazines around Los Angeles. "That's true across the board—motion graphics people as well as print people," staffers as well as freelancers. In fact, many free agents see themselves not as freewheeling soloists but as permatemps and content serfs.

ALABAMA NATIVE MATTHEW WAKE HAD paid his dues. After college, he'd worked as a short-order cook, waited tables, worked in construction, and clerked in record stores. While he was living in New Orleans, playing guitar in bands, a girlfriend suggested he might try something less financially risky than piling into a van to play small clubs across the South: music journalism.

Wake didn't walk right into a staff job—he wrote copy for a bank, freelanced for newspapers for free, sold ads, and sat through three-hour town-planning meetings, all ways to break in. After a few years he became a writer, and later an editor, at several southern newspapers. Finally, he became a staff writer at a weekly in Greenville, South Carolina. The paper was owned by Gannett—a famously profit-driven newspaper chain. Like other papers, his began to cut costs to hold on to market share and to keep its profits high. "Every quarter was like a *Friday the 13th* horror film," he said. "'Am I gonna be the guy that Freddie gets?'" One day in June of 2011, he and his colleagues were told the paper was eliminating its arts and entertainment staff: the weekly intended to recycle copy from other papers in the chain. It was one of about twenty thousand layoffs at Gannett under the CEO Craig Dubow, who retired in 2011 due to health issues—after seeing the company's stock prices plummet by about 700 percent. He left the company with a $37.1-million golden parachute.

"First," Wake said of his life post-job, "I went through my savings the way Jane's Addiction goes through bass players. I hit up tons and tons of publications—local, regional, national. What I've observed is that as times get tough, freelance is the first thing they cut." And publications are shrinking. "*Spin* just went bimonthly. The *Rolling Stone* I get in the mail is about as thin as a brochure. There will be more rats fighting for that same piece of cheese." (*Spin* magazine has since ceased print publication.)

Stressful as working for a Gannett paper could be, Wake had lived in a three-bedroom house, buying CDs or heading to bars when he wanted to. After he lost his job, he moved back to his hometown—Huntsville, Alabama—to a room in the house he grew up in, owned by his attorney brother. He wrote for pay when he could, and lived off what he makes taking care of a nonagenarian grandmother. "It gives me something to do so I don't have to go back to waiting tables," he said. "I just turned forty."

It became hard not to feel like he was going backward. When Wake had a job, he was able to start collecting art.

"Now I have the same Stones poster I had in college . . . ,"
he said. "Do I go into PR? Marketing? I go from interviewing Slash to writing copy for a Denny's menu? It's gonna be
a weird world for a while."

Typically, the Internet-cheerleader books—as well as
the websites of motivational branding coaches who urge
creative types to stop working for the Man and seize their
destiny—turn on rousing tales of success in the new economy. Pink's *Free Agent Nation,* for instance, opened and
closed with an inspiring sketch of Betty Fox, who ran a site
called GrandmaBetty.com and ended up with the kind of
big-money deal that most bloggers—the vast majority of
whom are unpaid—only dream of.

Jaron Lanier, who has been skeptical about the great
freeing benefits of the Internet economy, sees the reporting
on the new paradigm as driven by unlikely Horatio Alger
stories. "There are a few success stories," he said, "that create a false sense of hope." Because Radiohead can offer its
record free of charge, he argued, doesn't mean that bands
below the superstar level can. Similarly, the death of Apple
visionary Steve Jobs uncorked various rants about the value
of mavericks and how you can get it if you try hard enough.
Which means everyone who struggles in a post-boom, post-
bubble economy must be a loser. Lanier cited the example
of Kodak—a company that once employed 140,000 people
and supported an entire region of upstate New York—
which has been sold to Instagram, an online photo-sharing
service with thirteen employees. What happened to all those
middle-class jobs, he asks, all of that wealth? "So there's this
tiny token number of people who will get by from using
YouTube or Kickstarter, and everybody else lives on hope.

There's not a middle-class hump. It's an all-or-nothing society."

Today's gig economy is tough even for people accustomed to success. Dana Gioia served as a vice president at General Foods, and later as chairman of the NEA. But between those two stints, he worked for more than a decade as a freelance writer, poet, and critic. "When I quit my job in 1991, I had some tough years. I reviewed books, I did gigs for the BBC, I gave lectures. When a big piece appeared, people would invite me to give a speech. If you were willing to take a risk and float between gigs, you could make a living." By the time he took the NEA job, however, that was becoming impossible. "Electronic entertainment has taken over people's lives," he said. "You see it with lower rates of reading, with people not going to performances— it's all down. People not going means it's harder for the artists to make a living; it's very difficult for a jazz musician, for instance, to become well-known enough to get gigs. And political support for the arts is down." He no longer thinks it's possible to make a living as a freelance man of letters, like his heroes from midcentury. "There are fewer gigs," he said. The number of newspapers with stand-alone book or ideas sections is down substantially; serious magazines are half the size they used to be. "If I'd quit my job this year, I don't think I could have made it as a literary freelancer. The problem isn't the decline of the economy, though that doesn't help. The problem is the collapse of culture."

To what extent will that culture survive these changes? Human beings have been making art at least since one of our Paleolithic ancestors painted bison and deer on French and Spanish caves at least thirty thousand years ago. Stone sculptures of busty women, and music made originally using animal bones, are likely even older; as the late scholar Denis Dutton argued in his book *The Art Instinct,* creativity was hard-wired into the human race during our thousands of generations of evolution. So, some of us will always do this. Modern life has allowed specialization that Stone Age man did not enjoy, but it's never been easy to survive as an artist. Still, for generations to come, young people with trust funds will head to urban centers to make it as writers, visual artists, musicians, and filmmakers. A few—especially those with copious subsidies from parents—will strike gold and inspire the next generation to take a chance.

What's changed is the ability for people who didn't have the foresight to be born into wealthy families to earn a middle-class living in creative fields. Many cultural types are forced to go freelance because they are losing their jobs. A report shows that even well after the official end of the recession, slashed state budgets are making things much tougher, with a 16 percent drop in performing-arts jobs from 2010 to 2011. "For the performing arts," wrote economist and Progressive Policy Institute senior fellow Mike Mandel, "this is the moment where recession turns into depression." For authors, book advances are reported to be about half of what they were before the crash. That's easily the difference between a viable project and something you just can't afford to do without an inheritance.

And as the *New York Times* recently observed, the freelance musician has gone the way of the southern Democrat. "It was a good living. But the New York freelance musician —a bright thread in the fabric of the city—is dying out," wrote Daniel J. Wakin. "In an age of sampling, digitization and outsourcing, New York's soundtrack and advertising-jingle recording industry has essentially collapsed. Broadway jobs are in decline. Dance companies rely increasingly on recorded music. And many freelance orchestras, among the last steady deals, are cutting back on their seasons, sometimes to nothingness." This is all coming very soon after a surging discussion about how casual, "no collar" creative class, laptop-toting "knowledge workers," self-determining "free agents," and so on, would be redefining and reviving American life. Richard Florida's vaunted creative class was supposed to be pumping its mojo into American cities.

To Chris Ketcham, a freelance writer based in Brooklyn, it all comes down to living space. "Rent," he said, "is the basis of everything. For any artist or creator who wants to live with that dynamism of dense urban spaces, he can be saddled with rents so high that they take up 50 percent or more of his income. It's impossible to do things outside the marketplace because you're constantly working to pay rent."

Ketcham penned a long, impassioned article for *Orion* magazine, "The Reign of the One Percenters: Income Inequality and the Death of Culture in New York City," which coincides with some of the concerns of the Occupy Wall Street movement. "It goes back to the rise of the financial class, that top 1 percent," said Ketcham: "that takeover of New York by the very rich, which drives up the cost of land, of rents." His artist and filmmaker friends mostly have corporate jobs these days, he says. "They become servants to the corporate class."

With the recession fading and a supposed recovery at work, a rising cost of living in American cities becomes especially brutal to creatives whose work requires they have separate workspaces, like visual artists. The lack of affordable urban workspace makes it more difficult for artists to collect on the same blocks, where they can collaborate on projects and compare efforts. In 2013, almost fifty artists in the Industry City warehouse complex on the Brooklyn waterfront were forced to move because of rising rents. Many of them had moved to Sunset Park originally because escalating prices pushed them out of Manhattan and leafier, more central parts of Brooklyn; one had moved studios ten times over his career because of cascading costs. It's hardly the only place where artists help gentrify a neighborhood and then find themselves forced out. We have come a long way from Lascaux.

FREELANCERS PLYING THEIR TRADE IN the gig economy range widely—from artists sleeping in their cars and tapping electricity from streetlights to, until his death in 2012, Gore Vidal, living in luxury in the Hollywood Hills, and everything in between. One thing most freelancers—thriving or struggling—have in common is a complete lack of benefits. And that's especially true in the case of medical coverage. Steve Mirkin is a case in point. A longtime hard-working freelance writer, Mirkin has penned music and style stories for *Rolling Stone* and the *New York Times*. He's a sharp-witted Queens native with a fighter's temperament. "Ten years ago, I was making a good living as a freelancer—I was writing a story a day." With that work drying up, these days he's mostly a freelance researcher and writer for reality TV and game shows, which are now slowing as well. One thing these varied kinds of work have in common is the lack of health insurance. Mirkin doesn't like living without coverage. But money is tough as rates at both publications and in Hollywood fall—even the talent at *The Simpsons,* the longest-running show in television history, saw their pay being cut significantly—and he spent much of 2010 borrowing guest rooms and couches from friends across Los Angeles, later moving into a garage. "You worry every time you cough," he said, "that it could be very costly."

A few years ago, those costs suddenly became tangible. A sunny spring afternoon was interrupted by a kidney stone, and after a trip to the emergency room, Mirkin was hit with a bill for $30,000. "If you're not insured and you don't have the money," he said, "they charge you more." In Mirkin's case, luckily, a strong-willed relative intervened and got the cost reduced, but he's still fighting to survive. "I worked very hard to avoid having to declare bankruptcy."

His story is hardly unique. (Pink, to his credit, argued in *Free Agent Nation* that relying on employer-based medical insurance makes no sense in a world increasingly populated by the self-employed.) Radio producer Frances Anderton, an Englishwoman who moved to Southern California two decades ago, sometimes wonders if she lives in the land of the free. "The myth of America is about being mobile, and being entrepreneurial: this was a country where people moved around, renewing their lives. But the so-called countries of Old Europe end up being far more conducive to mobility and risk-taking because of their safety nets." This bind inhibits creative types, said Anderton, who produces KCRW's public radio show *DnA: Design and Architecture.* "Architects might have an idea to start a firm, or to buy a piece of land to develop a project, but they feel compelled to find a job with health care. People stay in jobs they don't like because they're terrified to leave. I know from my own experience of being a freelancer, medical coverage is staggeringly expensive. Throw in a partner and a child, and it becomes extremely daunting. What should be an exciting way to pursue one's career becomes fraught with peril."

The Patient Protection and Affordable Care Act was developed and passed into law in part because of the plight of people like this. It's only beginning to take effect, in the early months of 2014, some of it will take years to phase in completely, and one of our major political parties has dedicated itself to repealing and defunding it. The hatred of "Obamacare" on the radio and television airwaves is visceral. The degree to which it eases pressures for middle-class creatives, whether it is weakened by political attacks, or whether it survives at all, is currently hard to predict. But a health-care plan that applies to freelance workers, however imperfect its rollout and execution so far, is among rare good news the creative class has gotten in recent years. Despite our myths about the heroic or suffering artist, these people turn out to be made of flesh and blood after all. At the very least, this new legislation is a start.

For some people, the ever-changing alliances and environments of the gig economy add up to a better way to live and work. Some developments in the digital world have made that life easier. Kickstarter and other crowd-funding sites have created new possibilities: Kickstarter has already funded tens of thousands of projects, more than $400 million worth since its launch in 2009. (There's something for everyone: a Kickstarter for T-shirts, a Kickstarter for porn films, and on and on.) The most expensive of these projects is the Pebble smartwatch, which raised more than $10 million; many of the other biggest yields are video games or projects in which established celebrities pass the hat. But projects by such substantial figures as filmmaker Hal Hartley, novelist Neal Stephenson, and indie musician Stuart Murdoch have used Kickstarter, and in independent film, trying crowd-funding sites like IndieGoGo at the front end has become de rigueur. Some artists are uncomfortable with digital busking and the public exposure when a project fails to reach its funding goal; it has also made being friends with artists very expensive for some people. There have been plenty of abuses and flaws in the process. But just as a Band-Aid keeps a cut clean, these platforms have made good things possible.

Is this project-by-project process sustainable? Even observers excited about the digital economy are skeptical. "But how long can it last? Is there a limit to how many bike lights, iPhone cases, and slim wallets the crowd will back?" asked a 2013 story in *Wired*. "Crowd-funding is at a tipping point. We're about to discover whether it'll become endemic—a standard, behind-the-scenes, constant method of funding—or go the way of Groupon's daily deals, gradually fizzling out."

"Every single person I've ever talked to has said that doing Kickstarter is the hardest thing they've ever done," said the Brooklyn-based playwright and rock musician Stew. "You have to live it every day—you're not a songwriter anymore, you're planning, you're making promises, you're going to people's houses. . . . It becomes an all-consuming thing to get that money. It's like the grind of going on tour, without the joy of performing. You're setting things up to fulfill all the promises you made to everybody. And when it's done, you're still fulfilling the promises."

Crowd-sourcing, like the Web itself, works well for some temperaments and less well for others. The Web, for instance, has reduced the incentive for instrument teachers— why not just look that complicated chord voicing up on YouTube?—but has also allowed instructors in remote areas to offer lessons in a way they couldn't before.

"I've been a freelancer because that's what I fell into," said John Steinmetz, a composer, bassoon player, and educator who combines stints—teaching at UCLA, playing with the Los Angeles Master Chorale—even as he's watched music gigs dry up or move overseas. "I don't envy being married to the same group of people all the time. I like the variety; I still do."

But things have changed since he started out freelancing in the mid-'70s, and in 2011, he and his violist wife saw unpleasant trends—falling pensions, rising medical costs, a tougher freelance market—and decided to downsize and sell their house. When he left his position with the Los Angeles Opera, and his income dropped, they were glad they had. Some musician friends lost their homes.

Steinmetz sees the situation as part of what's sometimes called Baumol's curse, or "cost disease," after the work of the economist William Baumol in the 1960s. Baumol identified a mismatch between those whose labor would become more productive because of technology—assembly line workers, for instance—and those whose productivity stayed about the same. It takes just as long as it ever did to play a string quartet, or write a novel, or sculpt a statue. This creates a dilemma for employers, who are always looking to save money, and employees alike. And those older art forms, and those who practice them, are getting left behind in a twenty-first century in which other fields move much faster, Steinmetz fears.

"I used to have a confidence that there was a path available for people who were willing to work at it," he said. "But I'm not so sure about that anymore. If everybody's trying to crowd a deck of the last boat still afloat, there's not much room there." For many creatives seeking freedom, the free-agent economy has turned into another kind of trap.

4

INDIE ROCK'S ENDLESS ROAD

After the show [summer 2001 at UMass] we were invited to
a dorm room party, a Napster party. They weren't playing
records or compact discs. Instead, they had a high-speed
cable connection, provided free by the university, and they
had compiled a big long playlist on Napster. This was my first
exposure to the world of file sharing, to the dorm room jukebox
that would shake the music business to its core. A funny thing
happened in 2001. After years of going up and up and up, record
sales dropped 2.5 percent. The following year they dropped 6.8
percent, and they have continued to drop ever since, in ever
larger increments.

—Dean Wareham, *Black Postcards: A Memoir*

ONE CHARACTER INTIMATELY FAMILIAR WITH the plea-
sures and perils of making a living in the gig economy is the
indie rocker. A member of a once glamorous, if scruffy, sub-
class, the indie-rock musician has been hit especially hard

by the meltdown of the record industry and the ensuing transformation of cultural distribution. The music business was the first field to be swept by the waves that have recently overwhelmed the rest of the twenty-first century's culture makers, which made musicians, as the idiom has it, the earliest canaries in the creative-destruction coal mine. The indie rocker was the canary without corporate backing.

Part of what's startling, looking back, is to see that indie rockers were some of the earliest and most enthusiastic adopters of technology in general—the genre's key instrument, the electric guitar, was a technological product, and the music's '90s boom was produced in large part by the CD—and the digital world in particular. The very name indie rock refers to its musicians' rejection of major labels and much of the industry's corporate machinery: indie types were dedicated to DIY, doing it yourself. "People in the indie world thought technology was going to help them, give them more options," said Brooklyn music journalist Chris Ruen. "Independent artists were excited to see how this played out: it seemed *punk,* it was new—it was smashing the old idols, creating a new world." The DIY crowd seemed like natural cheerleaders for the self-branding, go-it-alone spirit of the new twenty-first century. So how are indie rock artists doing?

Mostly pretty poorly. A few musicians have benefited from the collapse of the record industry—Trent Reznor, Aimee Mann, and Amanda Palmer, for instance—and have found ways to connect directly with their audiences. James McKinley, Jr., of the *New York Times* calls this the conjunction of two trends, "the decline of record sales as part of the overall income of musicians and the rise of the artist as a branded commodity." Some musicians have used Kickstarter or direct sales to earn a living at a time when younger fans demand convenience and constant access instead of the hunting-and-gathering and thrill of the chase that earlier generations enjoyed. Indie arena-rockers Radiohead released a record online, with variable pricing. Licensing indie rock to television, movies, and advertising has become a source of revenue that barely existed two decades ago. And some indie labels, which tend to have lean staffs and generate strong commitments from fans, have not collapsed the same way major labels have; Chapel Hill's Merge Records, for instance, has shown that quality and stylistic range are possible in the new environment. But mostly, the financial structure—hammered by the downloading of recordings— has dropped out of indie rock as completely as it has from the larger music business, which in the final year of the twentieth century earned $14.6 billion in revenues for recordings. Those numbers fell to $5.35 billion in 2012—a loss of almost *two thirds* of its value in just over a decade.

Of course, there have always been starving artists and struggling musicians, and rock music in particular enjoys the mythology of the poor boy who comes out of nowhere, whether Liverpool or Detroit or the segregated South, to make it big. But even for some of the kings of the movement, the climate hardly suits royalty. Kyp Malone, the singer for TV on the Radio, a soul-meets-electronica combo that's become one of indie's most successful acts, said: "No one can get clean in dirty water—and we're all in it. In the meantime, I can't download my rent or my daughter's tuition." The Brooklyn band Grizzly Bear, for its part, puts out records that debut in the Billboard Top 10; they've recorded music for a Super Bowl commercial, landed a song on the *Twilight* soundtrack, performed regularly on late-night TV, and played the six-thousand-seat Radio City Music Hall. They are about a decade beyond the sleeping-on-friends'-floors, eating-beef-jerky-at-gas-stations stage of indie inauguration. But they're hardly living large: "Some of us have health insurance," said singer Ed Droste, who shares a small Brooklyn apartment, "some of us don't; we basically all live in the same places, no one's renting private jets." Guitarist Daniel Rossen sounds cautious, too: "If your livelihood is in songwriting," he says, "you never know when that's just gonna stop." They're aware that the business, as meager as it is today, could easily fade to a shadow within a decade. Across history, many musicians have spoken this way. But these are the *biggest winners* of the current scene.

Look beyond indie's most successful, and the figures are even more discouraging. Because the term "indie rock" refers, ambiguously, to both a guitar-based style and the connection to an independent label, this tribe is hard to quantify exactly. But because these acts are not playing arenas or signing with Sony, their earnings tend toward the low end of what's becoming a very steep curve. Chan Marshall, the singer behind Cat Power—probably the leading female artist in indie rock, whose album *Sun* snuck into the Billboard Top 10—went bankrupt and fell into foreclosure in 2012. "Young artists have to resort to stunts on YouTube," says veteran folk-rocker Richard Thompson. "How many people they can get to jump off Niagara Falls at the same time. Such ludicrous things to draw people's attention to your music."

What happens when everything depends on self-promotion? "Most likely they'll disappear, the reclusive artist replaced by one offering you a hoodie with her face on it," wrote Alina Simone, who put out two records on an indie that went out of business, and then tried flying solo. Without some kind of support or patronage, "Darwinism will probably ensure that only the musical entrepreneurs survive. I can't say if the world of music will be better or worse off if that happens, but it will certainly be a lot louder." Her label didn't bring Simone mountains of cash. "What I missed most about having a label wasn't the monetary investment, but the right to be quiet, the insulation provided from incessant self-promotion. I was a singer, not a saleswoman. Not everyone wants to be an entrepreneur."

A 2012 study of U.S.-based musicians and composers by the Future of Music Coalition, which involved a survey, interviews, and financial audits, found median earnings from music to be $34,455 gross, before expenses. The sources of this income include—in descending order of importance— live performance, teaching, salaried playing, composing, sound recordings, session work, "other," and merchandise. (Musicians earned, on average, 6 percent of their income from recordings.) Despite all the cheer in the blogosphere about the wonders of self-releasing music, musicians who self-release earned about half of what artists with a label deal made: the average gross for self-releasing musicians was $26,518. The study concluded, "The qualitative and quantitative data collected suggests that, while there are a handful of musicians who are wealthy, in general, US musicians are part of the working middle class." If a label deal is a remnant of the old days, like an appendix, and musicians are moving into a deal-free environment, most of them will land squarely in the *lower* middle class. (A study in 2013 showed that 43 percent of musicians lacked medical insurance, more than double the national average; most of the respondents who lacked insurance said they could not afford it.)

Some of these developments go beyond the world of indie. The playwright and musician known as Stew, who led the indie-rock band the Negro Problem and saw his Broadway play *Passing Strange* become a Spike Lee film, lives in a Brooklyn brownstone occupied primarily by musicians from pop to rock to the furthest edges of free jazz. "Artists are sort of stunned now that they have to do everything for themselves," he said—including, often, publicity and management. He was struck by the way his conversations with different kinds of musicians had become almost identical. "A decade ago, the free-jazz guy had nothing to do with someone playing pop. But now every band has to Tweet and [build a following on] Facebook. I know guys who play completely weird-ass, out-there stuff, and they have to Tweet, too. The club doesn't want you in there if you are not Tweeting all the time. Everything is mainstream these days. That creates a lot of stress in an artist, and it makes you into something different. It's all about bootstraps, about getting the private sector to support you. The grant-giving world is nowhere broad enough to encompass the breadth of the art being made."

The forces that have pushed a tiny sliver of Americans to capture the lion's share of U.S. wealth—and to thrive during a supposed recovery that has left the rest of the nation battered—have exerted themselves fiercely on the lives of rock musicians. A close examination of their plight sheds light on the predicament the creative class as a whole confronts.

"The music industry is a microcosm of what is happening

in the U.S. economy at large," White House chief economist Alan Krueger said in a speech at the Rock and Roll Hall of Fame in Cleveland in 2013. "We are increasingly becoming a 'winner-take-all economy,' a phenomenon that the music industry has long experienced."

NINETEEN EIGHTY-TWO CAN SERVE PRETTY well as the year indie rock began: the influential English band the Smiths formed, and R.E.M. signed to the IRS label and released its first EP, *Chronic Town*. (MTV, which would exert an effect nearly as strong on the rock-music industry as the coming of sound did on the movies, had just launched.) Indie was based on local scenes—often in outlying areas, like American college towns, the drizzly and provincial Pacific Northwest, and British cities reeling from deindustrialization—as well as tiny labels and small but dedicated fan bases. Whatever the ambitions of indie, larger forces were at work during its heyday that would become clear only later on. In '82, the top 1 percent of musicians earned a disproportionate share of concert revenues: 26 percent. Culture is never especially egalitarian: whether in the days of rockers or hippies or punks, pop music has always had a star system. But by 2003, the proportion earned by the top 1 percent had more than doubled, to 56 percent. During the same two-decade stretch, the cost of concert tickets increased steeply, and a few years into the Internet era, almost all of that money— nearly 90 percent—went to the top 5 percent of bands. (And lest skeptics say that rock music is a young man's game, between the Stones, Springsteen, the Eagles and others, the average age of the world's top ten tour-grossers is now in the mid-fifties.)

Part of the polarization has to do with the well-reported collapse of the record industry through illegal (piracy) and legal (iTunes, Spotify, etc.) means. Piracy brings musicians, of course, nothing at all, while services like Spotify and Pandora pay such minuscule royalties—which could, due to corporate lobbying, drop further—that musicians can have a hit song on one of these services and earn only pennies in compensation. ("You know how many hits you need on Spotify to make the minimum wage each month?" the roots-music singer and University of Wyoming economics professor Jason Shogren asked. "More than four million.") Part of it has to do with a nasty downturn and a supposed recovery that distributed its spoils only to the very top. "The major labels are happy, the consumer is happy and the CEOs of the web services are happy," David Byrne has written about label deals with Spotify and similar services. "All good, except no one is left to speak for those who actually make the stuff." Dave Allen of Gang of Four described the way musicians give their work to streaming services as "like applying the poison to your own dinner every night." Even musicians who've made their peace with the new world—Aimee Mann, Radiohead's Thom Yorke—feel ravaged by Pandora and Spotify. "It's like going back to 1890, before there were records, and the concert was the only musical experience," says Richard Thompson, whose songwriting royalties have fallen off a cliff: compared with twenty years ago, the royalty reports are "four times as thick for a quarter of the money. I'd be happy if they just shut Spotify down—if they're not gonna pay artists." To be fair, they do pay artists something, just not very much. The young, tech-savvy cellist Zoë Keating has done everything digital cheerleaders advocate:

she self-releases her music, has 1.2 million Twitter followers, and, in 2013, between two million YouTube views and 400,000 Spotify streams, earned from both services a total of about $3,000.

Some of these difficulties predate the industry's conquest by the Internet. The '90s saw the flowering of indie or "alternative" rock, and radio—which had been locked in a restrictive, repetitive "classic rock" format enforced by unadventurous programmers for at least two decades—had the chance to open up. "We won," Bay Area music journalist Gina Arnold wrote when Nirvana knocked Michael Jackson out of Billboard's Number 1 spot in 1991. American radio stations, in the early '90s, were owned by more than five thousand families and companies, and staffed with local deejays who largely picked their own music and in some cases had roots in regional music scenes. Some were good, most were bad, but with labels looking for the next Nirvana, it seemed like only a matter of time before commercial radio finally grew out of wildman posing and Boomer nostalgia.

But the possibility slammed shut with the Telecommunications Act of 1996, a gift to corporate consolidation, and especially to Clear Channel Communications. "Radio's big bully," as the journalist Eric Boehlert has dubbed the company, swallowed hundreds of stations and standardized their playlists; other consolidators followed suit. Commercial radio had always been safe and bland, but now any possibility of a fresh sound on the air was gone. If a song took too long for test audiences to recognize, it was eliminated—so the range of bands that listeners heard narrowed. Corporate consolidators began to vertically integrate, buying or "partnering" with TV stations, billboard companies, concert venues, radio promotion companies, and so on, while Washington slept. And it wasn't just musicians who didn't pass muster with dumbed-down "audience research" who paid the price for Clear Channel's spree—hundreds, maybe thousands, of deejays across the country were fired as corporations programmed countless stations from just a few locations. ("Thanks to clever digital editing," Boehlert wrote, "the show still often sounds local.")

Part of the issue, though, is cultural. That is, despite all the cheery talk about the liberating effects of the Internet, "the long tail," and the eclectic possibilities of these hierarchy-busting times, taste—with an assist from marketing and online algorithms—is converging to create a monopoly at the top. Pop music, which has always had its mix of stars, midlevel journeymen, and struggling or aspiring artists at the bottom end, now looks like the U.S. economy: a plutocracy heavily populated by serfs. As *New York* magazine documented in one of the few clear-eyed looks at this momentous change, in a single pre-Internet year—1986—thirty-one number-one songs came from twenty-nine different artists. By the Internet era, things were very different. Between 2008 and September 2012, a period of *almost five years,* there were only sixty-six number-one songs, and nearly half of them were turned out by just *six artists*—Katy Perry, Rihanna, Flo Rida, the Black Eyed Peas, Adele, and Lady Gaga. It's not just indie rock that's getting creamed: A single Adele record sold more than 70 percent of all of the classical albums sold in 2011, and more than 60 percent of all the jazz records. These bestselling artists may be prettier, but this is the equivalent of Donald Trump, Leona Helmsley, and a few others buying up all of America's real estate.

Of course, it's never been easy to land a hit record—even in the best of times, no musician could count on it. But recession-era rock has brought rewards to a smaller fraction of the artists than it did previously. Call it the music industry's one percent.

IMAGINE THE LIFE OF A musician who's worked for years to develop expertise as a player or songwriter, dutifully breaking into the club circuit and fighting to get the funding to record his or her songs. (And imagine this musician has found a way to pay for medical insurance, so he doesn't need to be saved from bankruptcy by one of those depressingly familiar benefit concerts.) It's never been a smooth road and most people are frozen out somewhere along the way, no matter how pure of heart. But today, a musician can wake up and find the album he just spent thousands of dollars recording is being peddled for free on PirateBay, and not be able to do a thing about it. Another artist can find her song's video on Facebook with an ad for BMW or the Newt Gingrich campaign attached—for which she is not paid. Or she can find her song available for illegal download alongside an advertisement for American Express. And while this kind of profiting from an uncompensated artist is illegal, all of the burden is on the artist to try to get their files taken down. In most cases, a pirate website can put the file or image of the band right back a few minutes after being ordered to take it down. (Unlike a musician signed to corporate labels, which police such things, the independent artist has to play this cat-and-mouse game on his own.) We're now in a world of brand-sponsored piracy. One of the late Lou Reed's last public acts was to complain about the way AT&T, Chevrolet, Domino's Pizza, and others took out ads alongside links to his pirated music.

Part of the way technology companies manage to shut down legislation—and even debate—around piracy and related issues (such as limiting the sale of counterfeit drugs on the Internet) is by shouting "censorship!" and spreading paranoia of a black-helicopter type government takeover of free expression. This became clear in late 2011 and early '12, as the Stop Online Piracy Act (SOPA) was introduced in the House of Representatives. As Bill Keller wrote in the *New York Times:* "The central purpose of the legislation—rather lost in the rhetorical cross fire and press coverage—was to extend the copyright laws that already protect content creators in the U.S. to offshore havens where the most egregious pirates have set up shop."

And while some of the legislation was overreaching and imperfect, the response was telling. When the Free Internet crowd—a collection of strange bedfellows—shut down SOPA after a Web blackout, they spoke publicly about how a ragtag bunch of cowboys ("an ad-hoc group of rank amateurs," in the words of one) had stood up to corporate Hollywood and those evil Washington bureaucrats. As with the uprising of the Tea Party, this was hardly a grassroots movement: Companies like Google, Facebook, eBay, Twitter, and others took out full-page newspaper ads and aggressively lobbied Congress. Google alone more than doubled its lobbying funds to $5 million in the first quarter of 2012, more than the lobbying budget of Hollywood's MPAA, the Recording Industry Association of America, Disney, and News Corporation put together. And many of the idealistic open-Internet nonprofits take money from Google and other corporate behemoths.

The roots of today's muddle go back to a pivotal moment more than a decade ago, when the music industry was flying high on the backs of fifteen-dollar CDs and a thriving economy, and indie rock still exerted a decent presence on the radio and the press. Then one day in May 2000, Lars Ulrich, the drummer for the band Metallica, pulled up in a chauffeured SUV—lawyers and two handlers in tow—to the faceless San Mateo office of the file-sharing service Napster. Ulrich, who had become the public face of one of rock's wealthiest groups and had a tendency to bluster, was there to deliver thirteen boxes, inside of which were the names of thousands of fans who had downloaded Metallica songs for free.

Some of those fans—and others who supported Napster—were there in San Mateo as well, and they were ready for Ulrich and his lawyers. Some jeered him as a greedy rocker; others smashed his band's CDs. Napster was at that point used by three-quarters of the nation's college students, and despite being owned primarily by a young programmer's wealthy venture-capitalist uncle, retained an outlaw cachet. "The sheer breadth of music available, combined with the opposition of major corporations," wrote journalist Robert Levine, "made Napster seem less like a technology company than a youth movement, complete with slogans and T-shirts."

The terms of the debate were largely established that day, and in the media coverage that followed the clash was typically framed as a David-versus-Goliath battle, the kids against the Man. The next few chapters, involving a poorly conceived lawsuit by the RIAA, and the op-ed shilling of high-cred rapper Chuck D—who called Napster a way to fight the power—did not make the industry look any better. And indie rockers, who had a history of mistrusting the big labels and the industry's infrastructure, did not jump in and come to the aid of the anti-downloading forces. "Anyone in my generation," writes Chris Ruen, then a Minnesota college student, "who paid attention to the litigious battles between Napster, Metallica, and the RIAA instinctively gleaned that *nothing* was less hip than getting uptight about music piracy. Doing so aligned one with multi-millionaire artists, greedy major labels, corporate scalawags, and thick-skulled Luddites."

Napster evaporated, succumbing to various legal challenges and bankruptcy in 2002. But the next year, Apple set up its iTunes store, and the issue was, at least for a while, settled. Music was now inexorably separated from a physical object, and recorded music was either free or awfully close to it. For some artists, this was no tragedy. Music has operated, they say, on the "gift economy"—in which a cultural artifact is freely given—for most of human history, and we were just back where we started. "The future of music is just like the past," said Kristin Hersh of indie pioneers Throwing Muses. "We wait on tables, we pass the hat, we write books, teach school, pass the hat again, maybe go a little hungry in order to fund our musical projects. Or we play only for the sky and we feel lucky to be able to do so."

A DECADE LATER, THESE CONFLICTS came to another head in a tussle that makes clear just how precarious is the entire ecology of music-making.

One of the disorienting things about technological change is the way it can take people who would otherwise be on the same side and pit them against one another. In this corner: a responsible and intelligent college radio DJ who loves Big Star and Yo La Tengo. In the other corner: a semi-famous indie rocker whose career playing skewed songs like "Sad Lovers Waltz" and "Teen Angst" depends on DJs and record buyers very much like his adversary. Were this the '80s or '90s, the two might have shown up mugging in a photo tacked to the college radio station's cluttered wall. But instead of being allies, Emily White, then an NPR intern and general manager at American University's WAMU in Washington, and the Camper Van Beethoven/ Cracker singer David Lowery—along with their followers— went after each other.

The dissonance here between fan and musician emerged from one of the key conflicts unleashed by Napster, iTunes, and their ilk: How should we pay for culture in the Internet era, and if we don't pay, what happens to the people who make it?

One weekend in 2012, White posted a piece on NPR's All Songs Considered blog called "I Never Owned Any Music to Begin With," in which she explained, in a reasonable, matter-of-fact tone, that despite being an enormous music fan, with a library of more than 11,000 songs, she had paid for almost none of it. White was not a culture-wants-to-be-free zealot, an unrepentant pirate, or a feckless, that's-just-the-way-I-roll Millennial. She seemed to suspect there's something wrong with this picture, but was not sure how wrong, and not sure how to fix it.

Lowery, a singer-guitarist who made his name back when

indie rock was called college radio, in the mid-'80s to early '90s, responded with a long post on the Trichordist, a community blog run by Artists for an Ethical Internet. He argued that by taking and listening to music without paying a record store or label or streaming service, White and her generational cohort were effectively cheating musicians out of the value of their work. If it's not literally piracy, he wrote, even folks who copy songs from friends, libraries, or radio station collections are depriving musicians of their property. And what's worse, he said, many of them were doing it with the assumption that the only damage they're inflicting was to the decadent and wasteful business model of the record industry. What you're doing instead, he said, is taking from artists—many of whom struggle—and giving their work to corporations bigger than anything left in the music business.

Lowery pointed out that what seems like innocent pilfering adds up to tangible real-world consequences for musicians like his friends Vic Chesnutt and Mark Linkous of Sparklehorse, both of whom killed themselves in the past few years in part out of frustration with the changing music business. (Both began to get exposure just as the traditional revenue model was falling apart, and Chesnutt had accumulated enormous medical debts.)

Who's right? In the broad sense, they both are. White is describing the way music sharing works among her generation, which came of age after the valorization of cover art, liner notes, and the physical qualities of records and CDs. (This said, some members of her generation have supported the vinyl revival, driven in part by a longing for a warmer and more expansive sound than what's on MP3s, but also by the old-school ritual of a brick-and-mortar shop, an in-formed and/or forbidding clerk, and the tangibility of the physical object.) She comes across as wanting to do what's right.

But Lowery's argument—despite a few misspellings and the jumble of both well-considered and rushed thoughts that the Web all but requires—is one of the more important meditations on the state of culture in our time. His argu-ment, in brief: The money being spent on music is not end-ing up in the hands of musicians, or even labels, or mem-bers of the creative class, from the record store clerk to a label president. It's going to Apple—which could, thanks to iTunes, buy every surviving label with pocket change—and other gargantuan technology companies.

Lowery's most compelling argument is an extended met-aphor about a lawless urban neighborhood—shades of the strange days during the 1992 L.A. riots—that never raised a police force. It's worth quoting at length:

So in this neighborhood people simply loot all the products from the shelves of the record store. People know it's wrong, but they do it because they know they will rarely be punished for doing so. What the commercial Free Culture movement . . . is saying is that instead of putting a police force in this neighbor-hood we should simply change our values and morality to accept this behavior. We should change our moral-ity and ethics to accept looting because it is simply possible to get away with it. And nothing says freedom like getting away with it, right?

But it's worse than that. It turns out that Verizon,

AT&T, Charter etc etc are charging a toll to get into this neighborhood to get the free stuff. Further, companies like Google are selling maps (search results) that tell you where the stuff is that you want to loot. . . . Further, in order to loot you need to have a $1,000 dollar laptop, a $500 dollar iPhone or $400 Samsumg [*sic*] tablet. It turns out the supposedly "free" stuff really isn't free. In fact it's an expensive way to get "free" music. . . . And none of that money goes to the artists!

There's a contrarian buzz on the blogosphere toward debunking Lowery's argument, calling him an old fogey or someone who won't let go of the old days. But his metaphor of the neighborhood that funnels money to technology corporations and takes it away from the artists actually writing and producing the music is accurate. And that tattered, corporate-sponsored neighborhood that could be one of Italo Calvino's bad dreams represents more than just the upending of the record industry.

The damage to culture generated by digital technology, the struggling economy, and changing habits can be seen in numerous places—the film market in Spain, where illegal downloads have made it almost impossible to sell DVDs, or New Orleans, where the newspaper that gave the most courageous coverage of Hurricane Katrina ended up laying off half of its staff. That abstract neighborhood is as real as the bookstore that used to exist down the street from the place you live or work, or the booksellers and managers who used to work there.

When you ask people why they steal music, or why they

don't care about the collapse of the record industry, the more informed ones talk about the decadence of the labels themselves. Lowery, who teaches a course on the economics of music at the University of Georgia's business school, describes his students' point of view this way: "It's OK not to pay for music because record companies rip off artists and do not pay artists anything." Nonsense, he says—some deals were unfair, but most allowed musicians to earn a living making music. As bad and wasteful as the labels could be, he's essentially right about this, and our new model, with its mix of iTunes and streaming and piracy, is no improvement.

But part of the blame for the state of affairs that White and Lowery are arguing over goes to the record industry itself, which slept as technology changed, then responded with lawsuits against Napster and collegiate downloaders rather than finding a way to accommodate new appetites and new capacities. We're back to the SUV in San Mateo. "The labels were the ones faced with this fork in the road," said Steve Knopper, a *Rolling Stone* contributor and author of *Appetite for Self-Destruction,* perhaps the best book about the record industry's suicide. "Come up with a new model, or ride CDs down into the ground. People on their own staffs were telling them, 'Do something with Napster, make a deal with them.' The labels, from top to bottom, said, 'We are going to rely on our CD-selling model, screw all these punk Napster people.'" And the real damage, he believes, was done in just a few years: from the emergence of Napster, in 1999, to 2003, when the iTunes store opened. "There was almost no legal way in that period, anywhere in the world, where someone could buy a download. That four-year period killed the labels. They had a deal on the table with Napster, but that deal collapsed. The majority of the people running the labels said, 'Screw this Internet stuff, we sell CDs. We're big, they're small.'" Part of what made labels vulnerable was the insularity of their leadership. "You had to prove that you went to clubs, had 'cred,' had worked with Elvis, that you had solid-gold ears, that you could hear a hit when no one else could." Not exactly the type given to thoughtful restructuring in the face of technological innovation.

The record industry was not alone. It resembled, for instance, the newspapers that covered it, as media companies allowed themselves to be upended by Craigslist and actually paid—thanks to the advocacy of starry-eyed futurists—to transfer content to the Web, where ad rates dropped tenfold. For a long time, the model for record labels and newspapers alike involved giving away something for a larger gain. With newspapers, said Knopper, "You'd sell your content incredibly cheap—like for 25 cents—but you'd also sell advertising. For decades, in music, the model has been, you listen to the music for free on the radio, and then it becomes, 'Oh, I love the single, I'll buy an expensive record or CD.'"

The anger and frustration, and plummeting revenues, we hear from musicians—and the disintegration of almost $10 billion in revenue each year—is the sound of what happens when the world changes and the leadership sleeps through it. Someone is making a lot of money from music, but it's not the labels. It's the tech companies. So with the music industry dropping the ball, is it fair to beat up on the musicians? Of course not, and that's why Lowery's argument resonates. Most of our pop images of musicians—whether Led Zeppelin trashing hotel rooms, Ozzy Osbourne in his Beverly Hills mansion, or hip-hoppers with Bentleys, bling, and bottles of Chivas—involve sudden wealth leading to profligate irresponsibility. In MTV's *Cribs,* musicians drive around in Ferraris; in rock biographies, touring is mostly about deflowering groupies and crashing Cadillacs into swimming pools. Rock music—unlike the folk and blues it came from—has always been aspirational and its rebel stance has often translated into materialism and narcissism. Elvis walked into Sun Studios a bashful truck driver, so shy he paced around the block several times before coming in; a few years later he was in front of the movie cameras wearing a gold lamé suit. Presley was not the last to travel this road.

But rock 'n' roll fantasy aside, the vast majority of musicians in any genre are working hard just to get by, and touring almost constantly for shrinking yields. The Internet has, with a few exceptions, not made things easier. And often a great deal worse.

Lowery, a former quant, or quantitative analyst, writes, "Of the 75,000 albums released in 2010 only . . . 1,000 sold more than 10,000 copies . . . the point where independent artists begin to go into the black on professional album production, marketing and promotion." That means the other 74,000 either broke even or lost money. It's the kind of thing you don't hear from Internet utopians who crow about the "democratization" the Web encourages and the way digital technology keeps us all "connected."

Here's what this kind of democratization actually means: "According to Nielsen," wrote Eduardo Porter of the *New York Times,* "75,300 albums were released in 2010, 25 percent more than in 2005. But new releases that sold more than 1,000 copies fell to about 4,700 from 8,000 during that time." That's selling more than just 1,000 copies. If, continued Porter, "professional musicians, movie directors and writers can't make money from their art, they will probably make less of it. Independent producers say piracy is already making it harder to raise money for small and mid-budget movies. Stopping piracy is about protecting creativity—and the many occupations it supports (think pop band or sound mixer). If we value what creative industries produce as much as we say we do, Congress will have to find a way to protect it without limiting speech."

Is there a way to make government regulations that satisfy Lowery, who wants artists to get paid for their intellectual property, and White, who insists on "the ability to listen to what I want, when I want, and how I want it"? Probably. It may take a few more public arguments—some perhaps less polite than this one—to get there.

LET'S LOOK AT TWO MUSICIANS who mark out the extremes of today's creative class and its plight. The first is the songwriter and producer Lukasz Gottwald, known as Dr. Luke, who works with Britney Spears, Katy Perry, Miley Cyrus, and Kesha. Clearly smart and musically gifted, he spent his early years in school boasting about his talents, dismissing jazz as simplistic, and skipping class at the expensive private schools his parents sent him to. "I remember being in class, and saying, 'I don't care about this, I don't need to know this.'"

Dr. Luke scored as many Number 1 hits in 2010 as the Beatles did in their best year. He lives large in the Hollywood Hills; due to a mansion renovation, he now operates out of a beach house he bought from Ozzy Osbourne. "The collapse of the album business—album sales hit historic lows this summer—has made Gottwald, who can reliably produce hit after hit, a sort of golden goose," John Seabrook wrote in the *New Yorker* in 2013. "He can make a song that's also a business plan."

In a culture that's post-record label, post-radio, and to some extent post-music press, how do singers break their music? Dr. Luke wills hits into being by asking members of his stable to tweet each other's song. Katy Perry has 30 million Twitter followers, so even if a tiny fraction picks up on the new Kesha track, it goes big fast. Pop music's creators and champions talk a lot about democracy and populism, and denounce those who don't like the music as the kind of elitists, snobs, and Puritans who would have dissed Irving Berlin or Elvis. And the hope that upbeat songs give listeners is part of the whole pop ideology as well. But this isn't democracy—it's the kind of monopoly capitalism Theodore Roosevelt hated, dressed up with bling and low-cut jeans. As for hope: synthed-out with gang choruses, or purplish and overwrought over lost love, Dr. Luke's songs sound like the music piped into the waiting room in hell.

Across town, on Los Angeles's scruffier Eastside, lives a Pennsylvania-born indie-rock musician named Chris Stroffolino. Is he an Everyman? Not really, but there are more like him. For most of the '90s and early 2000s, he published books of New York School–influenced poetry and a critical study of Shakespeare's *Twelfth Night*, taught at NYU and colleges in the Bay Area, and played piano on records like the Silver Jews' *American Water*—one of the highlights of the indie-rock movement. He never expected to get rich, but he lived for the energy of creating. He's articulate and impassioned—rumored by fellow musicians to know the chords to more songs than anyone else—but considers himself an introvert. "Carolyn Forché," he says of the poet and translator, "said the thing she feared about the Internet was that it would destroy the contemplative mode. It's about attention."

These days, Stroffolino comes across like a character in a Denis Johnson story. He's damaged, but also fierce and intelligent: there's something intense and pure about him. While biking one day a decade ago—he'd come west for a poet-in-residence position at St. Mary's College of California —he was hit by a car, and his leg was crushed. "So here I am in California with no support system." As he's alternated between pulling himself back up—teaching classes at a college in Oakland, playing at a recording studio—and falling back down again, largely because of a cascade of health problems, the network of small presses and indie record labels that kept him alive started to fray. And as college teaching started to tighten up, he found himself competing with his own students even for no-benefits, one-course-at-a-time adjunct jobs. He walks with a cane, apologizes for his dirty clothes, and calls himself, at forty-nine, "an old cripple."

Stroffolino sees his experience as part of a larger cultural collapse, and has started to write about the history of radio, the glories of Motown, of the racial context of '60s and '70 music, of the demise of the middle class. He's eagerly searching for new models for musicians and writers, and thinks digital technology could be part of the solution. He's recorded a few songs with Dean & Britta, but mostly plays piano in his van for tips, sometimes getting paid to play parties. "Now I'm living in my damn van," he says. "I hate my life. I'm sitting here chain smoking, trying to write my way out of it."

Internet optimists have a cheery solution to all of this: Musicians just need to "adjust" to these new conditions. They can do this with constant touring and through what's called *disintermediation,* or the removal of the middleman.

Live performance is indeed, for most musicians, the largest percentage of their income; in the 2012 Future of Music Coalition survey, musicians on a major or indie label made 30 percent of their music income from playing live; self-released artists made a whopping 38 percent. In both cases, this was roughly double that of their second-best source of income—teaching—and three or more times more than the money they make from recording. The touring argument goes like this: Sure, musicians aren't earning anything from selling records anymore, but they can tour! People are still going to concerts, the famous bands are earning fortunes on the road, and even smaller bands can sell T-shirts and stuff. So get going! Many of these advocates of endless touring also argue that musicians should have day jobs, never explaining how people can work full time and then take months off to pile into a van and drive from city to city. Fans look around a crowded club or concert hall and think, These guys must be raking it in!

Most of the musicians who are going it alone developed reputations during the label era and don't need the same kind of publicity support and investment labels used to offer. It's different for a younger group of artists. "How is the up-and-coming band going to quit their jobs and focus on music if they're not signed?" asks former White Stripe Jack White. "If the music is free and no one's buying the record, who's paying for it to be made? Who's paying for it to be recorded? Who's paying so that artist doesn't have to have a day job anymore and can dedicate himself to going on tour?"

Dean Wareham, who led the melodic New York band Luna, echoes Jack White's concern: "It's a minuscule number of bands that can make a living playing live, like Lenny Kravitz. Touring was something we did to support an album. I make money on some tours, but I barely break even on others. And how much touring can you realistically do? Those at the top are making good money on tour but this has never been particularly profitable for most bands." Wareham, by the way, does not get misty about the era of the big labels; he still owes hundreds of thousands of dollars to Elektra, a decade after his band quit.

In the old days, said John McCrea, lead singer of the Bay Area band Cake, "You'd go into debt to the label so you could afford to tour, with the hope that you might sell enough records to break even. It was tenuous at best. Now bands are being told they can make a living from touring, with potentially no money coming from record sales."

Even then, touring didn't guarantee a big yield for bands, with managers typically taking 15 percent and booking agents another 10 percent, not to mention money for truck-stop food. Drives were long then too, and days without showering just as unpleasant. Touring is even more financially precarious now that gas prices seem parked around four dollars a gallon. Driving a van from city to city can cost several hundred dollars a day just to fill the tank. As for those magical T-shirts: Clubs typically take between 25 and 35 percent of the grosses. Which means that for every twenty-dollar T-shirt sold, eight dollars could go into making it, and seven to the venue. The band ends up with five bucks for each one—not bad, but it's hardly enough to build a career on. And that's before you pay the girl working the merch table.

"Touring constantly will kill you after a couple of years if you are older than twenty," said McCrea. Most bands are not playing arenas of Bic-waving fans. "Most bands are middle class or lower-middle class. The T-shirts they sell are not enough to put gas in their van for a week. And you will burn out your audience—you can't go back to the same towns every six months. There is not an endless supply of people and free nights of the week."

Even though touring can be an important part of a musician's livelihood, it hardly guarantees a pot of gold. The Future of Music Coalition survey in 2012 found that expenses had gone up over the previous year in almost every major category—not just gasoline but vehicle rentals, hotel costs, and especially airline tickets. The survey research also revealed that, often, touring only allows musicians to run in place—they earn enough to keep them on the road, but the minute they park the van wherever home is, the clock starts ticking again, and they need more income and more material before they can play the next time. Without a pension or, in many cases, medical insurance, there's no time to waste. And for musicians who are not natural live performers, that revenue doesn't exist at all.

The Sisyphean nature of it all becomes especially stark

when musicians have children. "There are now a lot of family photographs on holidays, and I'm not in them," said McCrea, who had two small children just when he hoped the need for constant touring was easing. "That's starting to bother me. And as I plot the trajectory—the precipitous decline of recorded music—in five or ten years, it will be less than zero." The labels have been at war, he says, and they've used the musicians as human shields. He knows plenty of talented people who tried to stay in the game, but have given up. The ones who are touring constantly, he says, are seeing their marriages and families fray.

McCrea considers himself one of the lucky ones: he's able to do what he loves, his band has been together since the '90s, and in 2011 even scored a Number 1 album. Such apparent success doesn't go very far these days. "I'm *fine* not getting rich," he said. "But for a number-one record—an album costs a lot of money to record—we're certainly not swimming in money. Having a band is like a leaky bucket: You've got a lot of people to pay every month. I'm trying to get a month to write songs, or to record, or to do something creative." (McCrea has since helped found an advocacy group for musicians and other creatives, the Content Creators Coalition.)

Lowery was initially excited by all of the new technological possibilities. "We thought we'd make more money," he said, "through disintermediation and selling music directly to fans." When Facebook started its band pages, he saw the traffic on his Cracker and Camper Van Beethoven sites fall to about half what they had been. His musician friends found that they were experiencing the same thing. "Suddenly," he said, "the process of disintermediation started to reverse itself. I call it re-intermediation." But since the fans were already on Facebook, he figured, why *shouldn't* they connect to his band sites that way? So Cracker and Camper Van moved their fan pages to Facebook. "One day they told us, 'If you want your fans to see what you write, you have to pay us.' So we brought them all our fans, and now they're selling them back to us. That's classic exploitative re-intermediation. But we should have seen this coming— the people with the biggest computer servers, the biggest marketing budget, will win."

There's also a kind of distorting mirror at work here. Just as we hear more about U2 and Madonna and their extravagant stage shows (complete with wardrobe managers, multiple eighteen-wheelers, and so on) than about the huge number of bands whose tours did not involve building enormous science-fictional edifices, we see extensive media coverage whenever a musician beats the odds and makes money using new media. "If you hang out outside of a casino," said Lowery, "the people you're gonna hear about are the winners. You're not gonna hear from the vast number of people who are the losers." It's nice for the few who hit the jackpot. "But it's not a business model." It hardly suggests a prudent path for the rest of us.

The artists who can do without the array of middlemen that involves managers, label handlers, journalistic critics, and so on is quite small, wrote Errol Kolosine, who teaches music courses at New York University. "When you as an artist reach a point where your brand is as valuable as any label, then you are at the point where you can call your shots." If we want to keep musicians—and others in the creative class—alive, McCrea said, we have to start thinking and operating differently as a culture. "In a Walmart society that will buy slave labor if we can save twenty-five cents on a pair of socks, everyone is going to squeeze everybody else. I don't know that anyone is going to save us. I don't think anybody's really against technology. But the money to fund a Silicon Valley startup comes from Wall Street, or venture capital gets involved, and has its own demands. I get it; it's nothing personal. But it doesn't leave anything left over for the artist. And right now the artist doesn't have any way to fight back."

Until that happens, rock's road will be endless indeed. It's beginning, for many, to seem like a dead end.

5

THE ARCHITECTURE MELTDOWN

I grew up hearing over and over, to the point of tedium, that
"hard work" was the secret of success: "Work hard and you'll
get ahead" or "It's hard work that got us where we are."
No one ever said that you could work hard—harder than
you ever thought possible—and still find yourself sinking
ever deeper into poverty and debt.

—Barbara Ehrenreich, *Nickel and Dimed*

AROUND THE TIME THE Great Recession dawned in 2008,
architecture was serving as the glamour profession of the creative class. Extravagant, signature buildings—Frank Gehry's
titanium-clad Guggenheim Museum in Spain's Basque country, Richard Meier's white-travertine Getty Center in Los
Angeles, and multimillion-dollar concert halls opening from
Philadelphia to Orange County—drew not only press attention but the kind of architectural tourists who once visited
Irish castles or Italian duomos.

Brash, individualistic "starchitects"—cerebral urbanist Rem
Koolhaas, Iraq-born diva Zaha Hadid, gracious, serene Renzo
Piano, and others hailed in the press as visionaries—became
the new rock stars. Though much of the cast was international, architecture mania built on a longstanding idolatry
of the allegedly heroic architect in the United States, dating
back to the magnetic Frank Lloyd Wright and the valiant,
uncompromising Howard Roark in Ayn Rand's *The Foun-
tainhead*. New shelter magazines like *Dwell* brought sustainable and modernist design to a wider public, and websites
reveled in the eye candy.

For an era supposedly defined by bourgeois bohemianism,
architecture—a synthesis of aesthetics with hard-headed, pragmatic problem solving—was the perfect field. But soon after
the time Brad Pitt was hanging out with Frank Gehry—the
two met in 2001 and the actor began a kind of apprenticeship
—things began to change. For all its soaring lines and innovative solutions, architecture was exposed to the realities
of the marketplace like few other fields: the surging sense of
possibility that lasted through the '90s and the early 2000s
flagged when the housing market crashed and jolted the U.S.
economy. Gehry, whose Walt Disney Concert Hall quickly
became an iconic part of downtown Los Angeles and whose
widespread fame led him to a gig designing jewelry for Tif-
fany, complained about the lack of work in the States and
grumbled that he wished he could move his staff to China,
where there are more opportunities. Thom Mayne, the
Pritzker Prize–winning architect who has gone from one of
the field's rebels to one of its most successful figures, joked
grimly about the need for a party for depressed architects.
But it isn't just the celebrity figures who are frustrated. A

once thriving profession, one that required considerable education, dues-paying, and work ethic, and which has traditionally served a wide range of functions—designing mansions for the 1 percent as well as public libraries for the rest of us—is in trouble.

Architecture, of course, has always depended on wealthy patrons or the health of the surrounding economy, and some of its current travails are cyclical. With enough economic growth, building will return and some architects will work again. But the bust of 2008 was not followed by a boom that restored employment or stability. In fact, some of the larger trends, both inside and outside the profession, are discouraging. Among them are government austerity that leads to less high-end designing in the United States and Europe, corporate consolidation that squeezes out innovative small firms, and the diminishing fortunes of a middle class that once drove an important sector of home design. Sorting out which changes are cyclical and which are structural can be difficult while they're happening. What we can say for sure is that six years after the Wall Street crash, many architects are still struggling, and the field and the larger world seem to be changing in ways that will make the profession increasingly inaccessible.

"I don't feel like this is temporary," said architect Kevin Daly. "The immediate future will be more like now than it will be like it was [before the recession]. Until we make the decision as a society to invest in things—and I don't really see that happening."

These ups and downs became very tangible for Guy Horton, a Boston native who dropped out of a graduate program studying Chinese history and literature to become an architect, entranced by both the field's energy and its seeming stability. "I thought I was being pragmatic," he said. "Architecture was booming, the starchitects were getting a lot of attention. I was taken by the excitement of the field. Travels in China and around Asia, and stints living over there, got me more interested in cities and how they transform." After graduating from the cutting-edge Southern California Institute of Architecture in downtown Los Angeles, he was scooped up by the L.A. offices of a large international firm well regarded for its sustainable projects. In 2008, as the market was crashing, Horton was laid off. He bounced checks. He strained to pay student loans. Most of his income went to cover a health plan, but he avoided doctors or dentists because of high deductibles. He was pulled over by the police for his car's expired tags. He was demoralized and frightened for his family, which included a newly arrived baby daughter. After working hard to break into what seemed to be a burgeoning profession, Horton suddenly felt like he was being buried alive.

Horton wasn't alone. According to the U.S. Department of Labor, employment at architectural firms nationwide dropped from 224,500 to 184,600 between July and November of 2009, and the numbers kept falling for another year. In some cases, firms went dormant while remaining open. San Francisco–based Gensler, the nation's biggest firm, laid off 750 of a staff of about 3,000; British Pritzker-winner Norman Foster laid off a quarter of his London-based Foster + Partners. Gehry—whose Brooklyn Yards project in New York and condo/shopping hybrid in downtown Los Angeles wilted—cut Gehry Partners to ribbons, slicing more than half his staff of 250. The L.A. firm

Johnson Fain fell from 108 staffers to 40 within a year. All over the world, even in once vigorous regions, ambitious projects stalled. That process has continued, even with an economic recovery: in 2012, Gehry saw the projected Guggenheim Abu Dhabi museum go into deep freeze.

Many architects running smaller firms were lucky enough to keep their jobs but saw their fees—linked to falling construction costs—decline. Numbers are hard to come by and the upbeat American Institute of Architects does not track unemployment, but many thousands certainly left the field altogether. Sometimes they luck out: a former architect has become one of the best-loved baristas in Los Angeles; another runs the Coolhaus ice cream truck. Others have lost their homes and their medical insurance. Those who remain in the profession find design work scarce and are teaching, lecturing, or entering competitions, while others have moved into Hollywood production design. Such jobs have always been part of the profession, which revels in its synthesis of theory and practice, but the balance has shifted in a way that means architects are doing less and less architecture. "The recession has affected everyone, for sure," said Kevin Daly, an established Santa Monica architect whose firm, Daly Genik, employs ten people when at full strength. "Generally there's a lot less work than people are accustomed to having. Clients are doing feasibility studies and then keeping their options open."

Architect Marcelo Spina is a member of the creative class who serves the creative economy. His boutique firm, Patterns, designs art galleries and small museums, and had some early success. But many of those projects are drying up in a time of belt tightening. These days, he can only keep himself afloat through university teaching, and it's the same for his architect wife, Georgina Huljich. "It's a hugely important factor for us financially," he said. "We're proud academics, but we don't want to be purely academics—we don't want to be part of the paper architecture world. My colleagues are struggling the same way. Right now what you have is full-time employment with internship wages. There is much less meat for the same amount of animals. You see a whole lot of talented people not getting jobs." Spina is one of the lucky ones. He has strong connections in his native Argentina, where residential and civic projects have not died off, despite Argentina's currency woes. Because of a recent history of runaway inflation and credit busts, Argentine designers are usually paid with real money. "You know someone is going to show up with a bag of cash."

But those stuck working in the States are in a tight spot. In January 2012, the *New York Times* ran a piece called "Want a Job? Go to College, and Don't Major in Architecture." The article cited a report by Georgetown's Center on Education and the Workforce that showed architecture graduates, of all college majors, as the most likely to be out of work. The survey reported that a whopping 13.9 percent of architecture students between twenty-two and twenty-six were unemployed. Experience helped, but only slightly: among experienced architects between thirty and fifty-four, a full 9.2 percent remained out of work. Even humanities and arts majors—often the least career-obsessed of students—fared better. In May 2013, the center updated its findings in a way that suggests that the economic recovery will not restore the field's health. "Even as the housing bubble seems to be dissipating," the new report said, "unemployment rates for recent architecture graduates have remained high (12.8%). Graduate degrees and work experience did not shield these graduates from a sector-specific shock; graduates with experience in the field have the same jobless rates as the economy overall (9.3%)."

The *Times* story, Horton said, angered many of the architects he knew. "People were getting defensive about it. 'It's not *about* that—it's about the *passion!*' People were irate!" He knows younger architects who've left California, closed their firms, or moved back in with their parents. "People don't want to talk about unemployment anymore . . . we are supposed to be in recovery-optimistic-power mode." It's part of a professional ethos, he said, that stresses idealism, dues paying, hierarchy, optimism, and a heroic self-image while ignoring financial realities. It's something he's become intimately familiar with as he tries to chronicle the damage the recession has exacted on the field. "I'm trying to talk to architects about the economy. Forget it! It's hard to get real information. They're so conscious of PR—they're worried about what's going to get tweeted." Denial remains rampant among his brethren.

Part of the challenge of tracking the state of any creative-class employment is that the numbers don't tell the real tale. Neither do the Horatio Alger stories that so many newspapers and magazines love running about the handful of laid-off creatives who manage to "reinvent" themselves and turn their misfortune into an opportunity.

Not everyone is suffering. Eric Owen Moss and Barbara Bestor are very different kinds of designers, with sharply different lists of clients, but they show what is possible when talent and good fortune line up, even in hard times. Moss has some major advantages over even the typical successful architect: He is the director of an architecture school, which provides him with a hefty salary. He has connections in China and has several projects cooking in a country that considers a redesign of the coastline within the art of the possible. And he has an architectural patron who has financed a daring series of design projects—asymmetric office buildings and an "art tower" in Culver City—that earned a rave in the *New Yorker* in 2011. Though he calls himself "temperamentally optimistic," Moss knows what's happening around him. "If you look at the numbers, architecture graduates are looking for opportunities in other fields. Overall, commercial building has slowed to almost nothing."

Bestor, whose hair is cut in a kind of '70s shag, established herself as the indie queen of Silverlake, the bohemian neighborhood on L.A.'s east side; she's the author of a coffee-table book, *Bohemian Modern*, but somehow among the least smug people you will ever meet. Sitting in her retro-cool Airstream trailer, parked outside an open-plan plywood office that buzzes with activity, she compares herself to a culinary locavore: she's tapped into the neighborhood—its boutique small businesses and pop-culture spirit—and is the first call for cool coffee shops (Intelligentsia), wine bars (Lou), and record label offices (Dangerbird) in Hollywood and points east. "People know me; they know what I do." But even Bestor has struggled. After laying off most of her staff following the crash, she took a university teaching job in 2009, working, effectively, two full-time jobs. "Very much like an immigrant worker," she said. "I sold the house I had, bought a cheaper house and worked harder." She's coming back, but things are still tight. "It's a shell game: this will pay for that; this will pay for that this month."

Olivier Touraine, a Frenchman working in Los Angeles, helped design a Japanese airport for Renzo Piano soon after graduating from architecture school in the late '80s. He later taught at Columbia University and worked for future Pritzker winners Koolhaas and Jean Nouvel. In 2007, the *New York Times* profiled Touraine and his talented wife, Deborah Richmond, as a green-design power couple—and sometime professional rivals who had recently completed a home refurb for director Wim Wenders. Living in a sleek and sustainable new house made of redwood and corrugated steel that the couple designed, not far from Venice Beach, the gentlemanly, intellectual Touraine seemed like someone destined to thrive.

These days, however, "We are making less than a cleaning lady," Touraine says, sitting in Wurstküche, the high-design gastropub that serves the architecture students of SCI-Arc. He's exaggerating, of course, but the dried-up residential work hit his firm especially hard. "Architects' fees are based on construction costs—those are going down. When you do the math at the end, you end up with less. You have to get more work, but you have fewer employees. It was six employees, plus us. Now we have an intern two mornings a week." When he looks around at his colleagues, things don't look much brighter. "Everybody has been massively laying off." But the pain is not evenly distributed. "The bigger you are, the better you can pass through the storm. And if you are rich enough, even if [your firm] is very small, you can be okay, even if you are losing ridiculous money.

They are trust-fund babies: somehow the recession has been good for them; it has exterminated the competition."

Numbers are also deceptive because small firms often don't technically die. "They can't exactly close," he said. "They freeze. Or they close their professional space and move into their backyard or garage." Others buy cheap land in developing countries and design self-funded projects of their own to give clients a sense of forward motion. "It's completely staged." For small firms that keep struggling, the pain bleeds into a marriage. "I'm almost more surprised when I hear people are still together," said Touraine, who recently separated from his wife. "It's like having two guinea pigs in the same cage—night and day, you bring the stress back." Their firm, like their marriage, has since ended.

What's striking is that the troubles architecture has experienced have not been primarily driven by technology, as have the disruptions in many other creative fields. Architecture has certainly been reshaped by digital tools, especially those that make drawing and rendering easier—which caused job losses a generation ago. But technology doesn't seem to be putting large numbers of people out of work these days the way a slumping economy, state-sponsored austerity, and the instabilities of globalization are—at least, not yet. (Two decades ago, musicians, journalists, and photographers were enjoying what digital technology made possible, with little sense of how it would undercut their labor.) Despite architecture's trouble, the field's integrity has been defended, with varying degrees of success, by professional organizations and standards, most centrally the American Institute of Architects, the licensing process, graduate degrees, and so on. Architecture, in a sense, still has a guild.

To find a parallel field without these advantages, let's look to graphic design—another craft that has acquired a hip patina. Slammed by the great recession, the percentage of unemployed recent graduates lurked around 12 percent. But these grads are not, years into the recovery, the ones who need to worry the most: the lack of emphasis on traditional credentialing leaves graphic artists open to being undercut in a how-low-can-you-go economy. In the summer of 2013, the American Institute of Graphic Arts, the professional association for design, celebrated the fact that its "confidence index" was down by only a hair.

One designer who's seen the value of graphic arts training and experience fade is Eric Almendral, a native of Fort Worth who came to Los Angeles to work for the *New Times* weekly there. Laid off when the paper closed in 2002, Almendral— who has a clean, modern style, a passion for retro fonts, and an unshakably steady temperament—quickly found regular freelance work. But the money that makes a career in graphic design possible typically comes from a company's marketing or public relations budget, and those budgets were slashed or cut entirely. "It all started going away," he said. "It was immediate—there was no lag or delay. I was doing a project for Toyota—when they had their first bad quarter, they killed their marketing budget. I was done."

Many graphic artists lost their livelihoods with the decline of newspapers and magazines, and with the business slowdown of 2008–9. But the more enduring problem— and what's kept graphic design ailing even with a supposed recovery—is the place where technology collides with culture. The fall of print, and print values, has been as fatal to graphic artists as the recession. The software program

PowerPoint, for instance, convinced a lot of firms that they could do without graphic designers. "Millions of executives around the world are sitting there going, 'Arial? Times Roman? Twenty-four point? Eighteen point?'" Cathy Belleville, a graphic artist who later worked for PowerPoint, told the *New Yorker*. Some designers lose patience with the constant need to keep up with new software and hardware, financially and creatively: they feel like the technology is using them and not the other way around.

The root problem, Almendral said, is a new and pervasive ethos that cheaper is not only a good thing, it's the only thing. The ideology of Walmart and Amazon (where bots search for comparisons and set prices to undercut competition, even if it means losing money) has seeped into our psychology, making it harder to work as a skilled craftsman. "There are plenty of people," he noted,

> who are satisfied by something that they think looks "good enough," because they don't understand that a professional could be better than a kid who learned it off YouTube. What I hear a lot is, "Anyone could do that job if they learned the software." It's like saying, "If you learn all the keys on the piano, you can compose music." You can give someone a hammer and a pile of wood—that doesn't mean that they're Frank Lloyd Wright.
>
> People are confusing the tools with the work. That drives down prices and rates, and brings a lot of hucksters and phonies into the profession, because they work cheap. The technology has demystified the trade. Once you're sitting down in front of the same instru-

ment that everyone else has, the impression is that you are a software jockey—people don't see how that's different from doing an Excel spreadsheet.

The shift to a digital and online world has been good for some graphic artists—the Web, we were told, would open up limitless space for design, journalism, commentary, photography, and so on. But for a photographer or designer working on, say, album covers, the canvas has shrunk from the old twelve-by-twelve-inch vinyl LP to the CD case to the iPhone screen. This logic has asserted itself beyond the world of record jackets, and will not get any better even if the economy does. "I started out doing logos and icons, right out of college," said Felix Sockwell, an award-winning illustrator and onetime design director now based in New Jersey. "And now I'm back to doing that." Sockwell has produced illustrations for everyone from Blue Note Records to *Poetry* magazine to the Republican party. But the days when a full-page magazine illustration would pay enough to keep the lights on began to disappear at the dawn of the twenty-first century, and even established designers like Sockwell got slammed with the recession and the shrinking of magazines and papers.

When the economy began to come back, the work that returned paid less. Most online publications, he said, "spend almost no money on illustrations or photography." When Internet sites do hire graphic artists, he says, they pay 30 or 40 percent less than the same job had paid in print. One thing today's art departments have in common, whether for websites, magazines, or corporate clients, and whether for graphic designers or photographers, is their reluctance to pay in a timely manner. You have to all but subpoena some of them to get paid, Sockwell says. Between publications going under, business bankruptcies, and general economic instability, "I end up having to threaten people to pay: 'Here's my bank information, Wire the money to me by Friday or I will never work for you again.' It's a dog-eat-dog world: Everybody is being crushed right now."

Rebecca Johnson and Jeff Klarin are two midcareer graphic designers who've not only stayed employed, but made technology work for them. Klarin remembers working with X-Acto knives and paste-ups as a student, but now he talks about buying a new digital printer the way a teenager might rave about getting a Stratocaster for Christmas. Their firm, Bughouse, finds an ingenious Generation X solution to our current state: their homages to the analog world (wood surfaces with heightened grain, retro images of trees, worn old record jackets) are rendered mostly with digital tools. So they are neither doomsayers nor Luddites.

But they've also seen firsthand how parts of the field have been hollowed out: Design sites offer pre-made logos and templates for nothing, or close to it, which makes it nearly impossible for experienced designers to get work of that kind. A flood of recent graduates are willing to toil for close to free. An old client—a documentary film production company that hired Johnson and Klarin for motion graphics and titles—went out of business. A compositor friend— someone who arranges images for film composition—now trains dogs. "Ten years ago, everyone was doing really well," Johnson said of her creative-class peers. "Now I can't think of anybody who is. I don't know anybody who's doing 'really well' now—maybe our veterinarian friends, our lawyer friends." But Bughouse has found a way to adapt. As some aspects of their business have virtually disappeared, Bughouse has filled in the gaps by doing limited-edition artworks—silkscreens, sculptures, prints, some for set design. The people buying this stuff—entertainment industry executives, in many cases—are still wealthy. For now, that keeps them going. "We're just trying not to be poor," Klarin said. "Trying to hold on to our medical insurance," Johnson added.

Even Bestor, who is lucky enough to have boundless energy and talents that sync nicely with the state of the marketplace, worries about what awaits the younger generation of architects. Architecture has always been a tough field for newcomers. "Your salary starts at the schoolteacher level," she said, "but then you watch your friends who went to other professional schools go up and up, while yours stays the same. If they went to dental school they make more than you." It forces students to be cautious at the time in their careers when they should be stretching out and taking chances.

The current uncertainty makes the old model—poverty in youth, payday sometime in middle age—harder to count on. Bestor fears that after centuries as a profession, architecture will return to the patronage system, in an age of dwindling patrons. Or become a profession where "only rich kids can do quirky stuff and everyone else has to work for corporate firms."

Spooked by the marketplace, more and more students are going right into teaching from grad school, getting little or no professional experience. It's hard to blame students who graduate with significant financial pressure. Architecture differs from most creative-class fields by requiring extensive university training, and as university costs soar, financial aid dwindles, and student grants turn into enormous loans, entering the field will become an increasingly steep bet, and increasingly off-limits for the middle class. "If you go to a private school, you can easily come out with $100,000 in debt," Horton said. "For a graduate program, it's hardly unheard of to have $50,000 to $60,000. Then you have all the fees associated with getting your license."

Plus, thanks to an old-school ethos of paying your dues—as well as the freeze in building—today's students often wade through round after round of low-paying internships before getting a full-time job, only to find that salaries have declined or that the job doesn't last.

"It's not good for me," Touraine, who now teaches at USC, says of the field's sour state. "But I've had my good time. I probably won't be able to climb the way I wanted to. But I won't be homeless; I can teach. I'm really concerned about a generation that won't get a chance," who won't design a project that gets built. As for his generational peers, "We're pissed off, we're frustrated, we're overstressed. But as an educator, I feel like an ayatollah sending kids running into the minefield."

When he looks ahead, Touraine sees some hope in Japan, as well as some other countries still investing in housing and infrastructure, in contrast to the constriction in the United States. "There will be fewer and fewer firms, and they will all get bigger. The discipline of architecture will become more and more corporate. I can't imagine the Pritzker Prize will be going to American architects in fifteen or twenty years."

The crisis has implications beyond architects themselves, Touraine says. "It's much better in terms of competition and creativity to have five hundred firms of five people than five firms with five hundred people each," Touraine says. "Corporate America's firms are not that good, and they are often a lot more expensive. They've got effective monopolies, and they have very strong contacts because they have enormous marketing wings. That gives you a restricted choice, especially if it means commissions from China or the UAE," places where it's hard for an independent firm to get a hearing. Small firms, he said, which are typically more innovative, are increasingly at a disadvantage.

Horton thinks architects are deeply out of touch with economic reality and aren't leveling with students and young designers. "How do you keep the Kool-Aid and the boosterism flowing when there are no or few prospects after graduation?" he asked, describing what he called a lost generation. "But architecture just grinds on heroically, regardless."

People will always need houses, cities and nations will always need schools and libraries and civic buildings, and trendy restaurants will need redesigns. Architecture will never die completely. It's existed as a calling, in various forms, at least since the medieval master builder. Eric Owen Moss, who regretted having to lay off employees, said he's optimistic about the field. He expects to hire again in the near future—at lower pay and with less stability than he used to offer. Periods of tension sometimes produce fresher thinking. "Maybe there's an opening for new ideas."

The American Institute of Architects, which claims to represent the entire profession but is considered by some critics a cheerleader for corporate firms, has remained cautiously optimistic. The group, based in Washington, D.C., fights to make small advances sound like big victories. Despite bullish forecasts for 2013, the year saw some weak months, some strong ones. "This rebound is a good sign for the design and construction industry," the AIA chief economist, Kermit Baker, reported in June 2013, "and hopefully means that April's negative dip was a blip rather than a sign of challenging times to come. But there is a resounding sense of uncertainty in the marketplace—from clients to investors and an overall lack of confidence in the general economy—that is continuing to act as a governor on the business development engine for architecture firms." Despite predictions of resurgence, in early 2014 the group announced consecutive months of declining billing. Structural forces appear to be as strong as cyclical ones, holding back a revival within the profession.

The state of architecture, overall, reflects the larger story of the creative class in recent years. Security and artistic freedom exist only for those who are independently wealthy. Small independent companies absorb heavy casualties from the crashing of economic waves that large corporations are somewhat shielded from. The middle levels get hollowed out. Barriers to entry tighten. And there's a lingering sense that even as the recession lifts, these industry-wide problems will not abate. Record corporate profits, after all, have not led to a significant increase in design work or construction. These issues, of course, increasingly face the broader middle class in the postindustrial world as well.

Some smell trouble in architecture's sense of itself, as the most visible architects work for high fashion companies —Koolhaas's Prada stores, Gehry's $4,250 earrings for Tiffany and his hat for Lady Gaga—even as the profession suffers. This is part of a process by which the field orients itself around the top 1 percent and contributes to what the economist Michael J. Sandel calls the skyboxing of America. "Most architects in the '50s were building private houses— like the Case Study House project," Touraine said of the effort by *Arts & Architecture* magazine to design stylish, modest homes for the middle class. Even the ornery, individualistic California architect John Lautner, who designed extravagant homes, worked primarily for the middle class. (Even Lautner's signature flying saucer–like Chemosphere House in the Hollywood Hills, which has since become a showplace for wealthy owners, was done for a middle-class client, an aerospace engineer.) "But the idolatry of the starchitects has made it seem like architecture is only for exceptional buildings. Architecture is perceived as a luxury good. It can be—but it's not only that," Touraine said. His original ambition—to design stylish, sustainable homes for middle-class clients like himself—did not survive the move into a post-recession world where the middle has lost ground.

A decline in public spending—belt-tightening by U.S. cities and states, full-on austerity in Europe—kills off the civic projects that allow architects to develop reputations and make their payroll. Universities have slowed their building as well, as state support for both public and private higher education dwindles. The era in which a midcareer architect could jump to the next level by working on a new concert hall or a museum redesign now looks like a closed door—the bulk of this growth took place between 1994 and 2009, and there are few signs it will return.

AFTER TWO FULL YEARS OF pain, Horton got a new job, this time at what appeared to be a stable firm with ample business in China. "As it turned out, China was slowing down, and they weren't able to maintain a large staff anymore." He lost his job, again. For him personally, though, the recession and the blow it dealt his field has had a reasonably happy ending. He's now consulting for design firms, writing about the field, keeping his head above water, and trying not to worry that his family no longer has medical insurance. But he's less sanguine about where things are headed. "Architects are racing each other to the bottom, to get the few jobs that are coming back. Fees are going to take forever to climb back up," he said. "When work is abundant, you can roll with it and get work. You don't need a lot of business skill; you might need your lawyer to smooth things out. When times are bad, it's about business skills, BS, self-promotion. Architects are taking any kind of work they can get. 'I used to do custom houses, but now I'll do a warehouse.'" As the middle-level people at firms have been pushed out, "They bring in junior people who work longer hours. The pressure is on: 'Let's get as much work out of the people we have, instead of hiring.'" Some projects, he admits, are coming back as the economy gradually improves. But many of them are as flaky as housing-bubble financing. "They move from phase to phase, and get put on hold. The investors run out of money, or someone runs off to Macau. It makes an unstable, high-finance-driven field even more unstable." As the profession becomes increasingly globalized, it grows more dependent on China's boom-and-bust cycles, erratically emerging economies, and Middle Eastern oil money. In what could be a sign of things to come, more and more of the rendering and production work is being outsourced to China.

More broadly, the downturn has shown the contradictions of a field built on wait-your-turn hierarchy, a sense of self-importance, and a culture of sacrifice. And it showed that the world had changed from the postwar decades of professional loyalty.

"You had the economic bargain that Robert Reich talks about: You work, and you're taken care of," said Horton, who, born in 1968, is old enough to have seen the transition from the old model. "This bargain no longer exists—it's not unique to architecture. Architecture is a creative industry, but it's also reflective of shifting paradigms of the middle class. Architects are supposed to be serving society, but I think we're struggling to maintain our position in society."

Some things won't change. "There will always be the star architect smoking cigars," said Touraine. "That glamour is part of the image of the field, the iconic project and the iconic architect, the flair and fashion. It's the signature of the profession, but it doesn't represent the discipline at all." As the society that makes architecture possible changes, he says, "the discipline is transforming itself." As others in the creative class have found, coming out of a punishing recession has led not to a restoration of professional stability and health, but to a world that's been redrawn in ways more fundamental and lasting.

6

IDLE DREAMERS

CURSE OF THE CREATIVE CLASS

There was a siege going on: it had been going on for a
long time, but the besieged themselves were the last
to take it seriously.

—Paula Fox, *Desperate Characters*

THEY'RE PAMPERED, PRIVILEGED, INDULGED—part of
the "cultural elite." They spend all their time smoking pot
and sipping absinthe. To use a term that's acquired currency lately, they're *entitled*. And they're not—after all—real
Americans. This is what we often hear about artists, architects, musicians, writers, and others like them. And it's part
of the reason the struggles of the creative class in the opening years of the twenty-first century—a period in which an
economic crash, social shifts, and technological change have
put everyone from graphic artists to jazz musicians to book

publishers out of work—aren't being taken as seriously as they deserve to be. Or, worse, have been shrugged off.

Neil Young and Bruce Springsteen write anthems about the travails of the working man; we line up for the revival of *Death of a Salesman.* John Mellencamp and Willie Nelson hold festivals and fundraisers when farmers suffer. Taxpayers bail out the auto industry and Wall Street and the banks. There's a sense that manufacturing, or the agrarian economy, is what America is really about. But culture was, for a while, what America did best: we produce and export creativity around the world. So why aren't we lamenting the plight of its practitioners? The Bureau of Labor Statistics confirms that creative industries have been some of the hardest hit, beginning during the George W. Bush years and continuing through the Great Recession. But when someone employed in the world of culture loses a job, it's easier to dismiss or sneer at their plight than when it happens to, say, a steelworker or an auto worker. (Check out, for example, the cruelly unsympathetic online comments to the few stories that tackle the subject, or the backlash to HBO's *Girls* for daring to focus on young New Yorkers with artistic dreams and good educations.)

The musicians, actors, and other artists we hear about tend to be fabulously successful. But the daily reality for the vast majority of the working artists in America has little to do with bling. *Artists in the Workforce,* a report released by the National Endowment for the Arts in 2008, before the Great Recession sliced and diced this class, showed the reality of the creative life. Most of the artists surveyed had college degrees, but they earned less than the average professional, with a median income in 2003–5 of $34,800. Dancers, on average, made a mere $15,000. (More than a quarter of the artists in the eleven fields surveyed live in New York and California, two of the nation's most expensive states, where that money runs out fast. The report has not been updated since 2008.)

"What does it mean in America to be a successful artist?" asked Dana Gioia, the poet who oversaw the study while he was chairman of the NEA. "Essentially, these are working-class people—a lot of them have second jobs. They're highly trained—dancers, singers, actors—and they don't make a lot of money. They make tremendous sacrifices for their work. They're people who should have our respect, the same as a farmer. We don't want a society without them."

The visual art market is difficult to track, and remains mostly opaque. From a distance it looks glamorous and lush. "One thing that's clear regarding art fairs, auctions, and galleries," said New York–based performer and art journalist Alexis Clements, "the largest sales are often in the secondary markets. The artist is not getting any of that money. And artists, like freelancers, have a lot of trouble getting paid; some of them are suing their galleries. Because of all the attention to the glitz and glamour of the visual arts, there's an assumption that it trickles down."

Nonprofit galleries and organizations aren't always an improvement. "People don't realize that when they walk into a museum show, the artist makes nothing," Clements said. A survey of visual artists by the group Working Artists and the Greater Economy revealed that 58 percent of re-spondents who had shown in nonprofit spaces in New York earned nothing from their exhibitions, not even expenses. Others earned *close* to nothing. Many artists and performers, in fact, are effectively entrepreneurs, but have little of the regard of the lavishly paid, mythically potent CEO. A working artist is seen neither as the salt of the earth by the left, nor as a "job creator" by the right—but as a kind of self-indulgent parasite by both sides. Why the disconnect?

"There's always this sense that art is just play," said Peter Plagens, a New York painter and art critic. "Art is what children do and what retired people do. Your mom puts your work up on the refrigerator. Or the way Dwight Eisenhower said, 'Now that I've fought my battles, I can put my easel up outside.'"

The reality is different. An ecology of churches, chamber series, libraries, on-call studio work, and small and mid-size orchestras that neither pay a salary nor offer medical coverage keep musicians like Adriana Zoppo going. A hard-working freelance violinist who performs across Southern California, she's played, over a twelve-month period, at a church chamber series, on *American Idol,* on a Glenn Frey recording of standards, in the background music for a scene of *Mad Men,* and with her own baroque chamber group. She's also a regular player in the Santa Barbara Symphony (a city so expensive they often have to import their musicians), driving a hundred miles each way for four rehearsals and two concerts a month. "I just do a lot of driving, like every freelancer I know," she said. Every week students come to her apartment for lessons. The economy—and the loss of audience and donors—mean her work is down by about a third. "There's more and more time between jobs." It's even tougher, she noted, for people who rely on the movie studios. "Even before the economy went down, studios started doing more outside California; a lot of it is in eastern Europe." For those who made their living playing on records and movie soundtracks, "All of a sudden, they're making about 60 percent of what they did. What I see is a lot of people looking for things outside music—a lot of people have gotten real estate licenses. I know people who've added massage therapist" to their list of occupations. Some have dropped medical coverage they can't afford, taking their chances.

Of course, those who continue to work in the creative class are the lucky ones. Employment numbers from the Bureau of Labor Statistics show just how badly the press and media have missed the story. For some fields, the damage tracks, in an extreme way, along with the Great Recession. Jobs in graphic design, photographic services, and architectural services all peaked before the market crashed, falling 19.8 percent over the next four years for graphic design, 25.6 percent over seven years for photography, and a brutal 29.8 percent over just three years for architecture. (The bureau's categories count all of the jobs in a given field, including the people who, say, answer the phone at a design studio.) The category of "theater, dance, and other performing arts companies," which includes everything from Celine Dion's shows in Vegas to small groups that put on Pinter plays in boxy rooms, were down 21 percent between 2006 and 2011. These numbers tell an even harsher tale when we consider that U.S. population grew by 26.5 million people between 2000 and 2010: these fields would have had to increase by a percentage point or two each year just to keep up with the added supply in the job market.

Other fields show how the recession aggravated existing trends, but reveal that an implosion arrived before the market crash and has continued through our supposed recovery. "Musical groups and artists" plummeted by 45.3 percent between August 2002 and August 2011. "Newspaper, book, and directory publishers" are down 35.9 percent between January 2002 and a decade later; jobs among "periodical publishers" fell by 31.6 percent during the same period. So why hasn't this predicament gotten more attention?

Perhaps creative types, we suspect, are supposed to struggle. Artists themselves often romanticize their fraught beginnings: Patti Smith's resonant memoir of her early years with the photographer Robert Mapplethorpe, *Just Kids,* and the film and theatrical versions of the busker's tale *Once* show how powerful this can be. But these stories often stop before the reality that follows artistic inspiration begins: Smith was ultimately able to commit her life to music because of an infrastructure, a network of clubs, music labels, and publishers. And however romantic life on the edge seems when viewed from a distance, *Once*'s Guy can't keep busking forever.

Yes, the Internet makes it possible to connect artists directly to fans and patrons. There are stories of fans funding the next album by a favorite musician—but those musicians, as well, acquired that audience in part through the now-melted creative-class infrastructure that boosted Smith. And yes, there have been success stories on Kickstarter, as well—but even Kickstarter accepts just 60 percent of all proposals, and only about 43 percent of those end up being crowdfunded.

Our image of the creative class comes from a strange mix of sources, among them faux-populist politics, changing values, technological rewiring, and the media's relationship to culture—as well as good old-fashioned American anti-intellectualism. But perhaps the image is rooted in the ancient past. After all, it was only relatively late in the evolution of the species—after we settled down into cities and began to accumulate private property—that food surpluses, and with them, specialization, developed and allowed the existence of a creative class for the first time. The resentment may have started there, in the Bronze Age.

We'll probably never know its deepest origins, but we can clearly document the roots of anti-aestheticism in the very founding of the United States. The Puritans who settled on the shores of the Atlantic were austerity-loving religious fanatics who saw art not just as frivolous or womanly, but as idolatry. Before sailing to the new world they'd become notorious across England for smashing stained-glass windows and ripping the benches from church choirs. Much of this aggression was directed against the Catholic church, but the Puritans were no more fond of the church's support for painting and music than they were of other instances of popery. And while much of the landed gentry who led the nation were intellectuals and aesthetes, the frontier myth resonates much more loudly. The real American founding father is the "noble savage"–loving Jean-Jacques Rousseau, the critic Leslie Fiedler wrote, and our early literature is about men fleeing civilization and book learnin' for an unmediated experience with nature at its most raw. When—decades later—vaudeville, circuses, and early motion pictures began to spread, they were denounced for their corrupting influence on the young and working classes. "They were considered a threat to the American way of life," said the popular culture historian Robert J. Thompson.

Europeans, Plagens pointed out, have a very different relationship to the arts because of a high culture going back to the Renaissance and before. "Over here, America is more tied to pragmatism—clearing the land, putting the railroad through. . . . And artists don't really help with that, so we're suspect." The novelist Jonathan Lethem, whose father was what the writer described as "a non-famous artist," sees the American artist as living in internal exile. American history is stamped with "a distrust of the urban, the historical, the bookish in favor of a fantasy of frontier libertarian purity. And the Protestant work ethic has a distrust of what's perceived as decadence."

We don't wear buckles on our hats anymore; even coonskin caps have fallen out of style. But these latent notions in human nature and the American mind have taken a great step forward—or backward—recently. Richard Nixon and Spiro Agnew were demonizing long-haired bohemians, know-it-all professors, journalists, and other seditious types since around the time of Woodstock. (The origins of this kind of right-populism seem to go back to the segregationist hero George Wallace, the Alabama governor who denounced civil rights workers as "pointy-headed intellectuals." Agnew added "effete corps of impudent snobs" and "media elite" to the language.) But these seeds of suspicion and antipathy really blossomed with the invention of the term "cultural elite." During the Murphy Brown wars of 1992, Vice President Dan Quayle spoke at the Commonwealth Club of California, connecting the Los Angeles riots to a group sitting "in newsrooms, sitcom studios, and faculty lounges all over America," jeering at regular people. "We have two cultures," he said, "the cultural elite and the rest of us." Thus was the very word—"elite"—severed from its previous associations (many of them positive) with skill and accomplishment, or wealth and explicit power. (And Quayle was, after all, not only a vice president but a wealthy man who came from several generations of money.) Such attacks on the elite also oriented the resented group around education, culinary tastes (critics always seemed to describe these elites as drinking white wine or lattes), and attraction to culture. Presumably this cultural elite was driving to the opera in its Volvos—somehow managing to both sip a cappuccino and laugh at regular people at the same time—while dreaming up ways to undermine the American way. While the cultural left has led assaults on the literary canon, or the race and gender of artists whose work hangs in museums, and so on, it's rarely duplicated the anti-intellectual populism of the far right quite so well. " 'Cultural elite,' " says Lethem, is "a code word for people who are getting away with something for far too long. It's a term of distrust —you can almost hear a plan for vengeance in it. Republican politics hardened these impulses and made them more virulent and paranoid."

The theater critic and impresario Robert Brustein sees anti-elitism as more bipartisan. "That's where the left and right seem to meet," said Brustein, founder of the Yale Repertory Theatre and the American Repertory Theater. "The word 'elitism,' I think, is one of the most pernicious words ever introduced to the English language. Imagine to use that as an expletive! What it means is leadership, and without leaders you don't have any arts—without people who don't have ideas that nobody's had before."

If someone who takes in culture—or who writes about it or teaches it, as in Quayle's original formulation—is somehow "not like us," the only person more discredited is someone who spends his life producing this stuff. "There is a pampered class of artists in the United States," conceded Gioia. "But it's tiny. And they make insignificant money compared to sports people. We have this Puritan, practical tradition in the United States. Puritans would give to the poor, but not to the idle. Artists are seen as these idle dreamers." More typical than a celebrity artist feasting on enormous grants, he said, is someone like Morten Lauridsen, who is now one of the most performed living composers—after decades of scraping by, teaching and writing choral works. Or a writer like Kay Ryan, who until becoming U.S. poet laureate in 2008 was known to only a small few. "She never applied for a grant, never taught writing," Gioia said. "She taught remedial reading at a community college."

It was the Coast Guard Academy band, in New London, Connecticut, that allowed Kelli O'Connor, a conservatory-trained clarinet and saxophone player, to make a living. These days she's a principal in a nearby regional orchestra, plays with a chamber group at a Boston church, coaches at area high schools, and teaches at the University of Rhode Island. None of these pay a full salary or significant benefits. "Freelancing is a hustle all the time," she said. "You master the art of scheduling. Squeezing in as much as possible. There are some days when I'm not done until 11 or 12 at night, and then I have to get up at 7 in the morning." Like most musicians, she teaches private lessons, but her students have dwindled by more than half. "Because of the economy, it's really gone downhill. People are afraid to spend their money. You're constantly sending your C.V. to local schools to stir up interest."

"More than any other group of artists, musicians are getting a raw deal," said a rare story on the crisis, in *Crain's New York Business.* The story of the struggling musician is nothing new, but with smaller orchestras like the Long Island Philharmonic and the Queens Symphony scaling back, and musicals and dance productions using fewer players or none at all, professional musicians—many who studied for years at prestigious schools like Juilliard—are facing an increasingly tough time. They are being forced to piece together bits of freelance work, take on heavy teaching schedules, or leave the business altogether. Over the past decade, the number of members of the Associated Musicians of Greater New York Local 802 has shrunk to 8,500 from about 15,000. Tino Gagliardi, president of Local 802, told *Crain's,* "There are fewer opportunities for musicians, and as the work diminishes, people move on."

It's not just the recession, or just classical players; even as the larger economy has begun to come back, the creative class continues to dissipate. Musicians in Hollywood used to be able to make a decent living working for movies and television shows in studios by day, and then take their artistic chances in smaller combos playing clubs at night. Studio employment provided the fuel for the West Coast jazz movement of the 1940s and '50s, and for players of all kinds in decades after that. But from 2007 to 2014 Hollywood studio musicians have seen their earnings cut approximately

in half—a loss of $15 million—according to the American
Federation of Musicians Local 47. With their earnings collapsing, the entire ecology withers.

MOST PEOPLE GET THEIR IDEAS about artists and entertainers from the media—TV, the newspapers, radio, and so
on. When we see actors, musicians, and architects on the
covers of magazines or on television, we think we're getting an intimate look at the creative class. But most often,
we don't see them at all. Newspapers, especially, have long
felt a romanticism, and sense of duty, toward a "man in
the street," a kind of salt-of-the-earth figure who could—
depending on the location or era—come out of Springsteen
or Steinbeck. "There's the old saw about afflicting the comfortable and comforting the afflicted," said James Rainey,
who reports on the press for the *Los Angeles Times* and is
one of few journalists who has written well on the damage
to his own industry.

Coverage of the most vulnerable is among the noble
things that what remains of the press still does. But it means
that some strata get overlooked. When papers have written
about the recession, for instance, they've leaned heavily on
coverage of the poor and working class; professionals, say,
losing their homes because of the unemployment or falling
housing values hardly show up. One mainstay in recession-
era stories about the creative class has been pieces about
artists who have "reinvented" themselves—an architect
brewing a perfect cup of coffee—in difficult times. Or artsy
types who have pursued their "Plan B"—making vegan
cupcakes or running a groovy ice cream truck. Fun to read,

counterintuitive, more colorful than dreary unemployment statistics—and deeply unrepresentative of the reality that is gripping an entire class.

More representative—and harder to find—is the kind of thing veteran food writer Amanda Hesser conceded on the blog Food52: that she can no longer advise even talented and diligent young journalists to follow her path. "Except for a very small group of people (some of whom are clinging to jobs at magazines that pay more than the magazines' business models can actually afford), it's nearly impossible to make a living as a food writer," she wrote, "and I think it's only going to get worse."

One side of the equation, though, is well covered. The celebrity-industrial complex has all but exploded since the 1980s. Rainey recently spoke to a magazine editor who complained about being held hostage by a marketplace that demanded more and more coverage of people famous for being famous. "Part of this is because there are so many more news outlets than thirty years ago," he said. "When I started out, you didn't have *Us, OK,* so many supermarket tabloids that are big sellers and all about celebrity. On the TV side, there are hundreds of channels about celebrities, and you've got TMZ on the Web, Perez Hilton. . . . That's pulled some of the mainstream outlets in that direction."

But newspapers, which by some estimates have laid off as many as 80 percent of their arts writers since the turn of the century, may not be in the best position to document the crumbling of non-corporate culture outside Hollywood and television (which together consume the lion's share of media coverage). In their anxiety not to seem elitist, they may shy away from the struggles of folks in the fine and performing arts especially. They're busy keeping up with the Kardashians or deconstructing Robin Thicke. It's nothing as craven or cynical as "media bias," but the full picture of culture in the United States doesn't get told. Rainey agreed: "There's more attention to celebrities than to everyday people who put together productions, or who struggle to make a living in the arts." As a result, to most Americans, this middle class of the creative class might as well be invisible.

Technology has reshaped this issue in another way. "The stereotype of the creative genius has not let go when we look at people out of the past," said Thompson, the Syracuse University historian. He cited a number of costume-drama images—crazy-brilliant figures like Mozart and Van Gogh—whose prestige is undiminished and whose work is still widely revered. "But we are much less willing to apply this to people who are still alive. Because distribution has been democratized by the Internet, we tend to think that talent has been democratized as well." If everyone can post their videos on YouTube, why are some filmmakers richer and more famous than others? "I think it's changed the way we look at the contemporary creative class. A lot of it is resentment: Why are you up there when I can do this too?"

The prejudice against the creative class is part of a larger revolt against experts and expertise. When was the last time we saw an artist or an intellectual in a mainstream film, set in the present rather than a romanticized past, who was not evil or pretentious? Look at even B movies from the 1950s and you see another world. The writer Phillip Lopate called intellectual seriousness "the last taboo" in an essay that looked at how filmmakers and studio bosses who had come from Broadway or German-speaking Europe gave way to a movie landscape in which mature intelligence exists only to be mocked or undercut. "Of course, intelligence has always been associated with villainy (Mephistopheles, Iago), and simpler minds with virtue," he observed. But the process has amplified in our time. "Why is 'dumb' such a powerful metaphor for the American mood? Conversely, why has it become so rare nowadays to see onscreen a lively, functioning intelligence—an articulate, educated, self-aware character with an inner life? . . . The struggle to lead an unillusioned life is nowhere visible on our screens." We've come a long way since the time of Sputnik, when education and intelligence were valorized in a burst of Cold War chauvinism.

Steve Jobs and technological heroes are still worshiped, said Thompson, but it doesn't translate to creative people who do things that are intangible or hard to understand. "I've seen people walk into a museum and say, 'I can do that,'" he said. "They can't, of course. But when their computer breaks down, they know they can't fix it. Creativity is a form of expertise," something that we, as a democracy, have never been entirely comfortable with.

There are other changes in sensibility besides rabid faux-populism that spell hostility to the arts and those who work in them. One of them is a kind of market fundamentalism—the idea that everything, whether education, culture, or the state of our souls, can be bought, sold, and measured. "What isn't for sale?" asked a recent book by the political philosopher Michael J. Sandel. (You can now buy "access to the car pool lane while driving solo," rent a woman's womb, "shoot an endangered black rhino," and get your doctor's cellphone number if you're willing to pay for it, Sandel pointed out in *What Money Can't Buy.* The growth of for-profit hospitals, warfare, community security, and universities—which have recently gotten a sweet tax break— show how far we've gone in the past few decades.) "The market will give you a voice, empower you to do whatever you want to do," Thomas Frank wrote in his summary of today's rah-rah neoliberalism, "and if you have any doubts about that, then the market will crush you and everything you've ever known."

We see this same point of view—without the irony—in economic impact studies of the arts and the push for what's called "cultural tourism"—museums and philharmonics arguing for their worth based on the capital they generate. You see it, from the opposite side, when a cultural entity goes bankrupt. When a Kentucky newspaper reported the Chapter 11 filings of the Louisville Orchestra, the reader comments generated by the story gave a sense of the way many people think about culture and the market (reproduced here in all their typo-filled glory): "Get rid of them, the Ballet and any other useless tax funded 'entertainment' that isnt self supporting," one said. "Pack up your fiddles and go home boys and girls. Maybe find real jobs. Go to Nashville and vie for some sessions work." A third: "Sale all of assets to pay these people off, fire them all and get rid of the Orchestra. It isnt popular with the residents or they would have packed crowds and not have to worry about $$$." And unambiguous in its market fundamentalism: "The orchestra creates a product. That product has lost public appeal. Just like any business, this one needs to shut down. If your product isn't selling there is no reason to continue in business." Needless to say, classical music and other art forms originated and evolved in the age of patronage, well before the full-fledged market economy. Such prejudices re-call Oscar Wilde's assessment: "A cynic is a man who knows the price of everything and the value of nothing."

"Everything now has to be fully accountable," said Plagens. "An English department has to show it brings in enough money, that it holds its own with the business side. Pub-lic schools are held accountable in various bean-counting ways. The senator can point to the 'pointy-headed profes-sor' teaching poetry and ask, 'Is this doing any good? Can we measure this?' It's a culture now measured by quantities rather than qualities. We don't have any faith any more in the experts when they say, 'Trust us.'" Lethem added: "These days everything has to have a clear market value, a proven use for mercantile culture. Well, art doesn't pass that test very naturally. You can make the art gesture into something the marketplace values. But it's always distorting and grotesque." (The awkward fit reminds him of the Philip K. Dick story "The Preserving Machine," about a scientist who tries to convert treasured musical scores into animals that can survive an apocalypse—with unpleasant results.)

In some ways, the obsession with economics—both in-side and outside the arts—is driven by economics itself. "Forty years ago," said Plagens, who chronicled the West Coast art scene of the '60s and '70s in a gem of a book, *Sunshine Muse,* "you rented an art gallery for not much money, and bought a few gallons of white paint. Now you need investors and backers and all sorts of digital technol-ogy. So there's a bigger emphasis on having a business plan than the old bohemian model."

Despite the crisis in the creative fields in general, mass-distributed entertainment is booming. (Movies, because they cost consumers less than most live entertainment, are typically countercyclical.) "Popular art and commercial art is a form of escape," said Plagens. "It's what people want, especially in hard times; it's what you got in the '30s, with movies about the heiress who disguises herself as a poor working girl, and so on," which he sees as the precursor to today's tidal wave of sequels, remakes, and lame romantic comedies. "Serious art—novels, what you have in the galleries—brings you back to reality and makes you look at your life. Serious art makes people uncomfortable—and during these times, we don't need more discomfort."

The final irony is that these are times—disoriented, characterized by information overload and eroding certainties—when we most need the arts. But we seem strangely resistant to culture and the people who produce and disseminate it.

7

THE END OF PRINT

What Orwell feared were those who would ban books.
What Huxley feared was that there would be no reason to ban
a book, for there would be no one who wanted to read one.
Orwell feared those who would deprive us of information.
Huxley feared those who would give us so much we would be
reduced to passivity and egoism. Orwell feared that the truth
would be concealed from us. Huxley feared the truth would
be drowned in a sea of irrelevance.

—Neil Postman, *Amusing Ourselves to Death*

THE LUSH JUNGLE VILLAGE OF Macondo, with its shards
of ice like diamonds and stones like dinosaur eggs, and the
woman who levitated to heaven; the Great Plains and dry
Nebraska prairies of the pioneers; rough dogs pulling sleds
across Alaska's tundra; America's open road of fellowship
and possibility, from the Brooklyn docks to the waves of the

Pacific; a woman on a bridge in World War I Milan, selling roasted chestnuts.

They're all images we have because of novelists and poets—Gabriel García Márquez, Willa Cather, Jack London, Walt Whitman, Ernest Hemingway—who did some of their crucial early work writing for newspapers and magazines. Since the 1960s, the alternative press has produced its own talents, and we could add nearly an entire recent generation of British writers—Martin Amis, the late Christopher Hitchens, and James Fenton among them—who came up through the *New Statesman* alone. This list goes on forever. Suffice to say, journalistic training has been a crucial stage, and sometimes more than that, for numerous imaginative writers, allowing aspiring or apprentice novelists or poets to see parts of the world that would otherwise be unavailable to them, to learn to think critically about wars and crime and politics, or simply to sharpen their writing of sentences, deepen their sense of the language.

Journalism has a deceptive relationship to the creative class. The man in the fedora with the press card in its brim seems far removed from the composer of symphonies, the painter of canvases, or even the record-store dude in his vintage duds. But newspapers and magazines have not only served as training grounds, they've been part of the same ecology as publishing houses, museums, and concert halls: critics and cultural journalists have helped shape culture and bring prestige to its makers for five centuries. And increasingly, the plight of a newspaper reporter, magazine illustrator, or photojournalist has followed the same gloomy trajectory as the rest of the creative class. Despite superficial differences—journalists are less likely to have tattoos than indie rockers—people who work for publications fit very squarely among creatives. However pragmatic they may have seen themselves as in decades past, in the twenty-first century, journalists are nearly as likely to be struggling or underemployed as a modern dancer, cellist, or stage actor. Journalists are caught in the same trap as the "content creators" they chronicle. And while the high-end literary journalist or art critic sits most comfortably next to a playwright or a poet, all reporters worth their salt are first and foremost storytellers. It's not just technology, or the recession, but also anti-elite rage, market populism, and corporate consolidation that have led their own stories to run out.

First, the good news. "There's more great content published now than ever before," said David Daley, who became the editor in chief of the site Salon.com after years writing and editing for newspapers in Hartford, Louisville, and suburban New York. "There's a reason why the Internet so quickly reduced some of these papers to irrelevance, aided by the incompetence of some of our leading newspaper chains. The Internet collects groups of people and allows them to pursue their interests in previously unheard of ways: If you were interested in anything from deep political analysis of bills on Capitol Hill, to University of Colorado football, you better hope you live in Washington or Denver." Now, geography is banished.

Book coverage, in particular, he said, has improved, with sites like *The Millions, The Rumpus,* and the *Los Angeles Review of Books* (some of which don't pay or offer only a token fee to writers) creating a lively review ecology even as newspapers and magazines slash book sections and literary-minded weeklies go under. For the budding Edmund Wilsons and Mary McCarthys, there have never been more places to write for. The problem only arrives if the writer has rent to pay or food to buy. "In some ways it's a golden age for the reader. But it's not a golden age for the journalist," Daley said. (Book coverage also shows how vulnerable friendly, organic fan communities are to corporate hijacking: the good-hearted site GoodReads was bought in 2013 by Amazon.)

"We don't have a journalism problem," said Kit Rachlis, the well-regarded editor who once headed the *Village Voice*, *Los Angeles* magazine, and the now imploding *American Prospect*. "We have a business-model problem." An exact count is hard to reach, but journalism has almost certainly lost tens of thousands of jobs since the onset of the recession. The St. Louis–based blogger Erica Smith has tracked newspaper layoffs and buyouts on her Paper Cuts site, documenting almost sixteen thousand job losses in 2008 and roughly seventeen thousand the following year. The damage has been widespread but not equally distributed. Reporting from Washington and foreign bureaus—the kinds of places not likely to pay for themselves with advertising—have been slashed. Since 2000, nearly 80 percent of the reporters and critics covering the arts for print publications have lost their jobs, according to Doug McLennan of ArtsJournal .com—who calls it "a bloodbath"—with severe slashing at Portland's *Oregonian* and London's *Independent,* as well as on the Web at deep-pocketed MSN (owned by Microsoft, with its $78 billion in revenues), which killed its entire freelance arts and entertainment budget. Among the losses at the once-great *Village Voice* alone were Robert Christgau, Nat Hentoff, and J. Hoberman. Similarly, "Only two of America's top 100 magazines have a writer or an editor assigned to art," Tyler Green writes in *Modern Art Notes;* according to Suzanne Carbonneau of the NEA, "There are now only two full-time staff dance critics in all of America." Between MSN and the *Voice,* Christgau has now effectively been laid off twice. Science journalism, which also requires expertise and does not attract movie or plastic-surgery ads, has been hit similarly hard.

Approximately three hundred newspapers fell in 2009 alone. "When a newspaper dies in America," essayist Richard Rodriguez wrote, "it is not simply that a commercial enterprise has failed; a sense of place has failed." In a single month of 2008, the Newark (New Jersey) *Star-Ledger* reduced its staff by almost half. The leading paper in a rich, populous, and famously corrupt state, the *Star-Ledger* took its statehouse bureau down from thirteen reporters to four. (Even in this diminished state, the paper was able to break the Chris Christie bridge scandal, but we'll never know what stories the *Star-Ledger* and others aren't able to discover.) The San Francisco Bay Area has seen its reporting corps cut almost by half over the past decade, even as the region has boomed.

Some things have popped up online to offer hope for those who lost their jobs. A few superstar journalists—Andrew Sullivan, Ezra Klein, Nate Silver—have developed strong identities and followings online that don't depend on institutions. The website Grantland offers smart sports and pop culture coverage, driven by ESPN money. Websites, of course, have proliferated. Some sites do good work and pay a living wage. But most of them are aggregators, sites that sell journalism—the illusion of it, anyway—without journalists.

They simply repackage existing "content," competing in the same ad marketplace with the publications that actually conceived, reported, and edited the stories they steal. Author Robert Levine breaks the arrangement down this way: "You've got two outlets competing to sell ads. The one that doesn't invest makes money. The one that does, doesn't."

Demand Media is a content mill that pays fifteen dollars for stories and selects them based on advertiser demand; they call it "listening to the consumer." Associated Content calls itself "The People's Media Company" and functions like a temp agency. Pasadena Now covers the refined California city . . . with freelancers churning out copy from India and parts unknown, with made-up Anglo bylines. Journatic pays reporters in the Philippines thirty-five to forty cents for "250 pieces/week minimum." And Automated Insights has taken outsourcing one step further: it removes human labor completely, using algorithms to repurpose statistics into articles for sports and real estate sites.

As print has suffered, futurists hailed two larger trends: The news would migrate online, and it would become "hyperlocal," in emulation of the foodie commitment to locavore cuisine. These two trends came together with AOL's Patch, which required an underpaid army of reporters to file, according to AOL's CEO Tim Armstrong, "five to ten stories per day," chosen to stimulate advertising. In 2013, AOL dropped about half of Patch's staff. That's not the first of the post-print solutions that was going to show musty print types how backward they were. In 2011, Rupert Murdoch began the high-end iPad app the Daily, with a staff that included serious journalists. It folded the following year. Tina Brown's reboot of *Newsweek*—purchased in

2010 for a dollar—and the online Daily Beast seemed like a great idea, but by 2013 the magazine had ceased printing and Brown had moved on to other things. (A print *Newsweek* was revived in 2014, though it's unclear how long it can last. The Beast, meanwhile, has cut staff.)

In general, the Web has put downward pressure on freelance rates and salaries. Some magazines now pay staffers half what they used to; some pay literally nothing for contributions to their websites, others close to it. It is possible to extend the logic of the unpaid internship—free labor exchanged for prestige that pays off somewhere down the line—well into midcareer. Newspapers have laid off experienced staff and replaced them with poorly paid bloggers. Even some of the best national websites typically pay less than what an alternative weekly paid in the '90s. Some have joined a group, inspired by the writing of Jaron Lanier and aimed at "freelance content providers," called Stop Working for Free. "Deciding to become a rock writer makes about as much sense as sleeping with a hooker," journalist Peter Gerstenzang wrote recently. "You usually wake up broke." Once again, the superstars and the serfs are still there—it's what used to be the broad middle that's dropping out.

Even the better sites are no replacement for solid print outlets. The Huffington Post, for instance, is a site that has won a well-deserved Pulitzer Prize for a series on wounded veterans. But much of the site is based on volunteer labor and content from elsewhere. "The Huffington Post is a brilliantly packaged product with a particular flair for addressing the cultural and entertainment tastes of its overwhelmingly liberal audience," journalist Tim Rutten wrote after it was purchased by AOL for $315 million. He went on to say:

To grasp its business model, though, you need to picture a galley rowed by slaves and commanded by pirates. Given the fact that its founder, [Arianna] Huffington, reportedly will walk away from this acquisition with a personal profit of as much as $100 million, it makes all the Post's raging against Wall Street plutocrats, crony capitalism and the Bush and Obama administrations' insensitivities to the middle class and the unemployed a bit much.

The fact is that AOL and the Huffington Post simply recapitulate in the new media many of the worst abuses of the old economy's industrial capitalism—the sweatshop, the speedup and piecework; huge profits for the owners; desperation, drudgery and exploitation for the workers. No child labor, yet, but if there were more page views in it . . .

The sites that do create original content and aim high in their delivery have perilous business models: Salon.com, with its mix of sophisticated content and attention-seeking framing, and the smart, often contrarian Slate.com have struggled to achieve profitability. ("People don't even unpack anymore," Slate editor Jacob Weisberg said as he moved into his ninth office in fourteen years.) Politico does good work covering Washington politics, but reportedly earns most of its revenue on its print edition.

More than with other sectors of the creative class, the woes of journalists resonate beyond their own personal circumstances. The decline of print has consequences not just for our culture, but for our democracy. In 2010, the Pew Research Center released an assessment of the way the press and media worked in Baltimore, "The Study of the News Ecosystem of One American City." It showed that print—primarily the *Baltimore Sun*—originated about 95 percent of news stories. And this was after a period of staff cutting in which the *Sun*'s ability to produce original work was down 73 percent from two decades previous.

Studies also show the level of trust toward journalism and the media in general to be at an all-time low. Some of this comes from demagoguery. But the *New York Times*' credulousness in the run-up to the Iraq War and the free-market cheerleading of the financial press ahead of the biggest market collapse since 1929 didn't help.

The original dream of the Internet promised a rich diversity of voices—the mainstream media's monopoly, despised by left and right alike, would be shattered. But as Michael Wolff has documented in *Wired,* "The top 10 Web sites accounted for 31 percent of U.S. pageviews in 2001, 40 percent in 2006, and about 75 percent in 2010." These days, Google, Microsoft, Yahoo, and Facebook garner two-thirds of online ad revenue. As digital outlets proliferate into the space opened up by the closing of newspapers, some kinds of news have thrived, especially specialty sites dedicated to porn, political extremism, paparazzi-style celebrity coverage, and conspiracy theory. Twenty-nine percent of Louisiana Republicans, in a 2013 poll, blamed Barack Obama for the government's ineffective response to Hurricane Katrina in 2005, more than those who faulted the man who was actually president at the time. Since 2008, the proportion of conservative Republicans who believe the president is a Muslim—it is now 34 percent—has doubled. Fox News and rant radio help churn this kind of nonsense on the right, but it's easy to find on the extreme left as well, where some are convinced that President George W. Bush arranged the attacks of September 11, 2001.

Technophiles say that websites—and there are certainly some good ones—make print media obsolete. But in the age of the Internet, we're becoming drastically less informed. Or rather, news junkies know more than ever, but the gap between the most informed and the least has become stark. The percentage of Americans believing in man-made climate change was 75 percent in 2001, and down to 44 percent by 2012. Belief in evolution is lower than it was in the early '80s—46 percent of Americans believe in creationism, according to a 2012 Gallup Poll. A misunderstanding of deficits has had brutal political outcomes; in the case of public health, misinformation about vaccines and other issues has fatal consequences. There are numerous reasons for all this—the revolt against expertise of all kinds, post-Watergate distrust of institutions, the rise of science-hating religious fundamentalism—but part of what's happened is due to the loss of a consensus news source as a thousand websites bloom. If you are seeking confirmation for any wild theory—the Holocaust was a Jewish conspiracy, the Apollo moonwalk was set in a soundstage, the earth is flat— there is a site out there for you. For children growing up in the post-print world, many in schools without librarians, the long-term consequences are especially serious.

The Internet is not the only home of misinformation and propaganda. The army of flacks and spinmeisters has grown in the years that the number of journalists has declined; the former now outnumber the latter by approximately three to one. With the unlimited campaign spending unleashed by the Supreme Court's *Citizens United* decision in 2010, and the fourfold increase in spending on elections, Americans see more and more information about politics, the majority of it now bought and sold by interested parties and appearing without disclosure of its origins. (Similarly, lobbyists in the nation's capital—a $3.31 billion industry, according to the Center for Responsible Politics—now exceed twelve thousand.) One recent innovation, the video news report, or VNR, has a bright future, according to media critic Douglas Rushkoff, as television news deals with its own crisis.

> VNRs have been used by the pharmaceutical industry to sell new drugs, by the oil companies to present themselves as environmentally friendly, and even by the Bush White House in its effort to change public opinion about the postwar effort in Iraq. What makes VNRs ethically questionable is the lack of disclosure. It's one thing to buy a television advertisement; it's another to pass off one's commercial as reported, balanced news. Local TV stations, suffering budget cuts while striving to improve ratings, have little choice but to accept the free, celebrity-rich footage.

There are certainly subcultures for whom the current journalistic climate is very good indeed: crooked politicians and fraudulent business executives. "The next ten to fifteen years will be halcyon days for local corruption," journalist

David Simon told the U.S. Senate in 2009. "It's going to be a great time to be a corrupt politician."

SINCE THE RISE OF MERCHANTS and burghers in the late Middle Ages, the market economy has been a major driver of culture in the West. The Renaissance took off in Italy partly because of the wealth and international trade that were there. Since the breakup of the old aristocracy in the eighteenth century, the market has served as the primary foundation for the creation of music, literature, art, and much else. If epic poetry, as a German historian once wrote, is inconceivable in the world of the printing press, so artistic careers as rich and complex as those of Charles Dickens, the Marx Brothers, Miles Davis, and the Beatles are impossible to imagine without consumer-driven capitalism. (That is, book sales and movie tickets and record sales—rather than patronage or subsidy—supported these figures. The wide reception of this work, and the ability of its creators to keep making more, has certainly been assisted by nonmarket investments like public education.) Markets have brought us much good and plenty bad, but they've at least *functioned* much of the time. In some fields—New York publishing in the 1920s and '30s, Hollywood around midcentury, British rock music in the '60s—the commercial economy worked quite well. For other things—genres that came into being before modern capitalism, such as classical music and opera, say—it's proven less well suited. For yet other forms, this complicated marriage thrived for decades or even centuries, and then, at some point, went bad, even becoming a downright and unredeemed disaster. Like any disastrous marriage, the implosion can lead the two sides to wonder what on earth they ever saw in each other.

That seems to be the case, a decade or so into the twenty-first century, with American journalism. A number of unrelated factors came together around 2008, and most of them are not simple. But taking the long view, the troubles with journalism show the limits and perils of the relationship of commerce and culture. Shorn of its details, the story could be a Marxist parable about market failure, the exploitation of labor, free riders, and the tragedy of the commons.

These days, digital utopians will tell you that the means of transmission—whether we read something in print or online—doesn't matter. But America was a pure product of the print-besotted Enlightenment, and its revolution was jolted into action in part by newspapers and broadsides. It's useful to wonder: How would the United States have turned out if it had been founded before the era of mass literacy? Or by a Mediterranean, Catholic culture? From West to East, rather than East to West? What if it happened in an age dominated by images and pseudo-events, perhaps developing, as Norman Mailer once said of Los Angeles, as if it had been "built by television sets giving orders to men"?

Instead, the nation's formative years came roughly halfway into the four centuries dominated by the printed word. "From the early seventeenth century, when Western culture undertook to reorganize itself to accommodate the printing press," wrote Neil Postman, "until the mid-nineteenth century, no significant technologies were introduced that altered the *form, volume,* or *speed* of information." (What Daniel Boorstin has called the Graphic Revolution, including photography, didn't arrive until then.)

As a consequence, Western culture had more than two hundred years to accustom itself to the new information conditions created by the press. It developed new institutions, such as the school and representative government. It developed new conceptions of knowledge and intelligence, and a heightened respect for reason and privacy. It developed new forms of economic activity, such as mechanized production and corporate capitalism, and even gave articulate expression to the possibilities of a humane socialism. New forms of public discourse came into being through newspapers, pamphlets, broadsides, and books. It is no wonder that the eighteenth century gave us our standard of excellence in the use of reason. . . . America was the first nation ever to be argued into existence in print.

The Founders, who put speech and the press in the very beginning of the Bill of Rights, did not just propose a free press as an inalienable right—something they forbade the government to constrain. They insisted that a free press needed to be protected, and not only from a predatory state. The Founders considered dissent, against any kind of wealth or power, and the circulation of ideas to be crucial to their young democracy. The Postal Act of 1792 was created largely to allow newspapers to circulate freely—in the days before junk mail and electric bills, the postal service existed almost entirely for the sake of publications, and other subsidies and exemptions developed over the years. It's worth emphasizing: The news didn't start out as purely capitalistic by any means, although the usual telling of American history has made it sound like a vigorous, rough-and-tumble nation born the same year as Adam Smith's *Wealth of Nations* was synonymous with the free market itself. The press historian Robert McChesney has referred to the notion that the press was born from the free-market economy as the "immaculate conception" theory of journalism's early days.

It worked reasonably well for a couple of centuries, despite some unpleasant characters and bouts of yellow journalism. Let's pick up the story at a year that's rich with symbolism. By 1984, newspapers hit a landmark: 63.3 million copies a day were sold that year. American population would rise significantly, by about 83 million people through 2013—but the newspaper circulation number would never go up in those thirty years. And by the '80s, a time of great gains by corporations and finance, the corporate era was moving in earnest: *USA Today*—sold from a box that looked like a TV set and dedicated to what it called "the journalism of hope"—made its debut in 1982. The *Chicago Tribune* went public in 1983; the Cowles family sold the *Des Moines Register* to Gannett in 1985, the same year the Bingham family ceded them the *Louisville Courier-Journal;* the family-owned *Baltimore Sun* went to Times-Mirror in 1986.

The cascade, of course, continued into the '90s, until a genuinely family-owned paper, or one following anything but the corporate model, became an anomaly. Despite their protests of attitude and groovy independence, soon enough it became equally true of alternative weeklies as well. Papers had numerous meanings for their employees and readers, but for their ownership, they were essentially cash cows. Profit margins were above 20 percent for most of the decade —above 30 percent for many Gannett papers—and newspapers sold $44 billion in ads in 1998 alone.

The '90s were the peak years of journalistic employment, especially for newspapers. To media scholar Clay Shirky, the whole edifice was predicated on the logic of the printing press, and the way its operating costs created barriers to entry and other economic structures.

The expense of printing created an environment where Walmart was willing to subsidize the Baghdad bureau. This wasn't because of any deep link between advertising and reporting, nor was it about any real desire on the part of Walmart to have their marketing budget go to international correspondents. It was just an accident. Advertisers had little choice other than to have their money used that way, since they didn't really have any other vehicle for display ads.

Seismic as the ownership changes were, it was hard, initially, to discern how the pressures on publications changed. "What happened when newspapers got acquired by corporations?" asked John Carroll, who covered the Vietnam War as a young reporter and later helmed the *Baltimore Sun* and the *Los Angeles Times*. "At first it went pretty well. The money was very good—the corporations kept their shareholders happy but also threw a few dollars to the newsroom." Traditionally, publishers and many of those working on the business side—in circulation, ad sales, and so on—had some experience with the newsroom, and had inhaled a bit of its values, a deceptive mix of wise-cracking cynicism with a sense of giant-killing and professional idealism. But gradually, publishers and others on the business side—circulation people, advertising and marketing direc-

tors, a cereal-company executive turned newspaper CEO—
came from the world of business schools, management theory, and free-market ideology.

The career of Al Neuharth, the executive who built the
Gannett chain into the largest U.S. newspaper publisher
and later founded *USA Today*, revealed the shape of things
to come. He played up his folksy midwestern roots, railed
against stuffy "elitists" and "intellectual snobs," boasting
that his management "would trade profits over Pulitzers any
day." *USA Today*, he said, was different: "It doesn't dictate.
We don't force unwanted objects down unwilling throats."
He started something called the Freedom Forum—who
could be against that? "Since the 'journalism of hope' requires little more than press-release rewriting and virtually
mandates favorable coverage of local businesses," Thomas
Frank pointed out, "it can be done both cheaply and with
an eye to cultivating advertisers." Things were less hope-
ful for the employees and readers. When Gannett bought
a paper in Detroit, it turned its energy on its workers,
provoking a crippling strike that lasted a year and a half.
In Nashville, where Gannett owned one paper, it bought
the city's second daily—to shut it down. As time went on,
management-theory fables about moving cheese or melting
icebergs, corporate motivational speakers, and aboriginal
talking sticks would begin penetrating media-company
boardrooms. And the Gannett ethos moved, gradually, from
the bottom of the journalistic world to the top.

"Editors like me learned not to go into a budget meeting
talking about public service," said Carroll, who recalls corporate brass in the '90s referring to editors as "the priesthood." It wasn't a compliment. "This is very different from

the model of private ownership. Private owners ranged from horrible to great. But the newspaper was allowed to have a purpose outside short-term shareholder value." Often, old-school publishers were driven by their egos. "Your ego might be motivated by someone telling you you're putting out a great publication. Being publisher made you a big wheel in your community. When you had local owners, part of it was about what it could do for society. Also in the way it could help friends and punish enemies." For the corporate owners, "It was about *this* quarter. The long-term didn't exist."

Part of the importance of this period grows from the way another mass-media industry responded to changing demographics and its own ambitions by making different choices. Television was originally free to just about everyone, and like newspapers, each network was obsessed with its reach, since a larger audience brought higher advertising rates. But during newspapers' corporate era, cable television began asking people to pay to watch TV. At first it was mostly a few dozen channels with "bad movies and boxing," in the words of David Simon, the *Baltimore Sun* reporter turned television impresario; HBO was founded in 1972, Showtime four years later, with their penetration spiking in the '80s. "But ultimately, the quantitative increase in programming was accompanied by a qualitative improvement. You paid more, you got more. . . . More channels, more programming, more revenue—indeed, a revenue stream where none had existed." Newspapers, by contrast, sent their profits—which were fulsome—to shareholders and Wall Street, rather than investing in what they did, planning for the future, adjusting to the present, or anything else. "Advertising, not content, was all." (James Fallows uses a different but equally apt parallel: "In the early 1970s, control of the auto companies had passed from 'car men,' who had been trained to design and build automobiles, to 'money men,' who knew all about quarterly profits and stock options but very little about making cars. In the face of Japanese competition, the Big Three floundered until they put 'car men' back in charge.")

Since advertising, corporate shareholders, and an army of self-assured MBAs were running the show, was it any wonder that content—and what would later be called "content providers," the journalists themselves—was considered expendable? Layoffs and buyouts became common in the '90s, as wealthy media companies cried poverty. Simon took a buyout in 1995. "That's well before the Internet began to threaten the industry," he later wrote,

> before Craigslist and department store consolidation gutted the ad base, before any of the current economic conditions applied. In fact, when newspaper chains began cutting personnel and content, the industry was one of the most profitable yet discovered by Wall Street. We know now, because bankruptcy has opened the books, that the *Baltimore Sun* was eliminating the afternoon edition and trimming nearly a hundred reporters and editors in an era when the paper was achieving 37 percent profits.
>
> In short, my industry butchered itself, and we did so at the behest of the same unfettered free market logic that has proven so disastrous for so many American industries. Indeed, the original sin of American newspapering lies in going to Wall Street in the first place.

The Internet introduced itself to Americans as an avatar of freedom, and it was doubly true for the Net's entrée to media companies. Between a recession, shareholder pressures, declining penetration, the competition with television news, shouts of "bias," and so on, newspapers in particular were disoriented. They'd been hearing about the Web, and planning for it, superficially, since the early '90s; the ideology of "free" appealed to Silicon Valley types with sentimental attachments to hippie culture. Futurists and techno-visionaries told executives and editors that releasing their work free on the Web would attract new subscribers, especially those elusive young readers.

There were countless debates about print versus online—which one was better, which one was hipper, what kind of content went best where, and so on. The digital boys talked about how ink, newsprint, printing presses, kids on bicycles with early morning paper routes, all these expenses could be saved in the new regime. But in the long run, it turned out, it was really all about advertising. The Web, of course, offered unlimited space for ads, and increasingly crisp graphics. But the rates online were a small fraction of what they were in print. Adding one reader of the print edition—which allows a publication to get a marginally higher rate from an advertiser—made a very different impact to a publication's bottom line than adding an online reader. Robert Levine, in his book *Free Ride,* said it best:

> According to statistics from the Newspaper Association of America, a print reader is worth an average of about $539 in advertising alone, while an average online reader is worth $26. The money saved on printing

and distribution doesn't come close to covering the difference.

Logically, then, the dumbest move for newspapers would have been to convince their readers to abandon the print edition in favor of their Web site, where they're worth between a tenth and a twentieth as much. Yet this is exactly what most of them have done. They've poured resources into free sites full of extra blogs, video reporting, and data-driven presentations. By improving their online offerings—and often raising the price of the print edition to fund them—newspapers essentially encouraged readers to stop buying physical copies.

Of course, newspapers ran wild with this idea, and magazines absorbed the same ideology even if things played out a little differently for them. (In 2006, *Time* magazine, which typically put cultural and political luminaries on its cover, offered instead a mirror, with the cheery announcement that "You" were the Person of the Year. "For seizing the reins of the global media, for founding and framing the new digital democracy, for working for nothing and beating the pros at their own game, *Time*'s Person of the Year for 2006 is you.")

The digital utopians had not counted on what happened next. Newspaper profits remained fat even into the twenty-first century—peaking at an average of 22.3 percent in 2002—but employment started to fall. "When the money got tight because of competition from the Web," Carroll says, "the corporations showed their true colors." He resigned from the *L.A. Times* in 2005 after being asked to make a series of dramatic staff cuts. That year, the Tribune Company earned more than a billion dollars, for a profit of about 20 percent of revenues. The dark side of the corporate business model started to become clear, even during a pre-recession economy bolstered by a housing bubble. In 2006, Morgan Stanley tried to disrupt the *New York Times*'s two-tiered stock arrangement, which would have made the Gray Lady as vulnerable to takeover as any chain paper. An "activist" investor jolted a hedge fund's ownership of Knight-Ridder, the company whose Washington bureau had demonstrated the most independence and integrity in the runup to the two wars waged by George W. Bush; its publications were sold off and crumbled. Molly Ivins described it as "this most remarkable business plan: Newspaper owners look at one another and say, 'Our rate of return is slipping a bit; let's solve that problem by making our product smaller and less helpful and less interesting.'"

With all of these tensions starting to tear against one another, it didn't take long for things to go bad once the Great Recession hit. The bloodletting has been recounted elsewhere—papers failing in Denver and San Francisco and Seattle, magazines from *Gourmet* to *Vibe* to *Portfolio* to *Metropolitan Home* going belly-up. Even families and companies that worked to protect their journalism bled. The tale of one corporation—the Chicago-based Tribune Company—is extreme in a way that illustrates the larger structural problems. Its story ends with the transfer of nearly $600 million from reporters, editors, critics, photographers, graphic designers, and other members of the creative class to investment bankers and bankruptcy lawyers. (That is, enough to run several really good papers, for years.) Several executives got multimillion dollar golden parachutes. Meanwhile, thousands of people were put out of work, and a century-and-a-half-old company was left a smoking ruin.

AT LEAST A FEW NEWSPAPERS have survived better, one run by a famously liberal family, the other by a conservative corporation: the *New York Times* and the *Wall Street Journal* have also seen layoffs and pressures, but they seem bound to last. Still, today, the post-corporate era has begun. Publications are increasingly owned by wealthy businessmen, acquired by foundations or trusts, or shut down completely. Some publications enjoy a kind of contemporary patronage, operated for the sake of prestige; the *New Yorker* improved its circulation post-recession, but is likely losing money still. The *New York Review of Books,* oddly, continues to make money, perhaps because its readership manages to be, for the most part, both politically progressive and culturally conservative. Magazine subscriptions kept up with population growth from the '70s into the Great Recession, but these days most political magazines, whether on the left or the right, operate at a loss. Some serious magazines generate revenue from events and cruises. Others seem fairly sturdy: *Vanity Fair* will survive for as long as we have Ralph Lauren ads. Papers once owned by chains are now in the hands of hedge funds, private equity firms, and investment bankers expected to "harvest" various parts of them, the way organs are plucked from humans in Kazuo Ishiguro's novel *Never Let Me Go*.

Print publications still exist, and the pace of closing may have slowed, but people have begun to contemplate a world without newspapers, and some digital utopians even celebrate the possibility. When city halls or statehouses or corporate statements don't get attention from trained, fair-minded observers, what appalling development will we not hear about until it's too late? How will we learn about the next Watergate, or the next Enron, if no one is paying attention? We'd become like a lot of other countries, mostly unpleasant ones. "People do awful things to each other," a war photographer says in Tom Stoppard's play *Night and Day.* "But it's worse in places where everyone is kept in the dark."

Here's what John Carroll, speaking to the American Society of Newspaper Editors, imagines:

> If, at some point in America's newspaper-free future, the police decide that the guilt or innocence of murder suspects can be determined perfectly well by beating them until somebody confesses, who will sound the alarm, as the *Philadelphia Inquirer* did in 1977? Or, if those federal scientists who tell our doctors what drugs and what dosages are best for us are secretly allowed to take salaries and stock options from drug companies, how will we know it, if the *Los Angeles Times* is not there to tell us, as it did in 2003? Or, if some future president secretly decides to nullify the law and spy on American citizens without warrants, who—if the *New York Times* falls by the wayside—will sound the warning?

Carroll would like to see a return to the old model of local ownership, in which newspapers were owned by wealthy families for a mix of prestige, power, and civic commitment. "My hope is this could be restored," he says. "The newspaper owners who lived in the town where the paper was published felt an incessant pressure to put out a better paper, and to protect the health of the paper. They weren't looking at the next quarter—they were looking to give the paper to their grandchildren."

This could certainly happen, here and there. But there is no longer a feasible economic model for the newspaper—owning one becomes a commitment to losing money. And the days in which a wealthy local owner could bump into a fellow citizen on the way to the general store—a citizen who might praise or damn what was in the paper that week—are fading fast. Public spaces and any interaction between masters of the universe and the little people are at an all-time low. We're a long way past skyboxing—the very wealthy now live primarily in the air, in business class on their travels on the international conference circuit.

The evaporation of the very wealthy from the communities where they used to be grounded—the Carnegies in Pittsburgh, say—is quickening. At this point, as Chrystia Freeland documents in her 2012 book *Plutocrats,* some of them know their way around only one town: Davos, Switzerland, where it is too snowy and steep for the private drivers who chauffeur them around various financial capitals. When they buy publications, they are likely to be absentee owners. Their world and their readers' have very few points of intersection, and they're not getting any closer.

As newspapers have lost staff, some of their investigative roles have indeed been filled in with online alternatives. Two of the best regarded are the Voice of San Diego—which took off when a new owner turned the city's newspaper into something close to a flyer for the local chamber of commerce—and the MinnPost, which covers a state once well-served by the *Minneapolis Star-Tribune*. These and similar outlets, often with funding from foundations and local families, staffed with downsized print journalists, are doing high-quality work. The national nonprofit investigative site ProPublica operates similarly, often teaming with newspapers for ambitious projects, and has won several Pulitzers. But in many cases, they can be taken out by a single lawsuit or by an important donor changing his mind and deciding to invest his money elsewhere. Combine the serious American nonprofits doing investigative journalism, and you have something that adds up to a sliver of Apple's advertising budget.

In the United Kingdom, by contrast, the *Guardian* has managed to become, simultaneously, a money-losing print publication and a fantastically successful and enterprising website that recently helped break Edward Snowden's revelations of National Security Agency spying on the phone and Internet use of Americans and foreigners. The *Guardian* is able to do what it does—which includes losing about 100,000 British pounds per day—only because of the nonprofit trust that operates it. As vigorous a watchdog as it is, and despite operating the third most popular newspaper website in English, the market alone does not support what the *Guardian* does. ("A British newspaper wants to take its aggressive investigations global," read a *New Yorker* profile in 2013, "but money is running out.") Similarly, the strongest and highest-circulation paper in Florida, not long ago a hothouse of vibrant and competitive dailies, is now the *Tampa Bay Times*—known until recently as the *St. Petersburg Times*—which is owned by the deeply rooted non-profit Poynter Institute.

The troubles affect everyone who cares about an informed electorate and a democratic society. But the ailing state of journalism as it moves to the Web has even deeper implications for those who work in culture. When a newspaper's theater or classical music coverage disappears, sometimes the gap is filled by a blog that pops up on the same subject, written for insiders. The process resembles the removal of the arts from the public schools: they don't vanish but instead become a tiny subculture, losing their connection to a mass middle-class public, surrendering their ability to be discovered accidentally. As print goes, so does "middlebrow," the idea that culture can and should appeal to a broad readership.

The connections between print and culture don't have to be middlebrow in the scornful way the term has often been used, either. The indie rock movement of the '80s and early '90s arose not just because of new musical styles and bands like the Replacements and the Minutemen: it was also built, as Michael Azerrad documents in his definitive *Our Band Could Be Your Life,* on an underground network of clubs, college radio stations, and fanzines. The alt-country movement took its nickname from *No Depression,* the magazine, now defunct, that chronicled it. (The title originates with a Carter Family song.) The Pixies met through a classified ad in the *Boston Phoenix* (looking for musicians interested in melding "Husker Du and Peter, Paul and Mary.") The Pixies went on to become the leading influence on Nirvana; the *Phoenix* offered some of the nation's best music and culture coverage before collapsing in 2013.

There may be more music criticism online than there ever was in the heyday of indie 'zines and Robert Christgau's tenure at the *Village Voice,* or alt-rocking *Spin* magazine— all memories now—but it's far harder to trust. Lester Bangs may have been a bohemian wild man, but he and writers like him operated in what now seems like a quaint system of editorial independence. Many bloggers, by contrast, accept undisclosed advertising money for positive reviews of bands. It's hardly surprising that apostles of corporate synergy would find ways to bring their bands coverage in the publications they own. But the leading rock-criticism website, Pitchfork, surrendered its integrity after a "strategic partnership" with Fader Media and Cornerstone Promotions, lifestyle-marketing firms that generate cool branding for Pepsi, Levi's, and Reebok. Pitchfork's new section, journalist Chris Ruen writes, has become "a surreptitious space for Cornerstone to promote its projects while enjoying Pitchfork's 'Indie' stamp of approval among young *influencers.* Why try to convince an influential music site that they should cover your campaign when you can just as easily pay them to do so?" When traditional newspapers have been caught with this kind of undisclosed deal, people at the top are fired. The church-state wall between advertising and editorial content has been the key basis for press integrity since the beginnings of professional journalism; it is perhaps the most crucial casualty of the shift to online. In the new media world, when branding and journalism get tangled up together, anyone who notices is clearly reading from the old paradigm.

More broadly, the hybrid system with which a publication offered a blend of entertainment and the public good—some small part of democracy's infrastructure—may be history. One thing markets don't much produce is public goods—everyone enjoys fresh air and clean streets, but there's little market incentive to maintain them. Print advertising once did, however unintentionally. "Advertising now finds you online, wherever you are, like NSA surveillance," said McChesney. "It doesn't need content." The symbiosis was a historical fluke.

More profoundly, the end of print journalism—alongside similar pressures in book publishing that are not yet as highly developed but already are leading to consolidation and cutbacks—points to more than just turmoil in a few industries. Is it too soon to declare that the age of print has died? Probably. But the culture that goes back five or six centuries seems to be sputtering. It came to life in the decades following Johannes Gutenberg and may fade to black within a generation. Is there something special about words on paper? "Whenever language is the principal medium of communication—especially language controlled by the rigors of print—an idea, a fact, a claim is the inevitable result," Postman wrote.

> The idea may be banal, the fact irrelevant, the claim false, but there is no escape from meaning when language is the instrument guiding one's thought. Though one may accomplish it from time to time, it is very hard to say nothing when employing a written English sentence. What else is exposition good for? Words have very little to recommend them except as carriers of meaning.

In their sea of videos and pop-up ads and photo galleries, news websites use language as well, but it's language dislocated from the traditions print made possible. In a nonstop news cycle, when novels are written and read over cellphones and book reviews chopped into Twitter's bites, we may have reached not exactly the end of print, but the end of print culture or print thinking: the notion that we would stop, close the door, and frame a letter or story or novel or something with a firm, secure shape, a beginning, middle, and end—something aiming, even in vain, for permanence. The process works similarly for reader and writer. The novelist Junot Díaz described Facebook as "e-crack" and says he reads about thirty-six fewer books a year since he's begun to live online.

Print's residual prestige will never disappear completely—people still own harpsichords and typewriters and record players, if only for show, and fashion shoots and hotel lobbies use shelves of books for atmosphere—but the generation now in middle age, raised in the '70s and '80s, will be the last one that's native to print. "We are in some danger of believing that the speed and wizardry of our gadgets have freed us from the somewhat arduous work of turning pages in silence," Sven Birkerts wrote two decades ago, to both praise and oh-come-off-it ridicule, of a condition that has only accelerated. He looks at the way television has burned down our sense of the past—a process amplified by digital technology.

Through sheer omnipresence it has vanquished the possibility of comparative perspectives. We cannot see the role that television (or, for our purposes, all electronic communications) has assumed in our lives because there is no independent ledge where we might secure our footing. The medium has absorbed and eradicated the idea of a pretelevision past; in place of what used to be we get an ever-new and ever-renewable present. The only way we can hope to understand what is happening, or what has already happened, is by way of a severe and unnatural dissociation of sensibility.

In other words, it's become harder and harder to step outside of the swirl of commerce, the noise of marketing. For generations with no memory of a world before the Internet, there is no outside, no independent ledge, and as print goes down, some of what it takes with it will prove irreplaceable. The artist and the journalist, despite some obvious differences, have long been committed to uncovering truth—truth of the human condition, in the first case, and truth about human institutions in the other. They're not exactly the same things, but truth, of whatever kind, is often expensive. It's also, no matter what the cost, something we cannot live without.

8

SELF-INFLICTED WOUNDS

In the New History, nothing was judged—only counted. The
power of judging was then subtracted from what was necessary
for a man to learn to do. In the New History, the preferences
of a child carried as much weight as the preferences of an adult,
so the refining of preferences was subtracted from what it was
necessary for a man to learn to do.

—George W. S. Trow, *Within the Context of No Context*

THE MEANING OF HISTORY CHANGES as the forces it un-
leashes move through time, reshaping lives and assumptions.
How did we get to a place where Pomona College—an elite
California school that over the past decade included David
Foster Wallace and Jonathan Lethem among its faculty—
graduated only sixteen English majors in 2013? Where the
alternately prestigious and infamous Yale English department sees a drop of more than 60 percent from graduating
majors two decades ago? Even post-crash, Princeton now

187

sends nearly 40 percent of those who graduate with a job directly to Wall Street. (F. Scott Fitzgerald's alma mater, as well as Stanford, has begun a kind of affirmative action program to seek out high school students dedicated to studying the humanities.) "In response, a number of defenses have been mounted, none of them, so far, terribly persuasive even to one rooting for them to persuade," Adam Gopnik wrote in the *New Yorker*. "As the bromides roll by and the platitudes chase each other round the page, those in favor of ever more and better English majors feel a bit the way we Jets fans feel, every fall, when our offense trots out on the field: I'm cheering as loud as I can, but let's be honest—this is not working well."

All of these issues exert an effect on the creative class. This tale would seem very different if we told it in 1985, or 1999. But here's how it all looks from the second decade of the twenty-first century. Here's how we got the culture of culture we have now, and why it's so hard to get out of the ditch we seem to be in. And here's what's unpleasant to realize: in some ways, demonstrating the law of unintended consequences, members of the creative class created this mess by themselves.

Let's start with the way we've conceived, talked about, and transmitted culture for the past century and a half. One important thread of this story originates in the academy, into which "culture" strolled only fairly recently. Around the time culture-makers were struggling to adapt to the marketplace in the late nineteenth century, literature in English, followed gradually by the fine arts, sought shelter in the academy; the university became a kind of alternative to the bohemian garret. To study English literature, originally, often meant philology and rhetoric. But scholars developed moral and aesthetic ways of defining literature, which shifted over time but never quite gave up their insistence that something profound was at stake. For Matthew Arnold, writing in a Victorian society from which God seemed to be taking leave, literature was a civilizing influence, "the best that has been thought and said," providing "sweetness and light." For F. R. Leavis, whose point of view emanated influentially from 1930s Cambridge, Geoffrey Chaucer and Jane Austen and D. H. Lawrence had left us the timeless works that kept the English spirit whole in an age of mass society. American New Criticism, a bit later, borrowed the Leavisite emphasis on "close reading," crossing it with the ideas of T. S. Eliot and the defiant aestheticism of American southerners.

So, things changed over time. There was no stable, serene, golden age of unchanging aesthetic contemplation. First Dickens was out, for instance, then he was in. The value of literature was explained in numerous ways, some of them mutually exclusive. But that value itself, despite repeated redefinition, was never in doubt. The body of important works—even as the details changed—was accompanied by a sense that meaning or wisdom or depth or aesthetic triumph could be found within them.

The disruption began, to some extent, in the same place urban bohemia did: France. The work of a Swiss linguist and a French anthropologist brought a new system—with its emphasis on the workings of language, structure, and myth—to literary studies. Structuralism produced significant "schools" in various intellectual capitals—there was a Prague school, a Russian school, and the Toronto-based scholar Northrop Frye came up, in his book *The Anatomy of Criticism,* with a fascinating method based on archetype and the seasons. But its deepest impact was in 1960s France, where the literary culture was craving a replacement for a waning existentialism after the death of Albert Camus.

Structuralism later came in for some dismantling, but in the long term, it was successful beyond its wildest dreams. "To begin with, it represents a remorseless demystification of literature," Terry Eagleton, the British scholar who is the most lucid and sympathetic guide to contemporary literary theory, wrote in 1983.

> Loosely subjective talk was chastized by a criticism which recognized that the literary work, like any other product of language, is a construct, whose mechanisms could be classified and analysed like the object of any other science. The Romantic prejudice that the poem, like a person, harboured a vital essence, a soul which it was discourteous to tamper with, was rudely unmasked as a bit of disguised theology, a superstitious fear of reasoned enquiry which made a fetish of literature and reinforced the authority of a 'naturally' sensitive critical elite. Moreover, the structuralist method implicitly questioned literature's claim to be a unique form of discourse: since deep structures could be dug out of Mickey Spillane as well as Sir Philip Sidney, and no doubt the same ones at that, it was no longer easy to assign literature an ontologically privileged status.

Something, clearly, had happened to literature—now revealed as a nostalgic and elitist category. And something had happened to those charged with assessing what would become known as "texts," and interpreting them for students. "With the advent of structuralism," Eagleton continues, "the world of the great aestheticians and humanist literary scholars of twentieth-century Europe . . . seemed one whose hour had passed."

French intellectual culture changed in the postwar years as rapidly and violently as it had in the decades following the French Revolution. With the failure of the student/worker rebellions in 1968 Paris, structuralism became post-structuralism. Around this time, Jacques Derrida's "Structure, Sign, and Play in the Humanities" argued that there was nothing "behind" language but more language; "The Death of the Author," by Roland Barthes, separated the writer from his own literary work. Humanism itself—the tradition that stretched back to the Renaissance and extolled individualism, creativity, inquiry for its own sake, and the intertwined values of privacy and reflection—was now revealed as self-serving bourgeois illusion. "Literature," the canon, humanism—these were Trojan horses that looked good from afar but actually smuggled ideological poison inside the walls of the city.

As these scholars landed on American shores, the ideas stretched across English and comparative literature departments at Johns Hopkins, Yale, and elsewhere; in the Anglo-American world, the new school was often called "deconstruction" (which promptly became one of the most misused words in the language). Eventually these ideas would range as far afield as law schools. Feminism became a force on both sides of the Atlantic; the American Kate Millett took on D. H. Lawrence and Henry Miller and Norman Mailer in her 1970 book *Sexual Politics*. Each of these theories or intellectual styles, of course, was a bit different. Some of them were intellectually provocative in the best sense, and in some cases—Barthes in particular—these movements found formidable prose stylists. But these thinkers had at least two things in common.

First, these contemporary ways of looking at literature did not emulate the tweedy old traditions, based on hunches and personal responses and flashes of insight, but instead adopted the lab-coated methods of the sciences. Even though these critical schools came from the political left, in deep and unexamined ways they had less in common with Marx than they did with Frederick W. Taylor, whose *Principles of Scientific Management* from 1911 urged managers to "develop a science for each element of a man's work, which replaces the old rule-of-thumb method," and in doing so helped codify a kind of science envy and worship of technology that soon came to dominate the American soul. Neil Postman calls this development "Technopoly," describing Taylor's arguments this way: "These include the beliefs that the primary, if not the only, goal of human labor and thought is efficiency; that technical calculation is in all respects superior to human judgment; that in fact human judgment cannot be trusted, because it is plagued by laxity, ambiguity, and unnecessary complexity; that subjectivity is an obstacle to clear thinking; that what cannot be measured either does not exist or is of no value."

Second, and even more significant, these literary-critical movements were not particularly concerned with aesthetic worth. They were after something else. "Routing, or evading, literary value would have grave consequences for the public critic," the Irish scholar Ronan McDonald wrote in 2008:

But at the time, those in generational conflict with authority figures, flushed with the spirit of 1968, celebrated this de-mystification of the arts. Talk of canons, great traditions, or timeless beauty belonged to an older, fustier generation, like bowler hats or monocles. How refreshing to get past all that cloistered quasi-religious chatter, with its defense of elite sensibility and its palpable disdain for popular culture and the modern world.

To some, literature and the fine arts were simply outdated or irrelevant. But in the same way the creative class and its art got tangled up in earlier conflicts—medieval Christianity's war on pagan music, the Puritans' assault on Catholic idolatry—so "culture" was now a fighting word. Matthew Arnold's notion of literature and the arts as indicators of our humanity was now definitely over. "Not a performance should go by without disruption," the academic radical Louis Kampf wrote in 1969 of Lincoln Center. "The fountain should be dried with calcium chloride, the statuary pissed on, the walls smeared with shit." Kampf was later elected to the presidency of the Modern Language Association, the association of literature professors.

But a funny thing happened as the new schools of criticism, with their political energy, youthful vigor, and interest in the popular, came to American universities: students stopped caring. In the 1970s—not a decade known for pragmatism or narrow-minded acquisitiveness—the percentage of students studying English and the humanities, which had been rising for two decades, plummeted. Humanities majors went from 30 percent, in the 1970–71 academic year, to 16 percent by 2003–4.

"What are the causes for this decline?" asked William Chace, a Joyce scholar who has taught or served as president at Stanford, Wesleyan, and Emory. He wrote in *The American Scholar*:

> There are several, but at the root is the failure of departments of English across the country to champion, with passion, the books they teach and to make a strong case to undergraduates that the knowledge of those books and the tradition in which they exist is a human good in and of itself. What departments have done instead is dismember the curriculum, drift away from the notion that historical chronology is important, and substitute for the books themselves a scattered array of secondary considerations (identity studies, abstruse theory, sexuality, film and popular culture). In so doing, they have distanced themselves from the young people interested in good books.

Any sense of a common language was fading fast. To a lot of Chace's contemporaries, this might as well have been the squawking of a pterodactyl. But while advertisers—who had learned to connect with anti-authority impulses as early as the 1960s—were using the lingua franca, intellectuals were speaking in tongues.

MEANWHILE, JOURNALISM AND POPULAR CULTURE were experiencing a riot of their own. In some ways, this involved the same strains and tensions that were convulsing the academy: journalistic critics were picking up the giant-killing tone of society at large. But things played out a little differently at first.

Previous generations of intellectuals—the best of them perched on a precarious tightrope between journalism and the academy—had hardly been perfect citizens. They quarreled mercilessly with one another, often swinging from either side of the political spectrum to the other. But from the 1920s to the '60s, critics of literature and society like Edmund Wilson, Malcolm Cowley, C. Wright Mills, Irving Howe, and Jane Jacobs found substantial audiences for serious prose about the novel, capitalism, the city, and so on.

A new critic came along near the end of this period who changed the game. Full of tremendous energy, she loaded her essays with as many rapid-fire ideas as Charlie Parker packed into his solos, and she represented something new: female, defiantly Californian, anti-academic. Here, finally, was an intellectual who did not condescend to popular culture, who "got it." Her early essays and reviews of films like *Hud* and *Shoeshine* and *The Seven Samurai* were so full of passion that it's easy, when under her spell, to miss her fierce anti-intellectualism. Her work tackled outworn genres—the movie musical, the Serious Literary Adaptation—and championed new directors, Akira Kurosawa, François Truffaut, the American maverick cinema of the '70s. In almost every one of her early pieces she skirmished with other film reviewers. Critics and intellectuals have always fought with one another; historically, that heat has been the sign of a vital critical milieu. But this time was different.

It took decades for the consequences to become clear, but this writer, Pauline Kael, was not only knocking these old writers and their dusty standards, she was assaulting something that critics rarely tangled with: her natural readership and their notions of taste. She wrote several pieces on what she called "the art-house audience," none of them flattering. "I would like to suggest that the educated audience often uses 'art' films in much the same self-indulgent way as the mass audience uses the Hollywood 'product,' finding wish fulfillment in the form of cheap and easy congratulation on their sensitivities and their liberalism."

She hated what she called the "atmosphere of incense burning" that greeted some foreign films, and resented the kind of old-school cineaste who sat around discussing Bresson. Whenever the terms *poetry* or *art* or *depth* show up in her work, they're used to skewer any Puritan schmuck who would take them seriously. She denounced her employer, a Berkeley public radio station, for its dullsville "interviews with Quakers and Unitarians," and its fundraising. ("You're paying off the liberal debt. . . . They give you guilt. You give them money.") In the long run, Kael would champion "trash"—arguing that honest vulgarity was more valuable than earnest artiness—and come to ignore foreign cinema for the sake of American studio films. At first, it was gutsy and counterintuitive, but in the long run she was championing the kind of work that did not really need a critic's advocacy or interpretation, films that would later dominate world cinema. The "sensation" she extolled in her early work would become, in a dumbed-down form that Kael eventually disowned, the dominant style of the movies, eclipsing the art-house films she mocked. Kael also became one of the few critics since Edmund Wilson who made a mark not only on her peers but on the culture at large.

This would have all added up to one critic's idiosyncrasy if it had not been part of a larger, if uncoordinated, movement. Around the same time, a Los Angeles–born composer was writing pieces that destroyed the idea of artistic intention even more violently than the New Critics had, a French filmmaker was making films that blended art film and B-movie genre in unpredictable ways, architects were learning from Las Vegas, and a bashful New York illustrator, who had developed an unlikely cult of personality, was blurring the lines between art and commerce. What made art, or culture, special? he and the others asked, each in their own way. Some of this work made its mark in the most avant-garde and intellectually rarefied reaches of society; some was as popular and accessible as a Beatles record that challenged high culture's monopoly of complexity.

Much of what John Cage and Jean-Luc Godard and Robert Venturi and Andy Warhol produced was powerful and thrilling. But the net effect of this revolution was to destroy the middlebrow consensus—the sense that there was a shared body of artistic and intellectual touchstones that educated middle-class people should know about, that "serious" fare was somehow good for you, and that these works were to be passed down through education, journalistic coverage, and family rituals. It was the spirit that put John Cheever or George Balanchine on the cover of *Time* magazine, that had Leonard Bernstein on television, that made Rachel Carson famous, that provoked *Playboy* to commission profiles of Duke Ellington or Lester Young. And like the liberal consensus it largely overlapped with, the middlebrow consensus was attacked from both sides. It became collateral damage of the New Right's anger and the left's postmodern push, respectively.

The stakes weren't immediately clear. At first, the convulsive changes of the '60s and '70s called for an intellectual priesthood to interpret them. And across this period, several counterforces argued for the sanctity of culture, in their own ways. The writers at *Rolling Stone* and "underground" publications built a list of important artists, a counter-canon to classical music's three Bs, heavy on singer-songwriters and exemplars of instrumental virtuosity—Buddy Holly, Bob Dylan, Jimi Hendrix. Similarly, Susan Sontag—in some ways parallel to Kael, in other ways her opposite—seemed never to have received the memo that championing foreign films or difficult books was for squares or snobby Protestant men. (She argued for the difficult and obscure, for the sanctity of art, with a gusto that made her an outlier.) Good critics of classical music, painting, architecture, and other fields continued to work. For a while, things boomed. At times, it seemed like it would go on forever.

But as time went on, the changing culture—the fading of modernism, the middlebrow consensus, and the world around them—would leave the critics and intellectuals stranded. And the expansion of technology meant that teenage-corporate entertainment got bigger, louder, faster—how could poetry or paintings or piano sonatas compete with any of that?

As the philosopher Arthur Danto put it, art would continue to be made and interpreted, but after Andy Warhol, art history—as a discipline with a direction, a master narrative, a coherent meaning—became harder and harder to conceive or explain. A story was over. Nothing dies at once. It took a while to see just where this was all leading, as

Danto put it in a Mellon lecture at the National Gallery in 1995:

> The really important descriptions of events are often, even typically, unavailable to those who see those events happen. Who, knowing that Petrarch was ascending Mount Ventoux with a copy of St. Augustine in his hand, could have known that with that event the Renaissance had begun? Who, visiting the Stable Gallery on East 74th Street in Manhattan to see the Warhols, could have known that art had come to an end? . . . The structure of beginnings and endings, which almost defines historical representation construed narratively, is difficult to apply even in retrospect.

To Danto, the art history that began with the Renaissance, described by Giorgio Vasari as progressing through each major painter along technical advances that made more and fuller representation possible, had now concluded. For each art form, the story was a little different, and sometimes the death knells were premature—the novel was declared exhausted several times but always seemed to come roaring back. But something important had been broken.

The cultural critic had been an important player in both the middlebrow consensus and the avant-garde that broke it down. "These were the theologians," said Andras Szanto, who once headed the now shuttered arts journalism program at Columbia University, "the standard bearers, the keepers of the flame of a postwar master narrative—the modernist paradigm. It was based on a cultural and critical consensus of social progress, of breaking from tradition. There was a solidity to the culture, clear parameters." But the shattering of tradition ruptured their place as well. "What happens to the priests if there's no longer a catechism—when you have a splinter theology? Is this like the Protestant Reformation—every man's his own priest?"

Journalism responded, mostly, by picking up on the anti-intellectualism. By the '80s, demands for populist coverage were increasing. Coverage of classical music, theater, and other forms that didn't command a mass audience dropped, in the name of reaching a broader readership. An energized Christian right assaulted the arts as immoral and elitist. Not long after, people who ran newspapers and magazines, and who subscribed to Kael's hunger for sensation, would begin to get rid of books or fine-arts coverage altogether. A few held on to it, as long as the subject had become somehow "notorious." The media coverage of telegenic rebels and bad boy figures—what we could call the Marilyn Manson syndrome—simultaneously stirred up traditionalists and made everybody happy. The left reveled in the subversiveness of it all, while the right used the decadence of cultural figures as a wedge to lower taxes on the wealthy and defund the public sphere. "As a system, the backlash works," the social critic Thomas Frank wrote later. "The two adversaries feed off one another in a kind of inverted symbiosis: one mocks the other, and the other heaps even more power on the one. This arrangement should be the envy of every ruling class in the world."

And academia wasn't done yet. In the late '80s and '90s, the literary canon was attacked as being too white, too male, too straight, too Western. A few of the people making the attacks were actual reformers or dissenters who wanted to expand the sense of what was valuable. But many of these critics who found the sins of the world in the literature they were charged with teaching were like the politicians, who would arrive around the same time, campaigning for taxpayer-funded government positions on the basis of their fierce hatred of governing.

There was something else that both left and right were staring past. Katha Pollitt, writing in the *Nation* in 1991, described a "myopia."

Something is being overlooked: the state of reading, and books, and literature in our country at this time. Why, ask yourself, is everyone so hot under the collar about what to put on the required-reading shelf? It is because while we have been arguing so fiercely about which books make the best medicine, the patient has been slipping deeper and deeper into a coma.

Serious reading, it turned out—the kind people did when it wasn't required for school—was, outside a small minority, in trouble. (An NEA study showed the percentage of Americans reading fiction declining by 28 percent from 1982 to 2002, while time devoted to television, video games, electronic multitasking, and so on was increasing steeply.) Pollitt tried to imagine a nation in which reading novels was genuinely popular, something people did willingly at all phases of their lives. "In that other country of real readers—voluntary, active, self-determined readers—a debate like the current one over the canon would not be taking place. Or if it did, it would be as a kind of parlor game: What books would *you* take to a desert island?"

But why bother with dusty old books after all? A new academic field was picking up some of the advances of structuralism and its inheritors. *Cultural Studies*—a journal devoted to the new subject launched in 1987—did not bother with distinctions of quality, either, dismissing them as elitist in its passion for high-low mélanges. Anything could be described as a cultural practice, and consumers were as important as the producers; listening to pop was just as essential as composing a symphony. Semiotics, cyborg theory, Madonna studies, all experienced vogues. "But the more cultural studies looked at discos and detective fiction, *Cosmopolitan* and car advertisements," Ronan McDonald writes, "it seemed the general public drifted further and further away from the sorts of criticism the universities were producing."

Despite its engagement with the popular, and a political agenda devoted to broad social concerns, the prose of cultural studies managed a remarkable feat: it found a way to be even more impenetrable than the writing of the poststructuralists. A process that had been rolling for a decade or two—intellectuals now speaking only to fellow specialists —reached its apogee. Serious discourse, like the Anglo-American economy or public spaces, was on its way to being entirely privatized.

"What brings people back to books tends to be the belief that they offer something especially meaningful," Laura Miller succinctly put it in a *Salon* discussion of reading and critics in 2008. But "academic criticism has busied itself with undermining that belief for the past fifty years." Poststructuralism didn't help people with the meaning of their novels, or their lives, and neither did succeeding academic movements. "In cultural studies, whether or not a work by a member of a previously silenced group is 'good' or not is the wrong question: 'Good' is understood to be a suspect term based on the self-interested values of those in power."

Cultural studies drew some of its energy from the French sociologist Pierre Bourdieu, whose *Distinction: A Social Critique of the Judgment of Taste,* looked at the class roots of high culture, especially classical music. "Taste classifies, and it classifies the classifier," he wrote. Following his lead came sociologists who described the cultural "omnivore," who supplanted a crumbling "snob" culture. Sometimes, omnivorism encouraged people to range far and wide, high and low, for their cultural consumption, perusing the pioneering Sunday comics of Winsor McCay in the morning, reading Patricia Highsmith's novels by day, and taking in a Haydn quartet at night. Other times, it gave educated people reason to feel progressive by ignoring everything but mainstream entertainment.

WHERE ALL OF THESE TRENDS came together—where the pedal hit the cultural metal—was on the Internet. The critical style of Pauline Kael, long influential among film journalists in print, now became the default tone of Internet scribes and bloggers, though many lacked her intellectual depth or appetite for complexity and doubled down instead on her anti-elitist rage. The Internet encouraged dismissive "flaming" and anonymous takedowns. But one critical school arrived on the doorstep with what it claimed was good news.

Just as the earliest undercutting of the creative class had taken place in the world of recorded music, so music journalism was the first to see these trends all coalesce. Rock critics who had once championed scruffy, defiant rock bands on small labels—the Minutemen or Liz Phair—began blogging about every episode of *American Idol,* a TV show that played like a cruel satire of value judgment. To some of these scribes, *Idol*—in its earnest search for "raw, undiscovered talent"—was the program that gave their careers meaning, that captured the rags-to-riches possibilities of the new, wired economy. Although Simon Cowell, a judge on the show, came across as a parody of a mean Dwight Macdonald–style critic—and, rarely mentioned, one who made contestants sign over much of their future earnings—people wrote about the show as if it were a kind of populist utopia. ("America's in control," reported *Idol* executive producer Ken Warwick. "That's the secret of the phenomenon.") Those who resisted were dinosaurs, elitists, nostalgics, authenticity junkies.

These writers called themselves Poptimists, and they were dedicated to upending truths about music that had been accepted since the '60s and '70s, "reconsidering musicians (Tiny Tim, Dan Fogelberg, Phil Collins) and genres (blue-eyed soul, Muzak) long maligned in rock discourse," as one fellow traveler described it. Their quarrel was with the old sense that rock music—musicians playing songs they'd written themselves, usually involving guitars, and framed by albums meant to be taken as coherent artistic statements—had something transcendent about it. The search for the perfectly crafted pop single—what Brian Wilson, in an unconscious nod to cultural modernism, called "teenage symphonies to God"—did not concern them. The Poptimists aimed to topple a "rockist" canon, which they saw as full of outdated ideological assumptions, and sexist and racist to boot. This was odd, since earlier generations of rock critics had championed Mississippi sharecroppers, wise-ass Jewish punks, Rastafarian soul rebels, foppish British bisexuals, cosmic cowboys, at least one Canadian poetess, hillbilly drunks and other assorted drug addicts, and melancholy suicides and lost dreamers who seemed far from the WASP country club to which these critics likened the old order.

And all kinds of outlets, including ones that saw themselves as part of rock's rebel spirit, fell into a contrarian vogue for championing discredited musicians from the past—no matter how shallow. Instead of coverage of, say, the lost recordings of pioneering bebop guitarist Charlie Christian, or a tribute to the Appalachian string bands that laid the groundwork for country music, we read pieces "in defense of" blockbuster acts like the Eagles (the bestselling rock band in history), Billy Joel, Rush—groups whose songs, thanks to the iron lock big corporate labels and programmers had on radio in the '70s and '80s, it was once impossible to get away from. Some of these bands recovered from the critical dumpster are setting records for high-priced concert tickets on their inevitable reunion tours. Between irony, nostalgia, and critical reclamation projects, you could walk into an upscale coffee shop or expensive sporting event in the twenty-first century and hear the once compulsory AOR playlist as if it were still 1984, and the whole rebellion of punk, college radio, and indie rock never happened. It's as if citizens of the former Soviet Union pined for Siberian exile and endless queues for toilet paper.

But to the world of the Internet—which is interested in "hits" of a different kind and not critical discernment—there's no contradiction. To the print outlets that began to employ the Poptimists, this was a way to remain "relevant" in the online age. Who needed some tired old longhair going on about Captain Beefheart—it was time to bring in someone who knew what the kids were really listening to. And instead of telling readers to look to the edges of the marketplace, to a brooding singer-songwriter they might not hear on the radio but would find spiritually nourishing, or to an overlooked '60s garage band or '70s soul singer—the kind of thing rock journalists had done for decades—the Poptimists told you about what you already knew about, writing long, thoughtful pieces on Justin Bieber or boy bands or Beyoncé's genius for branding. So what if Britney didn't write her own songs—neither did Sinatra! And if 'N Sync were just prefab kids in matching uniforms, what about the Brian Epstein–era Beatles? If distinctions of quality didn't matter, who could tell the difference? The cry of "corporate rock sucks" was as dead as Matthew Arnold's grand claims for poetry. Like a celebrity magazine turboed up with a Ph.D., the educated, politically progressive Poptimists celebrated the gargantuan size of the market itself. This market populism was everywhere as the twentieth century turned into the twenty-first. A shift in hip-hop—from an earlier commitment to melodic ingenuity, black-music elder statesmen, and fight-the-power rabble-rousing to a gettin' paid corporate entrepreneurialism—tracked the very same changes.

Perhaps the most fascinating work to come out of this critical school was a short, often brilliant book by Toronto-based critic Carl Wilson. *Let's Talk About Love: A Journey to the End of Taste* dove headfirst into the world of Celine Dion, the Canadian chanteuse whose elaborately costumed

Vegas shows and machine-made music had drawn scorn from critics of the earlier school. Wilson delved into fandom, the shaping of taste, even his own early resistance to Dion and her music. (He had originally heard it as "bland monotony raised to a pitch of obnoxious bombast," until he thought more deeply about its cultural conditions.) Like his peers, Wilson's argument was indebted to academic theory, particularly Bourdieu's notion of personal taste as a smokescreen for class privilege. "If critics were so wrong about disco in the 1970s," he asks, "why not about Britney Spears now?" As writers like Wilson moved into positions at important journalistic outlets, we saw the triumph of the first critical school that did not want to distinguish between good and bad, better or worse, but to reflect people's preferences—and the marketing that shaped them—back to them. Everyone loves a winner, and rock critics had always written about stars and star-making. But here was a critical school devoted to extolling the handful of artists with the largest market share, and ignoring most of the rest. It was like the moment in *Family Feud* when Richard Dawson asked not for the right answer to the question, but to what a poll had shown most people *thought* the answer was.

And when it came down to it, Poptimists and their allies held the trump card: in the Internet age, any "lifestyle manager" or website operator could check the numbers, and see that the story on the battered troubadour Elliott Smith attracted a tiny fraction of the clicks as against a piece on the subversions of Lady Gaga or the rebel cool of *Idol* judge Steven Tyler. As for classical music or jazz or acoustic blues—subjects journalists had covered out of a sense that these genres were important, if still a minority interest—forget about it. For a weary suburban editor, stuck in charge of culture coverage despite having lost the spark himself, what could be better than journalists who wrote only about the stars who were showing up on TV, whose marketers were taking out the biggest ads? The hunter had been captured by the prey.

Just as talk radio has allowed faux-populist politics to thrive, coast to coast, so the Internet allowed a faux-populist sense of culture to spread much faster than previous critical movements. Instead of snarling about "bias," now it was *taste* that was considered treasonous. The novelist Rick Moody found this out when he wrote on *The Rumpus* and *Salon* about the young country singer Taylor Swift. At the time, Swift was being celebrated as a cross between Johnny Cash and Emmylou Harris, although much of the cheerleading concerned not her musical prowess or songwriting skills but the clues her lyrics gave to celebrity ex-boyfriends, or to celebrating the boldly feminist entrepreneurial spirit that had led her to promote her own fragrance. When Moody challenged her apotheosis, he was dismissed as an angry old sexist killjoy. Of course, there have always been people who consider critics scolds or grouches. But now it was critics themselves and other cultural gatekeepers urging their own to stop getting in the way of the winning team. Combine feckless critics, corporate marketers who had gotten even shrewder at shaping consumer taste, and the attention deficit disorder of the Web, Moody said, "and you do seem to have the perfect conditions for the growth and perpetuation of shallowness." As onetime theater critic Frank Rich put it, "The line between publicity—the whole *People* magazine,

Entertainment Tonight, In Touch gestalt—and reviews has been obliterated."

The sense that culture and the marketplace were essentially the same thing was not limited to the Poptimists. Instead of talking about quality—which had become speech in a dead language—publications and media outlets amplified their coverage of televised awards shows, devoting breathless attention to the horse race even months before the saddles went on. How long before a major print outlet, with a past commitment to the middlebrow consensus, hired a film critic who told you Michael Bay's films were better than Michael Haneke's, or a book critic who wrote an "in defense" piece on Tom Clancy at the expense of Alice Munro? Or an attention-getting art critic who knocked Claes Oldenburg and Georgia O'Keeffe, ignored the outsider artists, but argued that the "painter of light" Thomas Kinkade was a Picasso-sized genius and those pointy-heads were just too dour to admit it?

Market worship was not confined to cultural criticism. It was the lingua franca of the day, often crossed with technological utopianism. In the hyperventilating prose of George Gilder, we heard how computers would miraculously bring us insights, help shape our values. "Umm, insights and guides to value used to be among literature's jobs, didn't they?" the novelist David Foster Wallace wondered. But by now it was too late. After a while, even most principled conservatives opted out of the whole humanities game. Management theorist Peter Cohan had few doubts. "To fix this problem, the answer is simple enough: cut out the departments offering majors that make students unemployable." Governor Pat McGrory of North Carolina wanted to get rid of all those useless majors too: "I'm going to adjust my educational curriculum to what business and commerce needs." So much for conserving. "Maybe, in the past, conservatives stumped for some idealized core curriculum, or the Great Books of Western Civ," Thomas Frank wrote in *Harper's*, "but now the option of demolishing these disciplines is on the table, today's amped-up right rather likes the idea."

The visual artist who best exemplified the period—and drew idolization from young artists on both sides of the Atlantic—was a former stockbroker with an ironic oeuvre and a megawatt smile. Jeff Koons became famous for slyly "appropriating" work from others (an inflatable rabbit, balloon dog, Elvis) but then threatened legal action when his own work was pilfered. "The very people who brought us the death of originality," the critic Jed Perl noticed, "are increasingly preoccupied with the defense of their own originality." Among the most vital young filmmakers and rock musicians in the '90s extended the Kael-Warhol love of trash and hatred of Eurocentric seriousness into a kind of dumpster-diving aesthetic that led at first to triumphs—*Pulp Fiction, Odelay*—but both lost their way as the pop pastiches ran dry. The idea that art, or criticism, or the artist, needed to exist outside the culture to see it clearly and criticize it became indecipherable: everyone wanted to be on the inside.

In August of 2013, Amazon unveiled a new plan to sell visual art online. And even though, by now, art criticism had been marginalized, there was no shortage of wisdom-of-the-crowd comments by amateur reviewers, as documented by a *New York Times* arts blog:

> "Is there a Kindle edition available," asked one reviewer of Monet's 1868 portrait of his son Jean. "Pros" include "Looks good above my toilet" and "Fast shipping," another wrote. "Cons: Frame and painting looked used."
>
> "I think I'm going to touch this up a bit with some water colors I have laying around," the reviewer added. "Make the colors pop more." . . .
>
> Or one on a Warhol screen print of a Campbell's Golden Mushroom Soup can for just under $25,000, that directed other customers to the grocery section and noted: "This version is a much better price, and is delicious."

And if individual discernment, whether from an art critic in your newspaper or an obsessive clerk at your record store or your college English professor, is not important—if human judgment no longer matters—the replacement of people by computers becomes a lot less consequential. The decades-long assault on liberal humanism was a perfect prequel to the age of the algorithm.

"What we lose, when all is said and done, is an alternate system of valuation and achievement, besides price," said Szanto. "In the art market, the price reflected a co-existing critical consensus. There was some interplay that involved the critics, and there were other voices in the conversation. There could be manipulation, one-shot wonders, but by and large these valuations had grounding in a conversation about art. The great fear is that when we take away that critical element, we allow the issue—'what is art? what has value?'—to disappear. The only thing left is the market-place, and the value comes entirely from money, marketing, and everyday power."

WHAT DOES ALL THIS HAVE to do with the collapse of the creative class? Doesn't a broadening of what's good mean that more people can produce or sell culture? Doesn't the breakdown of hierarchy democratize the world of the arts and entertainment and journalism and everything else? Actually, the loss of nerve—the surrender of any sense of value—has dire implications for the creative class, some short-term, some longer.

Let's look at the academy first. One of the things a hu-manities education has traditionally done is excite young people about books and ideas, preparing them to become dedicated novel readers, museumgoers, theater frequenters, and so on. These are students who have chosen, after all, to study something less likely to lead directly to a lucrative field than their peers majoring in business or computer science, at a time of utilitarian education, neoliberal pragmatism, and high-stakes educational testing. If these numbers sink, the foundation for culture itself, and for the creative class that makes a living in and around culture, comes down, too. Literature, art, dance, and everything else depend on a supply-demand curve. Massive cuts in government support for both public and private universities, and the ensuing surge of tuition and loan burdens for students, have done enormous damage to the dream of an unfettered, wisdom-seeking liberal-arts experience.

"The American Freshman," a UCLA survey of incoming college students across the country, shows that young people have become far less interested in culture or learning for its own sake. A "meaningful philosophy of life" was very important to 86 percent of respondents in 1966, but by 2013 that number was cut in half. (Earning a lot of money surged as a priority during this period.) Surely, not all of this social shift can be laid at the door of academia. But the inability or unwillingness of academics—some, of course, excepted—to explain the value of their wares has also helped undercut the process of cultural transmission as well.

What happens when a significant proportion of those who guide students' relationship to books see them merely as "texts" to be interrogated, and tell you that anyone who loves, say, Rainer Maria Rilke or Virginia Woolf for their aesthetic qualities is a dinosaur? "If anything, literary enthusiasm can be a detriment if your job is to prosecute books for their ideological crimes," Laura Miller wrote of the shifting of critical priorities. "When even English professors won't stand up for literature, is it any wonder it's failing?"

Journalism has not responded to the rise of faux-populist critical schools by hiring more reviewers or music and arts journalists. In fact, journalistic arts criticism and reporting have continued to fall. There has been a rise in publications and sites that track the divorces, sex lives, court cases, and rehab visits of celebrities. The upper-middlebrow side of the press is not exempt: the *Los Angeles Times,* for instance, laid off half a dozen arts reporters and bolstered its coverage of fashion and "celebrity justice." More broadly, many genres—movies, pop music—are now being deemed "critic proof."

What's happened to the image of the critic? In 1950, the Addison DeWitt character in *All About Eve* was a cynic and an egoist, but also a sleekly charming and respected cultural authority. By the mid-'90s—after a few decades of intellectuals keeping their best conversation to themselves—the best-known critic in the world of movies and television was a cartoon endomorph, voiced by the nerdy Jon Lovitz, in the animated TV show *The Critic*. Anyone who had read Russell Jacoby's *The Last Intellectuals: American Culture in the Age of Academe* could hardly be surprised.

What happens to the arts when their shimmer fades, when it's all revealed—as Warhol told us—as a cynical game? "If we run this like every other business, it all falls to the ground," Szanto said. "If 'anything goes' aesthetically, we've liberated ourselves and we've taken out these arbiters, these goalies? If every shot can get into the net, what does it do to culture? What makes culture any different from anything else? Why does it need funding, education, nonprofit status?" The old critical-cultural alliance was imperfect, but it created a value system. "We clearly understood that art was one thing and lipstick was another thing. When you strip that away, you are left with another kind of entertainment. You can't put culture up against Hollywood—it's not a fair match."

As cultural authority has been discredited, distinctions of quality in the world of culture have now been dismissed as just personal preference. It's not only the highbrow snob who is frustrated. Neil Young, for instance, has complained about the terrible sound quality of digital music files, and how this leads to a culture of "good enough." Graphic designers grind their teeth when they are replaced by computer software. If quality is just an illusion, who's counting?

What happens if no one defends artists or cultural genres outside the pop marketplace? During a period in which powerhouse corporate marketers like Disney and Clear Channel had moved into the world of culture and the study of music and art had already been defunded from public schools? If we've freed ourselves from critical standards and the idea of a broad, middle-class connoisseurship disappears?

At least some proportion of American society still wanted to believe there's something exalted about creativity, and for these folks, there was an answer. Even as they drifted away from poems or classical music or taking rock songs seriously, they were told by a young writer named Jonah Lehrer that the corporate innovators who came up with the Swiffer, a mop made by Procter and Gamble, or the sticky note were exercising the same creative process as W. H. Auden or Yo-Yo Ma or Bob Dylan. Although the details of some of Lehrer's work were later revealed to be counterfeit, his synthesis of rah-rah management theory, *Wired* magazine gee-wiz, believe-in-yourself motivational speaking, and a bourgeois-bohemian brand of market worship made him perhaps the truest thinker of the age.

"If criticism forsakes evaluation," McDonald wrote in his book *The Death of the Critic,* "it also loses its connections with a wider public. This is why it is cultural studies, more than any other academic phenomenon, that has led to the death of the critic. To command wide public attention, the critic needs to write as if the stakes matter, that the arts are important and the questions to be arbitrated and judged upon are ones of some moment—not just politically but aesthetically (the two are interlaced). If we do not attend to value *in* the arts, then how can we attend to the value *of* the arts?"

Meanwhile, the notion of value—despite being revealed as a class-bound illusion—did not disappear. In fact, it thrived at just about every level of society. Russian robber barons dueled with Japanese technologists to capture the finest bottles of Bordeaux. Websites chased a subculture of fanboys and fangirls whose appetite for parsing the distinctions between superheroes knew no bounds. The kind of educated middle-class person who might once have been interested in a challenging novel in translation or an obscure band from the past now knew at what altitude level her coffee beans had grown, how the chickens he ate for dinner had been treated: the notion of cultural "taste" returned to its culinary roots. The chattering classes did not mind drawing distinctions over food, wine, and other consumables, nor did they avoid more expensive salad greens because they were tired of things that were "good for them." It looked for about a moment like this signaled a renewed, old-school respect for taste. "But what has happened is not that food has led to art," William Deresiewicz wrote in 2012, "but that it has replaced it. Foodism has taken on the sociological characteristics of what used to be known—in the days of the rising postwar middle class, when Mortimer Adler was peddling the Great Books and Leonard Bernstein was on television—as culture."

The Anglo-American world certainly ate better, and drank better beer. "But food, for all that, is not art. Both begin by addressing the senses, but that is where food stops.

. . . A good risotto is a fine thing, but it isn't going to give you insight into other people, allow you to see the world in a new way, or force you to take an inventory of your soul." A madeleine can be made with enough sugar and skill to provide momentary bliss, but it does not offer transcendence and meaning without Marcel Proust's language to frame it.

Godard once said that the youth culture of the '60s was the child of Karl Marx and Coca-Cola. Today, we are the bastard offspring of Reagan and Warhol. The collapse of the middlebrow consensus, the end of modernism, the demystification of culture, and the changing attitudes of the gatekeepers have all had profound and lasting consequences for the creative class.

9

LOST IN THE SUPERMARKET
WINNER-TAKE-ALL

No one can say when the unwinding began—when the coil
that held American life together in its secure and sometimes
stifling grip first gave way. Like any great change, the unwinding
began countless times, in countless ways—and at some moment
the country, always the same country, crossed a line of
history and became irretrievably different.

—George Packer, *The Unwinding:*
An Inner History of the New America

AS WE SURVEY THE STATE of the creative class, we can see
a few thriving and hear some creatives mouthing the words
of the prophets of disruption. But many—perhaps most—
are still struggling. Some have ceased to struggle: they are
simply flat on their backs. Like a series of microclimates that
seem to defy general description, there are bright spots, es-

pecially when it comes to some of the films and albums and novels being released. Between the Decemberists landing a Number 1 record, Noah Baumbach's films finding (briefly) their audience, and novels by Rachel Kushner and Junot Díaz reaching acclaim, the generation now hitting artistic maturity—the last generation raised before the Internet— has certainly produced important work, though it's not always easy to find. Television—at least if you keep the dial set on half-a-dozen high-end cable shows—has never been better. There are gems and good work in every field, from every generation.

But just as the suffocation of global warming doesn't cease because of a cold winter or the observer taking a Nordic holiday, the overall picture is less cheery. A wealth of exemplary cultural expression has not made it any easier for the creative class to ply its various trades. Moreover, its health is bound up with that of another class, which has had a tough time over the past few decades, as well, and whose future does not look any brighter than that of the creatives. That's the middle class, a group that Americans have been championing since the days of Thomas Paine—who is thought to have coined the term—as a source of wealth and stability; our American march toward broad-based equality as destiny manifest remains, as Vance Packard wrote a half-century ago, "deeply imbedded in our folklore." The British and other European nations have decided, more recently, that the middle is also the key to their republics. Despite longstanding tensions and denials on both sides, the bourgeois and the bohemians have been essentially members of the same class all the way back to nineteenth-century Paris.

(The best book on the subject, Jerrold Seigel's *Bohemian Paris: Culture, Politics, and the Boundaries of Bourgeois Life, 1830–1930,* makes their joint origins and ideology clear.)

Since then, young artists and their fellow travelers have tried to deny their membership in the middle class, and to establish real and symbolic distance from it. The late social critic Paul Fussell, in his influential topology of class behavior, referred to creative types as "category X," who had found in the pursuit of culture "the only escape from class." A skeptic and curmudgeon, Fussell had little sympathy for what he called "the young flocking to the cities to devote themselves to 'art,' 'writing,' 'creative work.' . . . Being an X person is like having much of the freedom and some of the power of a top-out-of-sight or upper-class person, but without the money. X category is a kind of unmonied aristocracy." (Their rumpled clothing sent the message: "I am more intelligent and interesting than you are: please do not bore me.")

We can think, too, of Stephen Dedalus in Joyce's *Portrait of the Artist as a Young Man,* soaring high above mainstream society as surely as his namesake did the world of antiquity. But artists, writers, composers, music critics, and cultural salesmen have not escaped the larger sociological, economic, and technological conditions that have undercut the rest of the middle class for three or four decades. ("You think you're so clever and classless and free," John Lennon sneered about a different class.) They're still caught in a winner-take-all culture that benefits those at the very top and undercuts the rest. Winner-take-all and steep income inequality are not exactly the same thing. But the former produces the latter, in both obvious and more subtle ways.

Creatives still live in a world where survival is increasingly stacked against people who aren't wealthy, and where a middle-class living is becoming harder to hold on to for the creative and conventional alike. If they're American, they still live in a world where four members of the Walton family (offspring of the founder of Walmart) own more wealth than the bottom 40 percent of their countrymen—more than 100 million people. *Citizens United,* the 2010 Supreme Court decision that dropped limits on political spending by corporations, means that plutocratic influence on U.S. politics will only increase. And guess what these groups typically ask for? More money, power, and influence for themselves—and a shredded safety net for the rest. With wages flat or falling for the middle class, the rising consumer spending that would drive us out of the slump (and lead to more purchases of records, books, and so on that would support creative careers) has not arrived.

In 1965, the average U.S. CEO made about 20 times more than his firm's average worker; at the time, it was the starkest differential in the civilized world. Now the ratio for Fortune 500 companies is 380 to 1, and climbing steeply. (That means the average worker in these firms must work for almost two months to make what the boss does in one *hour.* The CEO of Oracle, Larry Ellison, earns in an hour what the average American worker does in an entire year. Two years after the market crash of 2008, hedge-fund manager John Paulson made $2.4 million per hour.) The broad middle class that grew from the 1930s through most of the '70s, becoming the largest and strongest the world had seen, is turning into a mere niche: since about 1980, the middle class has worked harder for more hours, saved less, seen more personal bankruptcy, and lost both sleep and class mobility along the way. Productivity has skyrocketed, wages not at all. And this state of affairs existed before the Great Recession, which amplified a lot of these trends and tore apart what was supposed to be middle-class retirement savings, now increasingly handled by hedge funds.

What else has happened to the world the creative class operates in? In the United States, 60 percent of employers now check their potential employees' credit ratings, which keeps those hit hard by the recession from getting back on their feet. Rents have risen steeply in most regions even during a lousy economy, making it impossible for all but the wealthiest members of the creative class to live in and around Los Angeles, Washington, D.C., Seattle, Boston, and other cities that have traditionally served as hubs for art and music making. For all their creative cachet, San Francisco and New York are becoming cities without middle classes: writers and musicians lacking trust funds are being replaced by investment bankers and software jockeys, as well as a large servant class that commutes into town from poor precincts to clean their lavish kitchens and watch the children. (Lena Dunham has said that thanks to skyrocketing rents, her generation's Patti Smith will have to ditch Lower Manhattan for Tampa.) Home ownership is being made more difficult not just by the housing market being turned into a casino over the past decade and a half, but by speculators and Wall Street groups like Blackstone buying up foreclosed properties. The housing crisis that pushed so many out of their homes and destroyed their credit is not over. "The boom-bust-flip phenomenon," economics reporter Catherine Rampell wrote in the *New York Times* in 2013, "is just one of the most obvious ways that research suggests the financial crisis has benefited the upper class while brutalizing the middle class. Rents have risen at twice the pace of the overall cost-of-living index, partly because middle-class families can't get the credit they need to buy."

Speaking of the recession, do you really think it nailed everybody equally? Some bankers lost their seven-figure bonuses—some didn't. But the spoils of the recovery have gone almost entirely to the very top of the scale: 95 percent of the gains since 2009 have gone to the top 1 percent, with more than 60 percent of the recovery going to the top 0.1 percent, those whose annual income is almost $2 million or more. Meanwhile, the median American income has actually gone down. The lower 40 percent saw, even during a supposed recovery, their real income fall by 6 percent. "Basically," wrote Paul Krugman, "while the great majority of Americans are still living in a depressed economy, the rich have recovered just about all their losses and are powering ahead." For the vast majority of the nation, he argued, growth over the past few decades has been a spectator sport.

Even the *Economist,* the free-market magazine of the business class, has lamented the steep heights of American inequality. The CIA's World Factbook chart of the Gini coefficient— which measures the equality of income distribution—has the United States a little better than Uruguay and Jamaica, a little worse than Uganda, Cameroon, and Iran. (The World Bank's Gini index has the U.S. as the 112th most equal nation in the world.) This all comes after decades, by the way, of culturally populist, hierarchy-busting rhetoric from both sides of the political spectrum, market triumphalism by neoliberals, and boasting about the magic of the marketplace by conservatives, loud cheering for the empowered consumer, countless letting-you-be-you ads from Madison Avenue, vigorous motivational speaking about unleashing your potential, and endless democracy talk from digital utopians. It's hard for us to give up on the idea that our destiny is entirely in our own hands. But it's ceased to describe our reality.

Of course, for people to be able to work in the arts or entertainment at any level requires a number of culturally oriented wealthy people. The rich have kept culture alive in Western society for hundreds of years, and in some parts of American culture, especially the nonprofit arts, still do. They own most of our best political magazines and endow numerous university positions as well. But extreme polarization, wealth concentration, and the income cascades they provoke does not make it easier for the novelist or musician. People who challenge the dominance of the very rich are told, *These people are our job creators, they make our world go 'round, don't bark at them or they will flee to the Caymans or the Moon.* The mildest version of the reproach is, *Let the rich have their spoils—it doesn't affect you. Inequality is inevitable.* A harsher response is to accuse any critic of fomenting class warfare. But as Warren Buffett has famously stated, class warfare is alive and well, and his class is handily winning. The creative class has not been as fortunate.

"The situation is not unique to the United States," columnist Suzanne Moore wrote in the *Guardian,* "and in a world increasingly globalized, it will not stop with the Anglo-American nations." Whatever the limits of the burghers, "without this middle-class state of mind, this ever expanding inequality governed by aristocrats looks less like a democracy and more like a system that never shook off feudalism." That's almost literally true. An important study by two scholars at the Paris School of Economics, Thomas Piketty and Gabriel Zucman, is titled "Capital Is Back: Wealth-Income Ratios in Rich Countries, 1700–2010." They conclude, after looking at the United States, United Kingdom, Germany, and France: "In effect, today's ratios appear to be returning to the high values observed in Europe in the eighteenth and nineteenth centuries (600–700%)." Piketty, of course, became famous in early 2014 for his book *Capital in the Twenty-first Century,* which uses tax data for several nations to argue that extreme inequality is only just getting started. A century or two's progress toward equality has been vaporized in a bit more than a generation. Simon Johnson, former chief economist of the International Monetary Fund, described the triumph of the finance industry, at the expense of the rest of us, "the quiet coup."

To understand what's happened, where we are now, and how we can move out of this impasse, we need to look closely at two related issues, both with economic, technological, and cultural dimensions: First, surrounding the creative class exists a broader winner-take-all society of unforgiving limits. Second, a blockbuster culture has evolved from *inside* the creative class.

WINNER-TAKE-ALL STRUCTURES ARE associated with various Gilded Ages of the modern market economy. Income inequality was approximately as bad in 1928, right before the Great Crash, as it was in 2007, on the eve of the Great Recession. Many economists think the wealth concentration helped provoke the implosions; the imbalance is approximately as bad today. But the phenomenon goes back well before Gatsby's day, before nineteenth-century robber barons, before even the advent of capitalism. In fact, it goes back at least to one of the earliest heydays of the creative class. In ancient Greece we have some of the first documented evidence of winner-take-all mechanisms, in the Olympic Games that took place, in honor of Zeus, as far back as the eighth century B.C., and the Athenian contests of tragic drama during golden-age festivals of Dionysus, in which thirty thousand people would crowd in to watch plays by Aeschylus in between animal sacrifices and phallic parades. It's no surprise that winner-take-all markets are most common, across history, in sports and entertainment, and in some ways the larger story is their seeping out of those spheres into other aspects of life.

There may be something deep in human nature that responds to an all-or-nothing setup and the superstars it creates. In the folklore of most pre-modern societies there are records of popular contests involving animals. "Jumping frogs, racehorses, milk cows, show dogs and breeding bulls—all these animals and many more have been contestants in winner-take-all-markets," observed Cornell's Robert H. Frank, the economist who has done the most insightful work on the phenomenon, with Duke policy scholar Philip J. Cook. The very basis of our species—sexual selection and evolution—is itself a potentially winner-take-all arrangement, as passing down one's genes depends on a competition for mates that was, for most of human prehistory, anything but equitable. Since 85 percent of human societies—across the ages—are polygynous (in which men take multiple wives), there have been many men who've gone without mates while a few take dozens or hundreds. (One Moroccan emperor, three centuries ago, sired more than a thousand children. And in some species—seals, for instance—the ratio is even less reassuring.) Monogamy, which is enforced by law in some societies, is one of the most important and essential ways a society cuts against the workings of winner-take-all.

The key to a winner-take-all market is a reward for relative performance—sprinting a split-second faster than the runner-up, lifting a weight an ounce heavier than the competition, hitting a single home run more than another batter, selling one more record than another singer to earn a place on a Billboard chart. Economists, at least as far back as Adam Smith, mostly ignore these kinds of relative and context-based evaluations, emphasizing absolute goods and considering people as rational and independent actors instead of players in a web of cause and effect. Needless to say, the difference in performances and rewards in a winner-take-all market tends toward the steeply extreme. It goes against what intuition would predict. Here's Frank and Cook:

> It is one thing to say that people who work 10 percent harder or have 10 percent more talent should receive 10 percent more pay. But it is quite another to say that such small differences should cause pay to differ by 10,000 percent or more. Olympic gold medalists go on to receive millions in endorsements while the runners-up are quickly forgotten—even when the performance gap is almost too small to measure.

As James Gleick has noted, the career-destroying margin can be determined by something as slight as "a gust of wind or a different running shoe."

When it's this tight, there's an enormous incentive for competitors to take any edge they can—whether it's legal or ethical or not. The baseball player, in a world in which a few home runs can make the difference between a benchwarmer and a national star, has millions of reasons to take a performance-enhancing drug, and many fewer reasons not to. If enough players do, everyone who refuses to dope plays at a disadvantage, especially if a deregulated salary system creates a culture of superstar free agents. When the Soviets spent a crippling proportion of their revenues on bombs and missiles, the United States had to as well. The arms race meant more guns and less butter for everyone (except for those who built and sold the bombs). Frank and Cook describe this relationship, in which rational individual behavior does not serve the group, as "smart for one, dumb for all"—a classic tragedy of the commons. Behavioral psychologists know that positional relationships matter profoundly to people and have deep roots in our psyches and even our nervous systems. Some neoclassical economists and political commentators, though, lacking the language and interpretive tools to describe it, resort to chalking it up to "envy." But these positional arms races exert an invisible inflation on everyone caught in the same market.

This mechanism, then, goes way back historically. But it's taken on a new dimension in the post-Renaissance world, when smaller local markets have become united by exploration, travel, communications, and commerce. In the age of city-states, each German court could support a batch of musicians, perhaps even a small opera company, each pledging fealty to a local noble. When these states are all united into a nation or an empire, with a different economy of scale, there is suddenly only room for one. Same with railroads connecting previously isolated cities in nineteenth-century America. Like the Olympic runner who loses the race by a hundredth of a second, the company that once worked successfully in a single city is now out of luck. This is what came in the twenty-first century to be called, charmingly, "go big or go home."

Before scrutinizing the workings of winner-take-all markets in arts and entertainment, it's worth considering their traditional counterweights. If human societies seem to originate in this state (again, look at polygamy and the ancient Greek contests) and drift in this direction at other times (the rich-get-richer process of market capitalism) why don't we see winner-take-all cultures everywhere and at every time throughout human history? Some causes are economic and political, but our contemporary winner-take-all has a sociological dimension as well.

Traditionally, American society has included forces that balance winner-take-all effects. Some are very old (monogamy and a sense of public good or shared sacrifice predate the republic), while others go back approximately a century or more: progressive taxation, union protections for workers, restrictions on child labor, the trust-busting laws advocated by Theodore Roosevelt. In many societies, religious values and a culture of family (typically transmitted by women) spread the idea that there was something important outside self-interest and the marketplace. Others are more recent, like campaign financing laws that restrain the very wealthiest from controlling the political process and drowning out the voices of the less affluent. These all cut against—though do not entirely extinguish—the process by which the most powerful or wealthy or well-born consolidate their gains at the expense of the rest. During the middle decades of the twentieth century—the '40s, '50s, '60s, and most of the '70s—the United States did not have a winner-take-all society. It had instead what economists call the Great Compression, a structure of wages, government investment, and progressive taxation that led to a large and solid middle class, as well as steady economic growth. (The pattern in postwar Western Europe was similar.) A number of political commentators—Jacob Hacker, Timothy Noah, and Christopher Hayes among them—have shown how this compression was reversed. (Hayes points out that while the 1 percent has consolidated its gains substantially since the early '80s, members of Congress have become 260 percent richer as well.) But there were cultural forces at work, too.

The first of them may be the least tangible but among the most important for the existence of cultural institutions. That's the disappearance of a widespread idea of loss leaders, or noblesse oblige—a sense that some culture mattered for reasons outside its exchange value.

Take jazz, for example. Most of the businesspeople involved in music over the centuries have wanted a return on their investment. But not all. The jazz guitarist Kenny Burrell, for example, remembers recording in the '50s and '60s for label heads—at Blue Note, Prestige, Riverside— who saw the music as an art form. "Those guys *loved* the music," he recalled of the men who ran Blue Note, some of them refugees from Nazi Germany. "They were not concerned with making hits or making a million dollars." He saw the same spirit decades later. "I remember being in Europe, driving in a taxi, and seeing an ad for a radio station, where they said they played '500 years of great music.' And they listed Bach and Mozart, but also Ellington." Flash forward to America in the twenty-first century, where there are NFL wives who get more mainstream media coverage than every living jazz artist put together. The new economy was supposed to help niche cultures, but it has reinforced jazz's exile. "How do you promote this music if it's banned from radio, banned from television—and no longer reviewed in newspapers?" asked Gary Giddins, the former *Village Voice* critic, who remembered when things were different. (Burrell, who runs the jazz program at UCLA, has seen the real-world impact of all this. "Some students I know have gone to New York, struggled to pay the rent." Sometimes when he hears from old students—including talented and committed ones—they're living in their cars.)

But jazz isn't alone in its predicament. Big studios got behind movies that were not going to break box office records. Mainstream publishers took more chances. Even major labels signed odd or literary bands that seemed unlikely to recoup their investment. (Talking Heads on Sire, anyone?) "The idyllic example is Warner Bros. in the '60s [and early '70s]," says singer-songwriter Richard Thompson. "These guys were music people—and they earned income from the pop stuff, which helped them to finance the longer shots. And they worked on hunches: They weren't following marketing trends—'we need one of these, or one of these.' They said, This person Bonnie Raitt, I like her. This guy Randy Newman—he's gonna be good. This guy

Ry Cooder, this guy Van Dyke Parks. . . . If it takes ten years before he breaks even, that's okay. We'll try to see it sooner, but let's keep him around. Because we like to see ourselves as a broad-spectrum provider of music."

Of course, Anglo-American values changed, for reasons discussed elsewhere, and as a result, institutions changed as well. But one key was a changing culture not among the mass audience, or even the educated folk who tend to frequent jazz shows or buy poetry collections. Adam Smith saw this coming in the late eighteenth century: "The proprietor of land is necessarily a citizen of the particular country in which his estate lies," he wrote in *The Wealth of Nations*. "The proprietor of stock is properly a citizen of the world, and is not necessarily attached to any particular country." When the affluent class shifted from owning land to owning part of a business, the wealthy "proprietor" began to dislocate himself from a town or community. Multinational corporations took this a step beyond. When the world economy went global in the 1990s, and digital technology pushed it even further along, captains of industry and capital ended up starting timeshares for private jets and living everyplace-and-no-place that we know from the science fiction of Neal Stephenson. (The cultural equivalent of this class may be the rap and pop stars who fly around the world performing for dictators.)

The changing culture at the top—what Christopher Lasch called "The Revolt of the Elites"—leads to an abandonment of public spaces as well as the notion of a shared culture. That shift is the subject more recently of Chrystia Freeland's rigorously reported *Plutocrats: The Rise of the New Global Super-Rich and the Fall of Everyone Else*. Freeland spent time—in corporate boardrooms, on planes headed to business conferences, at the Davos summit—with numerous billionaires, many of whom come across as intelligent and decent. But these people—most of whom made their money with the opening of markets in the former Soviet Union and other newly privatized nations or during the digital gold rush—are very different from Henry Ford, who paid his assembly-line employees enough so that they could afford one of his cars, or Andrew Carnegie, who gave away all of his riches and built numerous libraries, concert halls, and other cultural outlets—especially in his adopted hometown of Pittsburgh. By contrast, plutocrats of the twenty-first century have no real hometown or home team of any kind. Their dedication is entirely to capital and to its frictionless international exchange.

It's hard to lament the fall of the Soviet Union—for decades one of the nastiest dictatorships the world has ever seen. But far more ambiguous is what its demise has done to us in the West. "That shift from state to private ownership is probably the single largest transfer of assets in human history," Freeland wrote, documenting how it created more twenty-first-century billionaires than Silicon Valley or Wall Street. In the '90s there was a lot of excited talk about "liberating" former centrally planned markets, and the "shock therapy" needed to do it. These days, Stalin is dead, but "Russia's oligarchs have done so well for themselves that inequality today is higher than it was under the tsars." This liberation accompanied a drop in GDP of about 40 percent, with businesses now run by Communist-reared jet-setters. Meanwhile, American communities have been transformed since the days when a local WASP or Jewish elite lived in the same city as the common folk and endowed the museum downtown. Is it any wonder that corporations are less likely to sponsor local arts events, or that local ownership of newspapers and magazines has been so hard to restore? If local prestige—someone who owns a publication and dines out on its quality in its sphere of influence—no longer matters, these things won't be coming back.

Another loss to the sense of noblesse oblige came with the end of the Cold War, when the U.S. government stopped underwriting culture, from tours of jazz artists overseas (which papered over racial tensions) or promotion of abstract expressionist painters (to demonstrate the rugged individualism of artists in a free society) to Nixon's doubling of the budget for the National Endowment for the Arts. (Lewis Hyde has pointed out the irony of a struggle with the Soviet Union pushing the United States toward a partially socialized, nonmarket arts policy.) Needless to say, before the Cold War, the Works Progress Administration kept writers, photographers, theater actors, and others alive during a difficult time. Despite the best efforts of our humanities and arts leaders, we see nothing like this today.

Cultural criticism is another traditional counterweight to the marketplace. Journalism and the market have a complex relationship; Pauline Kael called the critic "the only voice between the advertisers and the public," but critics, including Kael, also made stars. Critics or press coverage exerted, in the cultural sphere, the equivalent of journalism's old adage about comforting-the-afflicted and afflicting-the-comfortable. An obscure artist could leap to attention because of sympathetic press—Kael on Martin Scorsese's *Mean Streets,* for example—while megastars could see their reputations chipped away, even if not typically their accumulated wealth. But criticism is now gradually being replaced by marketing, at least in the genres now deemed "critic proof." Televised winner-take-all contests are part of the same process. *American Idol* makes it seem as if selecting overwrought crooners singing overplayed hits is the purest, most noble and egalitarian act of democracy. An art museum even based its biennial's $100,000 prize on the *Idol* model.

Winner-take-all contests have taken over not just pop music but coverage of movies as well. The Academy Awards and box office earnings were once information consigned to the back pages of newspaper culture sections. In the 1970s, for instance, the *New York Times* treated the Oscars like the gathering of Hollywood *alter kakers* it is. But by elevating the Academy Awards from a pseudo-event to a judgment of the gods—preceded by weeks and months of speculation—newspapers and magazines have created a massive grade inflation. Minor, low-credibility contests—the Golden Globes, Screen Actors Guild, and so on—now command breathless media attention and predictions because of the indications they give as to how the Oscars might go. Similarly, newspapers talk far more about the business side of the movies, putting box office figures—ubiquitous compared with even a decade ago—front and center. When the media want to discuss cinematic quality, they increasingly dispense with the aesthetic judgments altogether and instead ask—even well before awards season—what the Oscar voters on Olympus will judge.

A number of trends, all with their own origins and trajectories, are coming together now. Laissez-faire aesthetics is the philosophy in which visual art's value is derived from its connections to pop culture and its performance in the marketplace. (The term originates with the art critic Jed Perl, who has also written about how what he calls Warholism destroys nuance.) Anti-intellectualism—which tends to accompany market populism and hostility to culture—is another way an opposing system of value gets shut down. We get it first by destroying older systems of authority; television and advertising are quite good at this. Corporations have become "the tacit superheroes of consumer culture," media scholar Mark Crispin Miller said.

It's part of the official advertising worldview that your parents are creeps, teachers are nerds, and nobody can really understand kids but the corporate sponsor. They are busy selling the illusion that they are there to liberate the youth, to let them be free, to let them be themselves, to let them think different, and so on.

Look back at old movies and you'll see a time when even the hard-bitten studio bosses allowed educated people with inner lives, and some sense of the noncorporate arts, into their films. "Often, aspirations to high culture would be asserted through a ballet sequence, or a scene of the family gathered around the radio, listening to an opera program," Phillip Lopate wrote. "Certainly, we can smile today at the clumsy culture-mongering of those interludes; but the very naivete of those sequences reproaches us. For they point to a time in American movies when both high-culture and popular-culture references existed, where now only pop culture has the right to be alluded to." Mainstream movies often had an intellectual minor character, what he calls "a model of mature intelligence." In the '60s, even *Gilligan's Island* had the Professor. How many teachers or scholars on television are treated as anything but twits or villains today? Even residual prestige has evaporated.

The food writer Michael Pollan has written eloquently about what happens when context dies—when traditional ethnic rules about eating get worn away by modernization. Unless a society is careful, traditional habits of eating get replaced by fast food, phony nutritional supplements, and health problems. Similarly, as these old cultural figures and middlebrow tropes have been swept away, they've been replaced not by McDonald's, exactly, but by a culture of celebrity. Fame and celebrity, of course, are not new to our time: Leo Braudy has traced the phenomenon back to Alexander the Great. But with cultural hierarchy gone, most kinds of authority fading fast, and digital technology transforming our psychology, our culture and media have never been so dominated by celebrities. Celebrity culture—with its very limited room at the top—is another cause and effect of the winner-take-all society. The process and its effects remain baffling, but Karen Sternheimer—a sociologist at the University of Southern California who has studied fan magazines and the workings of fame going back to the early silent movie era—likens it to the adding of artificial sweeteners to food. "It's not like people said, 'Please, put more sweeteners in our salad dressing,'" she said. "But if you're going to give it to us, we like it. It's cheap content. And it becomes a vicious cycle," as media outlets offer more and more celebrity news and then, noticing that people consume it, double down.

Technological changes are a larger part of this phenomenon. Instead of waiting for *Entertainment Tonight* to come on, or the new issue of *Us* to arrive each week, you can find Hollywood gossip or lavish photos of Drake's baronial home anytime you want. "Or it finds you," Sternheimer said. "If you have a Yahoo email account, or go anywhere online, even onto a so-called legitimate news website, it's all over the place." These days, anyone can start a Twitter feed and become freelance paparazzi. You can get even closer: You can join the cast of a reality TV show and become a celebrity yourself. "Celebrity coverage has expanded to the degree to which journalism has been defunded," Sternheimer said. "It's so much more expensive to fund investigative journalism than to run something about a famous person getting married or divorced. 'Drama' becomes a replacement for journalism—it's a shiny object."

How does an obsession with *Lifestyles of the Rich and Famous* coverage persist in an age of stark inequality and stagnant middle-class wages? Fan magazines grew even more besotted with material bounty after the 1929 crash—typically ignoring or mocking directors and actors who'd been unable to make the transition to sound—and it's no different today. As Sternheimer wrote in her book *Celebrity Culture and the American Dream:*

> Celebrity and fame are unique manifestations of our sense of American social mobility: they provide the illusion that material wealth is possible for anyone. The American Dream, which shifts and mutates with changes in the economy and the political and social

backdrop, seems very real when we see the plethora of people who have entered the realm of celebrity.

An extroverted nonstop culture of celebrity also offers something reassuring to anyone who begins to doubt the promise of America during difficult times. Like Horatio Alger stories, the hyper-individualistic rags-to-riches tales that drive the celebrity narrative say: The system works. (Look at Britney! Jeremy Lin!) It's you who's failed.

Besides the larger society that has been shaped by a trickle-up economy, the world of culture includes mechanisms that create or reinforce monopolies at the top. Let's call it the blockbuster culture—the sociological equivalent of winner-take-all. Its roots are deep. "It's connected to our canonic ideas of greatness," said music historian Robert Fink. "Capitalism and the notion of the autonomous artist fit together to produce winner-take-all. The idea of the genius and capitalism work together beautifully. So the great artist is the one who sells a ton of records. Hip-hop is the genre that grew up in the Reagan '80s—the best rapper is the most popular one."

The term "blockbuster," which came into use in World War II, originally referred to bombs powerful enough to take out an entire city block. The cultural blockbuster has roots in the connection of previously independent markets. Elizabeth Billington, an English soprano at the dawn of the Industrial Revolution, became wealthy (earning in 1801 as much as five hundred farm workers) and internationally famous. She was a great talent, but she was also working at a time when transportation and communication were rapidly increasing, and industrialism was creating enormous wealth. If she had been born a century earlier, she would have been equally talented but far more provincial—and financially modest—in her following.

Instead, she lived at a time when talent and culture were being industrialized. We were on the road to what Walter Benjamin would call "the work of art in the age of mechanical reproduction." We arrived there, unmistakably, in the age of music recording and motion pictures. Charlie Chaplin became an enormously wealthy star when he made movies featuring the Tramp, and early recording artists—Enrico Caruso, Al Jolson, Paul Whiteman, Bessie Smith—could "perform" simultaneously all over the world thanks to the phonograph. This was, like most technological and economic advances, good for some, bad for the rest. If you were a local musician or actor, your audience could very likely spend its time and money taking in an industrial image of someone who lived thousands of miles—or dozens of years—away. "In 1900, nearly all spectator entertainment was provided by live performers," Chrystia Freeland wrote of what she called the birth of the superstar phenomenon. "By 1938, live acts accounted for just 8 percent of all public entertainment. In the mid-1920s, before the introduction of sound in movies, Americans spent $1.33 per capita on theater, versus $3.59 on movies; by 1938, the spending had further tilted in the direction of film—down to $0.45 on live performances and up to $5.11 at the movies." Whether you prefer movies to plays or vice versa, we were on the road to winner-take-all.

Some of these mechanisms seem innocent, even benign. The bestseller list, for instance, is the only book coverage some publications offer. The paper with the most sophisticated and influential cultural coverage in the nation, the *New York Times,* has made an institution out of its own list, which drives publisher promotion. Chain bookstores typically give discounts on books that land on the Top 10 or 15. There may be some trickle-down effect here—people come into a shop to buy a popular, heavily promoted thriller and find something else while browsing—but the list also acts like a regressive tax. The former *Washington Post* book critic Michael Dirda called the list "a disaster for literary and general culture." As he wrote in *BookForum:* "Above all, despite appearances, the best-seller list isn't populist; it's elitist. If there are a dozen slots, six are filled by the same old establishment names. For every James Patterson novel on the list, there's one fewer novel by someone else. This is a tight clubby little world." And it's a club dominated by celebrities that leaves new and unknown writers, poetry, essays, criticism, and other minority tastes out in the cold.

When Motown goes from a label with a dozen bands landing hits to one in which only Michael Jackson can create a megahit song, that's winner take all. When an Internet algorithm directs people only to the most popular work, that's winner take all. When the tax code is redrawn so that hedge fund guys pay less than you do, or corporate bosses pay a lower percentage than their secretaries, that's winner take all.

It's all good news for Dan Brown and Lady Gaga, but it's bad news for the creative middle class. In publishing, the death of the midlist started, probably, in the 1970s, and—despite a bump during the building of superstores—has accelerated since. The move to an all-or-nothing market for books became fiercest at the corporate presses that needed to satisfy shareholders each quarter and based their business model on Hollywood's. But even in the mostly pre-corporate days, the late Aaron Asher, who was the editor in chief at Farrar, Straus & Giroux, observed the process.

> Now more and more of these books are not being bought at all by the paperback houses. It's not merely that the mass-market publisher who has laid out a million dollars for a blockbuster can't afford the additional money to buy ten middle books for five thousand dollars apiece—that's a drop in the bucket to him. The *room* isn't there. The investment, the energy, all the thinking in a paperback house are geared to the book that it can make a killing on. Everything else is secondary.

Should it surprise us that the bestsellers' club has consolidated since the 1970s, the same way upper-income folks have taken over waterfront property? "Five of 1978's top-selling authors appeared among the top twenty in the previous five years," Frank and Cook noted, "compared to nine of the top ten in 1990." The process can be seen in nearly all markets. The blockbuster era—associated with the production of Hollywood films after the enormous success of *Jaws* and *Star Wars* brought the flourishing of small, smart auteur-style films to a close in the '70s—is now where we all live.

In film, it's actually gotten much worse. The closest thing to the '70s auteurs since *Star Wars* was the flourishing of independent films, in which Spike Lee and Steven Soderbergh and Hal Hartley made personal, eccentric movies never intended to break box office records. But like indie rock, which developed its own value system and counter-canon while the larger music industry became more fiercely corporate and then began to collapse, the '90s indie films were swept away by more powerful tides. (In a few cases, indie filmmakers became blockbuster directors, and the next generation of indie auteurs never arrived.) Part of the reason was, as with superstar sopranos and silent movie stars, the rise of technology and the merging of markets.

"We always exported our films," said film producer and industry critic Lynda Obst, "and our movie stars were always the world's stars." Many countries had their own thriving film industries. The balance changed, though, around the time the domestic DVD market lost steam. High-impact digital technology made mega-films like *Avatar* and the *Harry Potter* sequels possible, just as Russia and China were opening up to both capitalism and movies. These new markets went crazy for these films, and provided the studios with a tremendous financial jolt. Such movies also cost a hundred million dollars or more to produce and market. On the other side, there was a kind of film that didn't travel: anything with an original storyline, not taken from a comic book, video game, or theme-park ride, aimed at a grownup audience, and with more conversation or psychology than explosions. Foreign movie audiences "don't want writing or nuance," Obst said. "They don't want our jokes; they want jokes that are specific to their own cultures." What they want is "pre-awareness"—a movie about something they already know about. Like a superhero. Or a movie they saw last year, like one of the *Fast and the Furious* franchise.

These days, the Chinese market is either a physician jolting adrenaline into an ailing Hollywood, or a bully driving the grownup films away. Nearly ten new cinema screens *per day* are going up in China, most of them 3-D or Imax theaters, designed for blowout action movies. The market incentives are not geared to produce the next Eric Rohmer or Yasujiro Ozu.

Now that movie studios are content-providers for multinational corporations, "studios have to write P and L [profit and loss] statements," Obst said. "They can't write, 'I love this movie,' on it. That's not the way it works. These days, when every call is a $250 million call, they don't want to hear, 'I believe in this movie.' They want to hear, 'This will work in the international market, *because* . . . ' " They want a formula of special effects and Russian and Chinese action stars who can make the film huge. "You have to have a quantifiable algorithm." (Harvard Business School professor Anita Elberse has written in her book *Blockbusters* that even with several high-profile flops that some think could bring down the studios, the digital economy makes the search for megahits more valuable than ever for entertainment corporations.)

There's another side of the gulch where the middle used to be: thanks to low-cost digital technology, production of movies can now be done very cheaply, which means there are many no-budget films being made, at various levels of quality, but most of them never find distribution and hardly anyone gets paid. The middle has been so thoroughly hollowed out in film that Soderbergh recently said he's made his last movie. Even Steven Spielberg—hardly someone afraid of popularity or incapable of mass appeal—almost didn't get to make *Lincoln* because the studios, he said, are only interested in action-movie blockbusters.

What happens over time? In 1975, *Jaws*—which now seems like a model of intelligent, restrained, character-driven movie-making—opened on four hundred screens, at a time when films typically started out in the two or three biggest cities and rolled out gradually from there. By 2012, *The Dark Knight Rises*—directed by recovered indie filmmaker Christopher Nolan—opened on more than four thousand screens in the United States and ten thousand more worldwide, all on the same day. Comic book characters often start out as underdogs, but in today's pop culture they've become Leviathans. And for all the rhetoric that says that pop is really what "the people" want, the rollout strategy of a blockbuster artist like Lady Gaga resembles the plan to invade small countries. Her manager "arranged for 50 popular music bloggers to interview Gaga in the six months following the 'Just Dance' launch; during that period, these interviews alone totaled over 10 million impressions," Elberse wrote. "One key factor here is that people like winners —they prefer to consume entertainment products that are also chosen by others. As a result, a solid opening is often a huge factor in a rollout. For media products, initial success breeds further success, while a failure to achieve success early on frequently means having no chance to succeed at all."

Many members of the creative class get to work on a gargantuan comic-book or theme-park movie. But those blockbusters—as shown by high-profile flops that have led to multimillion dollar write-downs and Hollywood layoffs

—don't just marginalize the midsize films, which might otherwise have gone on those screens. The blockbuster model is about as sustainable a path for the creative class as a national economy where four lucky people—whose greatest accomplishment is an accident of birth—own as much as 100 million do.

The explosion of high-stakes contests in the arts and entertainment amplifies this process. "We live in a world of such celebrity that a lot is not celebrated at all," the musician Van Dyke Parks said. "Competition for me has no place in the arts. Art is not a contest!" These days, it most certainly is. There's only one winner at a time, and the winner takes all the chips.

What kind of a society do we get if a tiny group employs a combination of luck, skill, and hard work to take the vast majority of the spoils, while the broad remainder fight one another for the crumbs? We get a society a lot like where we live now—and an arrangement whose terms are visibly tightening. Even more clearly, we get the world in which today's creative class finds it ever harder to ply its craft, pay the rent, collect its meager revenues. We find ourselves halfway to a world where life has become so privatized that corporations plaster their names not only on football stadiums and concert halls but—as in David Foster Wallace's *Infinite Jest*—the years themselves are named for Glad bags and Depend adult undergarments.

Let's return to ancient Athens for a moment. The big winners of the festivals of Dionysus were Euripides, Sophocles, and Aeschylus. It's hard to imagine Western culture without these three, and it is likely that they were indeed the greatest playwrights of their era. But for various reasons, some having to do with a winner-take-all reward structure, some with the torching of the Alexandria library, we will never know. Their plays are the only tragic drama that's survived from the Greek golden age. It's as if the only surviving work from the music of the 1960s was the Beatles, the Rolling Stones, and Bob Dylan. No Aretha Franklin, no Kinks, no Zombies, no Love, no Byrds, no Otis Redding or Doc Watson or Miles Davis or Glenn Gould. We have only seven plays apiece from Aeschylus and Sophocles—so it's also like imagining the '60s without, say, *Rubber Soul* or *Blonde on Blonde* or *Between the Buttons*. That's the way corporate radio typically works. Winner-take-all exerts a relentless logic not just on our creative life, but on our cultural memory.

Let's also concede something: Cultural celebrity, and contests in the arts, are not always zero-sum games. A star can bring attention and excitement not just to his own career, but to an entire genre, as Maria Callas, Leonard Bernstein, and Wynton Marsalis did to theirs. The Van Cliburn and Thelonious Monk competitions bring media attention to classical piano and jazz playing. The Pulitzers, National Book Awards, and Booker Prize are sometimes the only chance novelists, poets, or composers have to land on the front page.

But when winner-take-all goes to its furthest extreme, its effects are relentless. People know this intuitively, as we see with the cult success of a film like *Searching for Sugar Man*, about the forgotten early-'70s folk singer Rodriguez, who became an inspiration in apartheid-era South Africa while laboring in obscurity as a carpenter in Detroit. (Once discovered, he went on to perform here, there, and everywhere, and to finally earn some money from his music.) The success of the film, and of Rodriguez's ensuing career, shows that people can be moved by the story of the unjustly overlooked artist. It's the kind of story, though, that could only happen in the pre-Internet, pre-globalized days in which national markets and music scenes were kept separate. All kinds of things could happen in the future, but a replay of this story will not likely be one of them. We've got inside us a love of the underdog, the beautiful loser, but those instincts seem like an evolutionary anomaly, like our tailbone, in what's becoming a ruthlessly quantified and globalized world.

WHAT CAN WE LOOK FORWARD to, then? Well, without significant structural change, current trends are likely to continue and get more extreme. What would that mean? Life is always complex, and no cultural change arises from a single cause; in fact, a study of plane crashes and reactor meltdowns shows that small, even tiny changes and unintended consequences can add up to unlikely and catastrophic conclusions. But taking the broadest view: We've spent several decades convinced that markets are the measure of all things. From speed-dating to Freakonomics to selfish genes to tipping points, this assumption crosses over to the vast majority of the political and intellectual spectrum and is now part of not just our market behavior but our most intimate and private lives. Post-Freud, it's the primary metaphor by which most of us think about our behavior and our relationships.

Markets work well for many things, both as metaphors and as mechanisms to direct goods. But they're often a mess for culture—especially the way we think about it—and market talk does little to explain the relative value of one painter or pianist or poet or newspaper over another. (For all their many differences, a purely market-driven culture is almost as bad as a purely state-driven one.) With the cultural and psychological triumph of the market, we've lost the very language by which we might express the worth of things. Instead, you hear something else: a cult of selfishness, in management theory and hip-hop, in Newt Gingrich and Oprah Winfrey and Sarah Palin. Though unbridled capitalism led to a fairly recent catastrophe, deregulation and the corporate model continues to spread. Public education has already succumbed, with predictable results. Hospitals and health care are on their way. The university system—where currently 76 percent of faculty members are adjuncts, part-timers, and others not on the tenure track—is on its way to becoming the next testing ground, as public funding is slashed and the professoriat is de-professionalized the same way journalism has been. A revenue obsession that has already led to a fascination with branding, digital technology, globalization, and self-serving democracy talk are leading us to MOOCs, which could very easily lead to a handful of academics becoming global stars while the rest drag their libraries and student loan documents from campus to campus for a few thousand here, a few thousand there. They'll join the rest of the creative class in the basement. Is it any wonder that market worship in the twenty-first century means the bestselling artists claim to be gods?

In the Anglo-American world, we think of ourselves in a number of sometimes contradictory ways. In the twenty-first century, we have reconciled them—at the expense of the culture and those who make it. Our impulse toward dissent and individualism—genuinely valuable and productive impulses—have been turned to the cult of the rebel consumer, or what the Clash called "turning rebellion into money." Young people buy a Jay-Z record and think they're raging against the machine; their parents gather around tables at their last surviving chain bookstore, with its stacks of volumes on how to unleash their inner corporate ninja. We're seeing record-breaking levels of poverty, but our cultural heroes are a long way from Steinbeck and Woody Guthrie. And we're all—in a society that has remained aspirational despite mounting evidence to the contrary—superstars waiting for our big break. "The [Jeremy] Lin story," David Carr of the *New York Times* wrote, "has broken out into the general culture because it is aspirational in the extreme, fulfilling notions that have nothing to do with basketball or race. Most of us are not superstars, but we believe we could be if only given the opportunity. We are, as a matter of practicality, a nation of supporting players, but who among us has not secretly thought we could be at the top of our business, company or team if the skies parted and we had our shot?"

This idea has a brother, too, in a culture that manages to reconcile individualism with conformity, to deny the role of larger forces and to regard history as simply something nasty that happens to other people. It says, if you are not a superstar, or a millionaire, you are either a step away or you're a loser. "A culture of arrogance, hubris, and winner-take-all was established," David Byrne has said. "It wasn't cool to be poor or struggling. The bully was celebrated and cheered." The former Talking Head is describing latter-day New York City. But it reminds us how since the Cold War much of the English-speaking world is coming to resemble post-Soviet Russia.

There are other visions of America or democratic Britain,

or have been in the not-too-distant past. In the fading years of the postwar boom, the political philosopher John Rawls tried to update the social contract in a way that synthesized both liberty and equality. The key to his notion is the sense that a working theory of justice must be dreamed up from behind a "veil of ignorance"; its architects must not know their position in the world they'd be born into, whether high, low, or in between. We need to think up a system that works if we win the lottery to superstardom, and also if we don't. It doesn't mean pure equality—but a system that is both substantially fair and substantially free.

Rawls's theory of justice has been assailed—like the liberal consensus and notion of the common good that it in some ways underlines—by both left and right. But it has hardly been supplanted as a model for a just society, especially for the creative class in the twenty-first century. What the past few decades have shown us is that we don't know—in an age of creative destruction—just where our seat at the ball will be. Will we be playing the violin for tips, dining on venison and claret, or scrubbing the floors? Will we be, as the Sinatra song has it, puppet or pauper, pirate or poet, pawn or king? We could move forward through that cast of characters, or we could move backward. If the twenty-first century has taught the creative class anything, it's that unless we have significant family wealth, we can be one, or all, or none at all.

For culture to work, we need a common language. The arts have historically drawn from a lingua franca, whether one made of images or words or sounds or narratives, and it's impossible to have one when we are becoming more culturally and economically divided every day. No wonder our common language has become celebrity gossip and reality TV. In the past, we've done better, and we can do better again. What we need to create—which means fighting against the assumptions we've inherited—is a world that is not predatory, not coddling, not made up exclusively of feudal lords and struggling serfs, but one that allows culture to serve human needs. And that includes culture's creators and assessors and street-level salesmen. It means smashing contemporary myths and adjusting to a new world that encourages a creative class that is robust, productive, and secure. It means being ornery, forward-looking, and wise.

EPILOGUE

Culture, for me, is the effort to provide a coherent set of answers
to the existential predicaments that confront all human beings in
the passage of their lives. . . . For this reason, tradition becomes
essential to the vitality of a culture, for it provides the continuity
of memory that teaches how one's forebears met the same
existential predicaments.

—Daniel Bell, *The Cultural Contradictions of Capitalism*

FROM VAN GOGH SLICING OFF his ear, Baudelaire expiring
in a dimly lit Parisian demimonde, Beethoven snubbing an
Austrian empress and striking a prince with a chair, or Hendrix torching his Stratocaster, our images of the artist are bold
and indelible. These tales of the very high and very low—
starving artists, radical transgressives, godlike superstars—
make great movies and feature stories. They also mislead us
mightily about the nature of art and artists themselves.

My quarter century as a cultural journalist has given me a wide window into the lives of creative people, one that's allowed me to peer beyond the myths and legends. In some cases I've merely met a painter or film director for an hour or two; in other cases, I've struck up long-term friendships with indie rockers or lyric poets. What I've found is that despite romantic myth, most artists and others who work in the world of culture come from the middle class and hope, after a few years of scrambling and bare-bones living, to return to it. This doesn't mean giving up their tastes or artistic dedication or even, in some cases, political commitment. But mostly, they want safety and stability, and the ability to keep working. Despite a sense that artistic work and the work ethic are in tension, the creative class defines itself by its labor. Creatives know as well as anyone what Barbara Ehrenreich calls the "secret hedonism of the middle class . . . a pleasure that cannot be commodified or marketed, that need not obsolesce or wane with time." These days, as I've documented, that work, and its ensuing pleasure, has become difficult to maintain.

Middle-class values show up in unlikely places. One of the founders of the underground comics movement, R. Crumb, is a notorious bohemian who lives in seclusion in the south of France. But the underground cartoonists I know, who work to varying degrees in Crumb's tradition of alienation and social criticism, are concerned not just with their necessarily obsessive art but with finding safe, affordable places to live, decent schools for their kids, and ways to continue working. Similarly, no one would call the neo-expressionist painter Eric Fischl *petit bourgeois*. His goal as an artist, however, is not to get rich or to appall the squares, but to paint canvases well and truly enough that he can keep painting, and to wrestle with the essentials of what we once called the human condition. Contemporary art based on shock and celebrity and vanguard cool has convinced most people that it's not for them. But art, he writes, "gives experience its meaning and its clarity." Culture, he argues, is something that allows us to transcend the pressures of the larger society, to get somewhere deeper than daily life allows.

What Fischl is describing here is what skeptics denounce as *middlebrow*—a term we hardly use anymore, but which has come in for its share of abuse over the years. It has deep connections to the middle class and the growth of the mass audience, though middlebrow aesthetics and the economic middle are not exactly the same things. Dwight Macdonald did his best to destroy middlebrow in his 1960 essay, "Masscult and Midcult." I adore much of Macdonald's work, including this impassioned essay, but he's wrong here, as he often was about political questions. Midcentury intellectuals who assailed middlebrow, especially its dream of engaging a broad audience with culture of some seriousness, did not realize how good we had it.

I know many artists and intellectuals alike whose passion for culture was sparked by something as middlebrow as a public library or Leonard Bernstein's Young People's Concerts, a newspaper profile of an obscure rock band, a high school art class, a foreign novel published by the Modern Library, or Time-Life books on famous painters. I was born in 1969, to parents shaped by an earlier era, so I was in the right place to see their world, and its accompanying assumptions, fade away like a pale ghost.

I should make my perspective clear here. Culture may

not make us better people; sometimes it does, sometimes it doesn't. But it does make our society better: more alert, more alive, more compassionate, more connected to both past and present. A wider dissemination of art and culture would benefit not only the broad society. It could help give the creative class a future.

WHY DOES ASSERTING THESE THINGS seem so unfashionable, or even, as one colleague has put it, positively radical? The answer becomes a bit clearer if we look at how our sense of culture—and our assumptions about it—was built. It's worth remembering that, throughout Western history, art-for-art's-sake existed for only very brief slivers: in fifth-century Athens, Renaissance Italy, France here and there, 1890s London, maybe Greenwich Village. Otherwise, art has always been *for* something else.

That *something else* changed repeatedly; it was never stable. Prehistoric humans painted images on cave walls not just for aesthetic contemplation, but so hunters could attract bison or deer. To the ancients, music took some of the sting out of blood sacrifices—a kind of aesthetic apology. Later on, the artist was a sort of magician. To the medieval mind, the artist mattered not at all—he was little different than a carpenter or cobbler—except to channel the glory of God. As the Renaissance got closer, musicians were stationed in towers outside towns: *Türmer* (in German, "tower men") and *Pifferi* (their Italian equivalents) were offered lodging and an instrument if they sounded their horn at the approach of marauders or fire. Later, painters and musicians became advertisements for prestige-seeking dukes and princes. Later still, major composers wore livery, alongside the footmen.

These old solutions to the question of what the arts are for seem silly or at least antique today. But they kept the wheels of culture rolling, and kept the creative class employed, in however subordinate a position. Those liveried composers were most decidedly "the help," but we remember their work today in a way we don't the edicts of their better-born employers.

As we moved into the early modern period, though, things changed decisively, and in some ways postmodernity is still struggling with the same tensions and questions. On the surface, it looked like the best of times—the eighteenth and nineteenth centuries were an era of great expansion in the audience for the creative arts, culture's growing accessibility, and burgeoning middle-class patronage. There was also a broadening of the creative class as photographers, publishers of music and books, journalists, art dealers, Barnum-like impresarios, and symphony orchestras took advantage of changes in technology and distribution. The growth of cities made possible a mass audience for the performing arts; heating and electricity made year-round theaters and concert halls possible. The widening of education—and the emancipation of middle-class women—provided a vast readership for the novel, especially. Engravings and posters made visual art accessible; paperbacks could be read on trains. Libraries, public galleries, and concert halls opened.

At the same time, an older way of life came to an often sudden end: church and court patronage collapsed definitively as small city-states merged into larger ones and the commercial classes displaced the nobility. The artist's new life—publishing, publicity, subscription concert series, the marketplace—had been established only in patches. At a time when the artist was already trying to adjust to mechanical reproduction, industry, and the marketplace, the great disruption of 1789 happened, and it was followed by more than a century of turmoil and revolution—especially in France, the center of cultural gravity. Artists were left stranded. Some—Byron and Beethoven and their followers —imagined themselves as nobles or dandies. Even more slid into the gutter. The ideology of the Parisian demimonde— bohemia's scorning of the bourgeoisie—succeeded all too well. The world of Flaubert and Berlioz, or Baudelaire and their contemporaries—like the Water Drinkers, artists too poor to afford wine—is still with us.

It would have been impossible for the creative class to come through all of these changes with its faith in progress and society intact. (The term *bourgeoisie* forever carries a sneer that the parallel word in German—*burgher*—never has. But the self-image of artists carried a similar baggage no matter where they lived.) The relentlessness of vanguardism, and the conflict of artists with the early-modern capitalist West, a world built on fame and the marketplace, was not limited to Paris. Walt Whitman and Emily Dickinson struggled in their very different ways to deal with this new world, and their near contemporary Edgar Allan Poe combined aristocratic pretensions with a beggar's lifestyle.

During the nineteenth century, then, artists lost their place in society—began going underground—and the arts themselves were dislocated from the class that increasingly supported them. In some cases, artists and their work became driven by contempt for the middle class. Before long, the feeling became mutual. Culture became a minority taste, and artists came to be defined by their melancholy, seclusion, alcohol consumption, and cult of the self. This was a long way from the days when the artists and culture had a central role, with the shaman holding forth around the tribe's communal fire, or massive ancient harvest festivals accompanied by tragic drama. From this point on, artists lived in their own neighborhoods, which started out as bohemia and became, in many cases, academia. Artists grew alienated not just from the bourgeoisie but from other generations and rival movements in their own art forms. The artist became an outsider.

After all this—and the great richness produced in nineteenth-century France and the modern movement that grew out of it—you'd think that culture and the middle class would never make peace again. But it happened, for a while at least. The machinery of middlebrow started as early as the 1920s, as modernism crested. Inspired by the notion of the American Century, and rising levels of education in the United States, Henry Luce, a missionary's son, founded *Time* magazine in 1923, with a youthful, Ivy League tone: David Halberstam later described it as bearing "more than a touch of young college kids in raccoon coats on their way to football games." Luce was certainly no angel. But publishers like him were not simply profit-driven Babbitts. "His greatest influence," Halberstam continued, "may have been in broadening American culture, in involving millions of middlebrow Americans in the arts, in theater, in religion and education." The *New Yorker,* a humor magazine that eventually defined upper-middlebrow cultural seriousness, began a few years later.

By the postwar years, we got a book club run by W. H. Auden, Jacques Barzun, and Lionel Trilling, the G.I. Bill that led to the cultural education of artists and audiences alike, the National Endowment for the Arts and the National Endowment for the Humanities, and the establishment of public broadcasting that led, by 1970, to PBS and NPR. Universities, many of them state schools, expanded faster than they ever had before, or since. Culture was, at this point, largely bipartisan: Eisenhower sent black jazz musicians around the world, Nixon supported the NEA. (Was some of this self-serving, politically expedient, or nationalistic chest-beating? Of course.) Britain had its own middlebrow push, with Kenneth Clark's *Civilisation* and Jacob Bronowski's *The Ascent of Man* appearing on television, and later inspiring Carl Sagan's *Cosmos,* perhaps the last gasp of America's original middlebrow moment.

For all the ups and downs of culture and the creative class, an old classical idea, dressed in different vestments each century, persisted: that drama, poetry, music, and art were not just a way to pass the time, or advertise one's might, but a path to truth and enlightenment. At its best, this was what the middlebrow consensus promised. Middlebrow said that culture was accessible to a wide strata of society, that people needed some but not much training to appreciate it, that there was a canon worth knowing, that art was not the same as entertainment, that the study of the liberal arts deepens you, and that those who make, assess, and disseminate the arts were somehow valuable for our society regardless of their impact on GDP. Today, every one of those statements goes against our post-industrial, technocratic grain.

WAS EVERYTHING BETTER IN MIDCENTURY? Of course not. I have no nostalgia for a world of legal segregation, the closet, or ironclad gender roles. But we got some things right. Just as the middle class grew during this period of relative equality that economists called the Great Compression, so the middlebrow consensus ensured that culture thrived as well. Both the creative class and the middle class have seen their stability undermined over the past few decades, and my sense is they will resurge together, or keep falling in tandem. What we need most decisively is to reconnect culture to the burghers and rebuild the institutions that made the connection work the last time around. It also means acknowledging that the creative class needs certain middle-class protections. Traditionally, protection has come from things like record labels, publishing houses, newspapers with strong subscription bases, and trade unions—all of these institutions aggregate risk while leaving the "content creator" relatively independent intellectually and creatively. In the age of disaggregation, their days are all numbered.

This has a political meaning, too, one that honest people on both sides of the spectrum should agree on: An artist or musician or journalist who relies on corporate patronage, rather than a real audience or a mixed economy, is not independent.

Of course, for nineteenth-century bohemians or early-twentieth-century modernists, the idea of seeking a stable middle-class life from which to produce art would have seemed like a joke. But let's consider today's scholars: Some conceive of themselves as truth-tellers doing work independent of the marketplace and state power. Others are more modest in their self-conception. But virtually all seek the stability afforded by tenure and steady institutional employment. Academia and the tenure system may need reform, but only the most heartless neoliberal would argue that teaching and scholarship will be better when academics are all "free agents."

Was the midcentury middlebrow idea a perfect and unimpeachable notion of how culture and society could fit together? Probably not. Were the attacks on it—by avant-gardists and lowbrows and highbrows alike—justified, and perhaps even fruitful in some cases? Sure. In the short term, those critiques may even have generated interest in culture and provided a one-time boost for the creative class. But they destroyed, intentionally or not, an important foundation, and its loss makes it hard to move forward. At some point, someone will come up with a conception better than middlebrow. Until then, it beats the alternatives—neoliberal utilitarianism that values culture only for the money it makes, reactionary conservatism that shuns it, faux-radical academia that sees its only value as its power for subversion. As surely as the financial deregulation that has helped erode the middle class, and shifting social norms that have taken the prestige out of the arts, the Internet and associated technology has pummeled the cultural middle. The marketplace gets more trivial and celebrity-obsessed and crassly commercial by the minute, and the high-culture avant-garde anchored in academia and foundations survives the way any gated community does, becoming a bit less accessible every day. But the middle is withering, like a garden starved for rain.

A dedication to supporting a cultural middle ground, shoring up a sturdy creative middle class, and disseminating culture as widely as possible does not mean the arts must be stifling or predictable. The culture I'm hoping for does not have to be narrow in the way suggested by the old curse "middlebrow." I'm not advocating that philharmonics offer only performances of Tchaikovsky symphonies and other warhorses, or that museums restrict themselves to blockbuster shows of familiar Impressionist masters. Independent film depends on mid-sized budgets; indie rock's musicians and audience come from the middle class, despite their protests to "alternative" status. The past decade's burgeoning of literary, ambitious television programs—*The Wire, Mad Men, Homeland*—is culturally middlebrow, and driven economically by something as old-fashioned as subscription series and bundling. (This means these shows don't have to pay for themselves.) The middle can be dynamic and unpredictable.

Clearly, we need some kind of canon—the common language that many on the cultural left resist. But everyone will speak and hear this language in their own dialect. We do not need an official consensus culture, whether the corporate-commercial version (the endless Foreigner and Huey Lewis heard on album-oriented rock radio) or the Stalinist equivalent (novels that climax with the pouring of cement, a dictator that persecuted Shostakovich for his eloquent dissonance). We do need reference points, though.

The three- or four-decade Age of Middlebrow—which seems now a Silver Age at the least—saw not only the safe and conventional work jeered by Dwight Macdonald, but challenging and idiosyncratic art as well. It's hard to imagine today, for instance, a musician as truly radical as Thelonious Monk appearing on the cover of *Time* (as he did in 1964) or a comparable mainstream magazine, or a classical artist as daring and imaginative as Glenn Gould maintaining the kind of following he had in the '50s and '60s. Harper Lee and Ray Bradbury were household names; even with a vastly smaller number of channels on television, Robert Frost and James Baldwin could be seen there. Could a magazine today lead a design program for boldly modernist middle-class homes the way *Arts and Architecture* did for its Case Study Houses from the late 1940s to the early '60s? None of this kept a more radical stripe of culture from fermenting alongside the center—including the Beats and Betty Friedan, Ornette Coleman and *Partisan Review.* "I don't think that Americans were smarter then, but American culture was," Dana Gioia said in his 2007 Stanford commencement speech. "Even the mass media placed a greater emphasis on presenting a broad range of human achievement."

Restoring the middle doesn't just mean promoting the mainstream. It means stirring passion for culture in schoolkids and college students. It means the media connecting to something besides "transgression" and luxury. It means academics caring about the fate of the discourse outside their institution's walls, and noticing how indecipherable their prose has become. While Edmund Wilson and Leslie Fiedler and Jane Jacobs did not likely think of themselves as middlebrow, they represent a style of public intellectual that will not return in the current climate. Even a Macdonald—a thinker seeking an audience outside the academy and avoiding academic affiliation—is nearly unimaginable today.

This restoration also depends on middle-sized institutions: news organizations that are large enough to take on serious projects and survive lawsuits but that don't require regional monopolies; movie studios that turn out mid-budget movies that are neither celebrity-packed blockbusters nor microbudget indies that never find distribution; a publishing ecology that allows midlist writers to make a living. Despite our rags-to-riches legends, much of the art that ends up being enduring is made by people who labor for years before something in them, or in the audience, allows a breakthrough to occur. With no middle ground, and with our relentless cult of efficiency, that breakthrough doesn't have time to arrive.

Arguing for a common cultural language is a sure way to get branded a conservative these days; making a case in favor of access for all will result in being denounced as a socialist. Part of what has led students away from studying the liberal arts, and kept middle-class adults from going to the theater, and steered news organizations away from substantial journalism is simple: it's money. Without public support for the things that matter, it will all drift away. That means arts funding that makes possible not only the exemplary mainstream work Gioia championed—Shakespeare, the Big Read, writing programs for returning veterans—but the avant-garde theater and experimental music that David Sefton presents at Australia's Adelaide Festival. Without a sturdy mainstream, the fringes wither.

I'm not advocating for a new WPA. But I am urging we multiply our support for culture, as well as journalism. Just as radio, nearly destroyed by corporate consolidation and automation, has been revived by public networks, so

our news sources need to be reinvigorated. If disaggregation—the separation of click-bait from thoughtful, rigorous
journalism—cannot be reversed, if the subscription model
cannot be restored, we will need to follow the path much of
northern Europe has. This doesn't mean a new Pravda, but
something like the public support Britain offers the BBC, or
that Nordic nations—which even the free-market *Economist*
calls the most democratic in the world—give to their news
outlets. This does not mean state control, but grounding
that leads to the press being more rather than less aggressive
in reporting on both public and private spheres. Subsidies
and similar supports were an important part of the early
years of the American press, and we cannot depend on a
few foundations or philanthropists to save us now. The total
money required for all of this, by the way, would be pocket
change compared to our military or surveillance budgets.

There's another middle that should be restored for a
healthy culture: cultural middlemen. Bookstore workers,
newspaper arts critics, radio deejays, librarians, and so on
are crucial to keeping culture circulating; most of them are
responsible for connecting the creative arts to a non-special-
ist audience. Their role is often overlooked, or demonized
as "elitist" by techno-utopians. "But gatekeepers are also
barriers against the complete commercialization of ideas,"
George Packer wrote, "allowing new talent the time to
develop and learn to tell difficult truths." Can digital technology help? Public-private partnerships? An expanded
nonprofit sector and a reworked tax code? Maybe.

Many of the challenges of the twenty-first century may be
unsolvable. Seismic technological and economic trends work
against the creative class and much of what I value, but some

things are within our control. The details are complicated, and because conditions are changing so fast it's probably pointless to provide specific solutions here.

But this is what I'd like to see: A world in which people who aren't poets read poetry and draw sustenance and wisdom from it. In which non-dancers attend dance concerts, and folks who are neither professional musicians nor foreign businessmen go to jazz shows. In which a growing, rather than a shrinking, number of people read and discuss novels, and can hear about authors and ideas in the press. Where adults, and not just children, learn to play instruments, supporting music schools and the musicians who teach there. Every decent-sized city would have an array of book and record stores and performance venues, as well as a good newspaper that could afford arts coverage and assertive watchdog journalism. In which ambitious, hard-working students could attend a good college, study something meaningful to them, and become the kind of adult who pays for culture and cares about its future. It means people who buy art or books or publications taking the effects of their purchases as seriously as they do their locally sourced greens or shade-grown coffee beans. It means cities where non-famous artists and other talented members of the creative class can support themselves if they work hard enough. It means a world, in short, very different from the one we have now, and even more different than the one we're headed toward. Without wishing, and passion, we'll certainly never get there. With nerve and follow-through and some luck, we just might.

BIBLIOGRAPHICAL ESSAY

Introduction: Down We Go Together

This section, like virtually all of the book, came from a combination of reporting and research. The introduction relies on a series of interviews I did for a *Salon* story, "The Creative Class Is a Lie," from October 1, 2011 (www.salon.com/2011/10/01/creative_class_is_a_lie/). I spoke to the critic Lee Siegel and the singer-songwriter Richard Thompson especially for this chapter.

The Borders Books statistics are from a *U.S. News and World Report* story, "Why Big Companies Are Axing Jobs," by Rick Newman, from September 16, 2011 (www.usnews.com/news/blogs/rick-new man/2011/09/16/why-big-companies-are-axing-jobs). Newman's previous *U.S. News* story, "12 Industries Still Losing Jobs," provided the figure about what he calls "traditional publishing" (http://money.usnews .com/money/blogs/flowchart/2010/11/10/12-industries-still-losing-jobs).

Robert McCrum's story about British novelists is from the *Guardian*, March 1, 2014, "From Bestseller to Bust: Is This the End of an Author's

Life?" (www.theguardian.com/books/2014/mar/02/bestseller-novel-to-bust-author-life).

David Byrne's quote comes from a 2013 *Salon* interview (www.salon.com/2013/12/21/david_byrne_do_you_really_think_people_are_going_to_keep_putting_time_and_effort_into_this_if_no_one_is_making_any_money/).

Jaime O'Neill's "Where's Today's Dorothea Lange?" appeared in the *Los Angeles Times* on September 12, 2011 (http://articles.latimes.com/2011/sep/12/opinion/la-oe-oneill-culture-20110912).

The Donald Justice lines appear in the title essay of *Oblivion: On Writers and Writing* (Storyline Press, 1998), and the Tobias Wolff quote from his introduction to the *Best American Short Stories, 1994* (Houghton Mifflin, 1994).

Though I disagree with some of his conclusions, Richard Florida's work is central to what I do in this book. His most important volume, for my purposes, is *The Rise of the Creative Class* (Basic Books, 2012 edition); *The Great Reset* (HarperCollins, 2010) also proved useful to me. Some other books with which I beg to differ in this introduction include Chris Anderson's *The Long Tail* (Hyperion, 2008) and *Free* (Hyperion, 2010), and David Brooks's *Bobos in Paradise* (Simon & Schuster, 2000).

While I read Jaron Lanier's books *You Are Not a Gadget* (Knopf, 2010) and *Who Owns the Future?* (Simon & Schuster, 2013), the quotes here come from our conversation. His work helped shape this book in numerous ways: a line from *Future*—"When machines get incredibly cheap to run, people seem correspondingly expensive"—could serve as an epigraph here. Similarly, I consulted Andrew Keen's *The Cult of the Amateur* (Doubleday, 2008), but his words here come from a phone interview.

The best research I know on the importance of the G.I. Bill and similar public support for the education of jazz musicians is in the invaluable social history by Marc Myers, *Why Jazz Happened* (University of California Press, 2012).

Finally, my understanding of bohemian Paris is indebted to Jerrold Seigel's *Bohemian Paris: Culture, Politics, and the Boundaries of Bourgeois Life, 1830–1930* (Viking, 1986).

Chapter 1. When Culture Works

Some of my general frame for this chapter comes from David Byrne's *How Music Works* (McSweeney's, 2012), Ted Gioia's *West Coast Jazz* (University of California Press, 1998), Rachel Cohen's *A Chance Meeting* (Random House, 2004), and Jane Jacobs's enduring *The Death and Life of Great American Cities* (Random House, 1961) as well as her lesser-known *The Economy of Cities* (Vintage, 1970). Bruno Latour's work on actor-network theory, though typically applied to the history of science, proved useful in the study of culture. *Bruno Latour: Hybrid Thoughts in a Hybrid World,* by Anders Blok and Torben Elgaard Jensen (Routledge, 2011), includes some of the most lucid assessments of his work available in English.

The quotes from musicologist Robert Fink, literary critic Adam Kirsch, graduate student David Blake, and arts presenter Kristy Edmunds came from phone interviews.

This chapter concerns three cultural flowerings. For the Boston section, the most important text was Peter Davison's memoir of the 1950s literary scene, *The Fading Smile* (Knopf, 1994). The poetry of Plath, Wilbur, Lowell, and the others was often in my ears as I wrote this.

Hunter Drohojowska-Philp's *Rebels in Paradise: The Los Angeles Art Scene and the 1960s* (Henry Holt, 2011) was my most important reference for the Los Angeles section; *Ed Ruscha's Los Angeles,* by Alexandra Schwartz (Massachusetts Institute of Technology Press, 2010), proved useful in putting the artist and his peers in context with Southern California's film, architecture, and design scenes.

I also spoke to the art critic and onetime Angeleno Dave Hickey, whose *Air Guitar* (Art Issues, 1997) and *The Invisible Dragon* (University of Chicago, 2009) served as background for my entire book.

For the section on Austin, my key text was a book whose rambling style matched the scene it described: Jan Reid's *The Improbable Rise of Redneck Rock* (University of Texas Press, 2004). In more than a decade of reading about the development of the alternative country scene, Peter Doggett's *Are You Ready for the Country* (Penguin, 2000) strikes me as the most comprehensive. Listening to this music, from the Byrds album *Sweetheart of the Rodeo* to the songs of Lucinda Williams, also informed my perspective. Interviews with these artists, especially Willie Nelson, are plentiful.

I also relied, for the Austin section, on conversations with music journalists David Menconi and Ed Ward.

Chapter 2. Disappearing Clerks and the Lost Sense of Place

The majority of the reporting for this chapter comes from a *Salon* story, "The Clerk, RIP," which ran on December 18, 2011 (www.salon .com/2011/12/18/the_clerk_rip/). I've also shadowed clerks at record stores and bookstores for two *Los Angeles Times* stories, "Lend Them Your Ear," August 25, 2003 (http://articles.latimes.com/2003/aug/25 /entertainment/et-timberg25), and "The Music Clerks Who Can Spin Your World," December 9, 2004 (http://articles.latimes.com/2004/ dec/09/news/wk-cover9). Some of that material appears here as well.

Nick Hornby's novel *High Fidelity,* the Stephen Frears film of the same name, and Kevin Smith's movie *Clerks* provided essential background, as did years of working as a cultural salesman myself (at Tower Records and two bookstores) and getting to know others who did.

Steve Knopper's chronicle of the record industry's meltdown, *Appetite for Self-Destruction* (Free Press, 2009), was helpful for this chapter as well as some of my later writing on indie rock.

Rebecca Solnit writes better than almost anyone about sense of place; I drew primarily from her books *Storming the Gates of Paradise* (University of California Press, 2007) and *Wanderlust: A History of Walking* (Viking, 2000) especially.

Michael Chabon's *Telegraph Avenue* (Harper, 2012) gets specifically at the sense of culture and community that can be made by a record store and its staff. Ray Oldenburg's book *The Great Good Place* (Paragon, 1989) sketches out how this works more generally.

Pico Iyer has written with enthusiasm about globalization, though in an email conversation with me—some of which I've quoted from—he describes its toll. An essay of his is included in the book *My Bookstore* (Black Dog and Leventhal, 2012), edited by Richard Russo, which I also quote from.

The two books by Andrew McAfee and Erik Brynjolfsson, *Race Against the Machine* (Digital Frontier Press, 2012) and *The Second Machine Age* (Norton, 2014), document the shift from human to computerized labor. I spoke to McAfee by phone on two occasions; his quotes come from the first of those conversations.

Wendell Berry's essays, with their focus on place and the land, have inspired me for a long time; his quote here comes from Wallace Stegner's 1992 essay, "A Sense of Place," in Stegner's *Where the Bluebird Sings to the Lemonade Springs* (Modern Library, 2002); both wrote eloquently about these topics.

Coverage of the Center for Household Financial Stability study can be found in "The Five-Year Mark: Stock Market Is Booming, but Most Households Have Not Regained Lost Wealth," by Mary Delach Leonard, *St. Louis Beacon*, September 19, 2013 (https://www.stlbeacon.org/#!/con tent/32792/household_snapshot_hourglass_091713). Information on the rising of San Francisco rents post-recession is available in "The San Francisco Rent Explosion," *Priceonomics*, July 18, 2013 (http://priceonom ics.com/the-san-francisco-rent-explosion/).

I refer to two novels in this chapter, Philip K. Dick's *Do Androids Dream of Electric Sheep?* (Doubleday, 1968) and Don DeLillo's *White Noise* (Viking, 1985).

Chapter 3. Of Permatemps and Content Serfs

This chapter on the gig economy has its origins in an October 13, 2011, story in *Salon* called "Why 'Branding' Won't Save the Creative Class" (www.salon.com/2011/10/13/why_branding_wont_save_the_creative_ class/).

Denis Dutton's *The Art Instinct* (Bloomsbury, 2009) proved useful for me in this and other chapters; I say this without agreeing with the late aesthetic philosopher's libertarian assessment of the history of culture. I refer in the chapter to Daniel Pink's book *Free Agent Nation* (Warner, 2001).

The quote from social critic Thomas Frank comes from a phone conversation, as do the quotes from the musician Stew and the Internet skeptic Jaron Lanier. (The Kodak versus Instagram information comes from his book *Who Owns the Future?* cited earlier.)

I also found useful information and quotations in *Wired*'s "Attack of the Kickstarter Clones" (www.wired.com/design/2013/05/kickstarter -knockoffs/).

The information on the departure of artists from Industry City comes from a *New York Times* story, "Rising Rents Leave New York Artists Out in the Cold," by Cara Buckley, March 7, 2014 (www.nytimes.com/ 2014/03/09/arts/design/rising-rents-leave-new-york-artists-out-in -the-cold.html).

Chapter 4. Indie Rock's Endless Road

The majority of this chapter on musicians came from phone and in-person interviews with musicians and writers: writers Chris Ruen, Robert Levine, and Steve Knopper, and musicians Dean Wareham, David Lowery, Kristin Hersh, Chris Stroffolino, John McCrea, Richard Thompson, and Mark Stewart, who goes by Stew. The section that recounts the battle between Emily White and David Lowery came from my 2012 *Salon* article "Steal This Album" (www.salon.com/2012/06/20/steal_ this_album_what_happens_if_no_one_pays_for_music/).

The Future of Music Coalition study, "Artist Revenue Streams" (http://money.futureofmusic.org), is packed with useful information; I learned a lot from conversations with the group's co-director Kristin Thomson. The group's more recent study, on musicians and medical coverage, is "Taking the Pulse in 2013" (http://futureofmusic.org/article /research/taking-pulse-2013-artists-and-health-insurance-survey-results).

Several books—Ruen's *Freeloading* (OR, 2012), Eduardo Porter's *The Price of Everything* (Penguin, 2011), Knopper's *Appetite for Self-Destruction* (cited earlier), and Astra Taylor's *The People's Platform* (Metropolitan, 2014)—proved invaluable in sketching the parameters of the crisis. Some of the quotes from musicians come from *Freeloading*. Dean Wareham's memoir, *Black Postcards* (Penguin, 2008), tracked the rise and fall of indie rock from one musician's point of view. Robert Levine's *Free Ride* (Doubleday, 2011) was an important source for this and other chapters.

Some of the best work on the economics of indie rock comes from *New York* magazine's issue on the subject, "Music's New Math," Sep-

tember 30, 2012 (http://nymag.com/arts/popmusic/features/grizzly
-bear-2012-10/), which included a number of charts and an in-depth
band profile, "Grizzly Bear Members Are Indie-Rock Royalty, But What
Does That Buy Them in 2012?" by Nitsuh Abebe (www.vulture.com
/2012/09/grizzly-bear-shields.html).

The essay by Alina Simone, "The End of Quiet Music," is from the
New York Times, September 25, 2013 (http://opinionator.blogs.nytimes
.com/2013/09/25/the-end-of-quiet-music/).

Alan Krueger's Cleveland speech—"Rock and Roll, Economics, and
Rebuilding the Middle Class"—can be found at www.whitehouse.gov/
blog/2013/06/12/rock-and-roll-economics-and-rebuilding-middle
-class.

The Pollstar data on the "1 percent" of touring acts is collected and ana-
lyzed here: www.digitalmusicnews.com/permalink/2013/07/05/onepct.

David Byrne's quote comes from his October 11, 2013, Guardian piece,
"The Internet Will Suck All the Creative Content Out of the World"
(www.theguardian.com/music/2013/oct/11/david-byrne-internet-con
tent-world).

Jason Shogren's line on Spotify is from a New York Times article by Michael Segell, from June 21, 2013 (www.nytimes.com/2013/06/23/arts
/music/roots-bands-in-the-wyoamericana-caravan-build-a-tour-them
selves.html). Dave Allen's line about Spotify originally came from his
conversation with Rick Moody on The Rumpus; Allen has since softened
his criticism of streaming services (http://therumpus.net/2013/07/swing
ing-modern-sounds-46-the-distribution-problem-part-two/).

The information about Zoë Keating appeared in a Guardian article
by Stuart Dredge, from February 24, 2014 (www.theguardian.com/tech
nology/2014/feb/24/zoe-keating-itunes-spotify-youtube-payouts).

Bill Keller's assessment of SOPA, which more or less matches mine,
is from his "Steal This Column," New York Times, February 5, 2012 (www
.nytimes.com/2012/02/06/opinion/steal-this-column.html?pagewanted
=all).

The data on lobbying budgets come from Levine's Free Ride.

The best work I know on Clear Channel, radio consolidation, and
cyber-jocking (creating the illusion of local deejays) is Eric Boehlert's

reporting in *Salon,* especially "Radio's Big Bully" (www.salon.com/2001 /04/30/clear_channel/).

The information on "Dr. Luke" comes from John Seabrook's *New Yorker* article "The Doctor Is In," from October 14, 2013.

The quote from Errol Kolosine comes from this June 21, 2013, *New York Times* story, "Who Needs the Critics? Go Cryptic Instead" (www. nytimes.com/2013/06/22/arts/music/who-needs-the-critics-go-cryp tic-instead.html).

Wendy Fonarow's *Empire of Dirt: The Aesthetics and Rituals of British Indie Music* (Wesleyan University Press, 2006) provides a useful anthropological look at the field.

Chapter 5. The Architecture Meltdown

Some of the reporting and research for this chapter came from my 2012 *Salon* story "The Architecture Meltdown" (www.salon.com/2012 /02/04/the_architecture_meltdown/). Updating that piece for the book required further interviews with its sources, and exchanges with James Chu, director of research for the American Institute of Architects. The work on graphic artists is original to this version. That included interviews with Eric Almendral, Rebecca Johnson, Jeff Klarin, and Felix Sockwell.

The quote from Kermit Baker comes from an AIA press release, "Strong Rebound for Architecture Billings Index," American Institute of Architects, June 19, 2013 (www.aia.org/press/releases/AIAB099230). The 2014 report of the new decline in billing is in a press release, "Another Decline for Architecture Billings Index," American Institute of Architects, January 22, 2014 (www.aia.org/press/releases/AIAB101427).

The statistic on unemployment among graphic-design majors comes from a Georgetown University study, "Hard Times: College Majors, Unemployment, and Earnings," by Anthony P. Carnevale and Ban Cheah, Georgetown Public Policy Institute, Center on Education and the Workforce, 2013 (http://www9.georgetown.edu/grad/gppi/hpi/cew/pdfs/ unemployment.final.update1.pdf).

The *New Yorker* story on Powerpoint is by Ian Parker, "Absolute Powerpoint" (www.newyorker.com/archive/2001/05/28/010528fa_fact_parker? currentPage=all).

Chapter 6. Idle Dreamers

The majority of this chapter originated in research and reporting I did for a 2012 *Salon* story, "No Sympathy for the Creative Class" (www.salon .com/2012/04/22/no_sympathy_for_the_creative_class/).

The NEA's *Artists in the Workforce* study served as the foundation for this chapter and a guide to my thinking in much of the rest of the book (http://arts.gov/publications/artists-workforce-1990-2005). The Bureau of Labor Statistics data were almost as important, from their reports on statistics by industry: www.bls.gov/bls/industry.htm. Besides the work for that story, I interviewed the artist and writer Alexis Clements and consulted the WAGE Survey of artists working in the nonprofit sector: www.wageforwork.com/resources/4/w.a.g.e.-survey-report -summary. Clements's article "How Are Artists Getting Paid?" ran in *HyperAllergic* in 2013: http://hyperallergic.com/75549/how-are-artists -getting-paid/.

Leslie Fiedler's ideas of Americans' self-conceptions are probably best described in his *Love and Death in the American Novel* (Anchor, 1992).

Robert Brustein's quote comes from my 2005 *L.A. Times* article "Critical Condition" (http://articles.latimes.com/2005/may/22/enter tainment/ca-critics22).

Phillip Lopate's essay "The Last Taboo" appeared in *Dumbing Down: Essays on the Strip-Mining of American Culture,* edited by Katharine Washburn and John Thornton (Norton, 1996).

Thomas Frank's parody of market worship comes from his prescient book *One Market Under God* (Doubleday, 2000).

The unsympathetic reception of the Louisville Orchestra's bankruptcy filing first came to my attention because of a piece by Tim Smith in the *Baltimore Sun,* January 4, 2011, about "fighting the anti-cultural crowd" (http:// weblogs.baltimoresun.com/entertainment/classicalmusic/2011/01/a_ tough_battle_for_2011_fighti.html).

The information about Hollywood musicians comes from Richard Verrier's story in the *Los Angeles Times* from May 27, 2014, "Discord in Hollywood: Musicians Implore Hollywood to Stop Scoring Films Overseas" (www.latimes.com/entertainment/envelope/cotown/la-et-ct-mu sicians-outsourcing-20140527-story.html).

Chapter 7. The End of Print

More than any of the other chapters here, "The End of Print" drew from my two decades as a writer and editor for dailies, weeklies, and magazines. My father, brother, wife, and many friends are full-time or freelance journalists, and their ideas helped inform this chapter as well. For this chapter I interviewed Kit Rachlis, Robert McChesney, Thomas Byrne Edsall, David Daley, Sasha Anawalt, Douglas McLennan, and John Carroll; conversations with Manohla Dargis, Robert Levine, Lynell George, Joe Mathews, R. J. Smith, Ramsey Flynn, Ted Gioia, Tony Ortega, and Maria Russo also helped orient me.

Much of my perspective and some of the data in here—including the ratio of spinners to journalists, and the statistic about Washington lobbyists —come from the updated version of *The Death and Life of American Journalism,* by Robert McChesney and John Nichols (Nation, 2010). Some of my information about Demand Media, Associated Content, and Journatic comes from this as well. The anthology McChesney edited with Victor Pickard, *Will the Last Reporter Please Turn Out the Lights* (New Press, 2011) was almost as valuable. I also consulted McChesney's *Salon* essay "Mainstream Media Meltdown" (www.salon.com/2013/03/03/ mainstream_media_meltdown/).

Richard Rodriguez's line comes from his book, *Darling: A Spiritual Autobiography* (Viking, 2013).

Tyler Green's quote about art writers is from "San Diego Wants Its Art Critic Back," in *Modern Art Notes* (found on *Blouin Art Info*), July 7, 2010 (http://blogs.artinfo.com/modernartnotes/2010/07/san-diego-wants -its-art-critic-back/), and Suzanne Carbonneau's line about dance critics was spoken to, and relayed by, Sasha Anawalt.

Tim Rutten's assessment of the Huffington Post is from an op-ed column in the *Los Angeles Times* titled "AOL? HuffPo. The Loser? Journalism," February 9, 2011 (http://articles.latimes.com/2011/feb/09/ opinion/la-oe-rutten-column-huffington-aol-20110209).

John Carroll's 2006 speech to the American Society of Newspaper Editors is adapted in "John S. Carroll on Why Newspapers Matter," *Nieman Watchdog,* Nieman Foundation for Journalism at Harvard University, April

28, 2006 (www.niemanwatchdog.org/index.cfm?fuseaction=ask_this
.view&askthisid=203).

Clay Shirky's important essay "Newspapers and Thinking the Un-
thinkable" ran originally on his blog, March 13, 2009 (www.shirky.com/
weblog/2009/03/newspapers-and-thinking-the-unthinkable/).

Douglas Rushkoff's words come from his *Life Inc.* (Random House,
2011).

Michael Wolff's information about pageviews comes from this *Wired*
article, "The Web Is Dead. Long Live the Internet," August 17, 2010
(www.wired.com/magazine/2010/08/ff_webrip/).

My description of misinformation in the age of Web journalism comes
from Christopher Hayes's *Twilight of the Elites* (Broadway, 2012).

Jacob Weisberg's quote comes from a *New York Observer* story by
Nick Summers, November 10, 2010 (http://observer.com/2010/11/
jacob-weisberg-was-a-web-pioneer-but-he-doesnt-much-care-for-what
-works-on-the-web-now-can-slate-recover/).

Erica Smith's *Paper Cuts* is online at http://newspaperlayoffs.com/.

Michael Azerrad's *Our Band Could Be Your Life* (Little, Brown, 2001)
gets at the role of the press in building the indie-rock movement.

Michael Schudson's *Discovering the News* (Basic, 1978) is a useful social history of newspapers, especially of the convention of objectivity and
changes in journalistic sensibility.

James Fallows's *Breaking the News* (Vintage, 1997) is another important book I consulted. Tom Standage's *Writing on the Wall. Social
Media—The First 2,000 Years* (Bloomsbury, 2013) provides a long-term
perspective on today's changes.

The *New Yorker* story on the *Guardian* I mention is from October
7, 2013 (www.newyorker.com/reporting/2013/10/07/131007fa_fact_aulet
ta?currentPage=all).

James O'Shea's *The Deal from Hell* (Public Affairs, 2011) provided
many of my details about the Tribune crackup.

The statistic about 2002 profit margins can be found in John Morton's
article "Buffeted," *American Journalism Review,* October–November
2007 (http://ajrarchive.org/article.asp?id=4416).

Morgan Stanley's attack on the *New York Times*'s stock structure is described in "New York Times Family Pulls Funds from Morgan Stanley," *DealBook,* February 2, 2007 (http://dealbook.nytimes.com/2007/02/02/ny-times-owners-pull-funds-from-morgan-stanley/).

David Simon's 2009 address to the United States Senate is here: www.reclaimthemedia.org/index.php?q=journalistic_practice/wire_creator_david_simon_testio719. Simon wrote about the parallels and differences between newspapers and cable television in a *Columbia Journalism Review* essay, "Build the Wall," July 21, 2009 (www.cjr.org/feature/build_the_wall_1.php?page=all).

Chrystia Freeland's *Plutocrats* (Penguin, 2012) served as useful background for this chapter and others.

Daniel Boorstin's *The Image* (Vintage, 1992) is a classic that continues to matter, and to become more true with time.

The comparison between nonprofit investigative journalism and Apple's budget comes from Astra Taylor's book *The People's Platform* (Metropolitan, 2014). The figures about the Bay Area come from the Greenslade Blog on the *Guardian,* by Roy Greenslade, "Fewer Journalists 'On the Beat,'" June 4, 2014 (www.theguardian.com/media/greenslade/2011/apr/13/us-press-publishing-newspapers).

The descriptions of Al Neuharth, and Thomas Frank's assessment, come from Frank's *Harper's* essay "Bright Frenetic Mills," from December 2010 (http://harpers.org/archive/2010/12/bright-frenetic-mills/).

The best writing on a return to payola and similar by rock music blogs and sites appears in Ruen's *Freeloading.* The journalist Jim DeRogatis did the earliest and most important work on how standards were changing as music journalism moved online; for example, "Pitchfork's Ryan Schreiber Talks About the New Future of the Site," *Chicago Sun-Times.com,* March 5, 2008 (http://blogs.suntimes.com/music/2008/03/pitchfork_founder_and_indieroc_1.html).

Junot Díaz's lament for time lost online is from Alex Mar, "One Hundred Seconds of Solitude," *New York Times Book Review,* March 8, 2013 (www.nytimes.com/2013/03/10/books/review/one-hundred-seconds-of-solitude.html?pagewanted=1&_r=1).

Two books by the late media historian Neil Postman inform this and other chapters, *Amusing Ourselves to Death* (Penguin, 1985) and *Technopoly* (Vintage, 1993). I quote from both in this chapter.

Sven Birkerts's quote came from *The Gutenberg Elegies* (Ballantine, 1994), a book that echoed through my entire project. Finally, the writing of Christopher Lasch, especially his essay "The Lost Art of Argument," also resonated for me, particularly: "When debate becomes a lost art, information, even though it may be readily available, makes no impression."

Chapter 8. Self-Inflicted Wounds

This chapter took me—a onetime Wesleyan student of postmodernism and French theory—to places I did not expect to go. For this chapter I spoke to Robert Fink, Ted Gioia, Andras Szanto, Tim Page, and Sasha Anawalt, and corresponded via email with Rick Moody.

The information about Pomona and other schools' English majors comes from Verlyn Klinkenborg, "The Decline and Fall of the English Major," *New York Times,* June 22, 2013 (www.nytimes.com/2013/06/23/opinion/sunday/the-decline-and-fall-of-the-english-major.html).

Adam Gopnik's quote comes from "Why Teach English?" posted on the *New Yorker* blog Page-Turner: On Books and the Writing Life, August 27, 2013 (www.newyorker.com/online/blogs/books/2013/08/why-teach-english.html).

Terry Eagleton, *Literary Theory: An Introduction* (Blackwell, 1983).

Postman's quote comes from *Technopoly* (cited above).

An important source for this whole chapter is a slim volume by Ronan McDonald, *The Death of the Critic* (Continuum, 2007). I found the Louis Kampf quote here.

The Thomas Frank quote on the backlash comes from *What's the Matter with Kansas?* (Henry Holt, 2004). His quote on the academic curriculum, and the quote from Peter Cohan, come from "Course Correction" in the October 2013 *Harper's.*

Most of the reviews I describe by Pauline Kael (whose work, by the way, I adore) appear in *I Lost It at the Movies* (Little, Brown, 1965).

William M. Chace, "The Decline of the English Department," *The American Scholar,* Autumn 2009 (http://theamericanscholar.org/the-decline-of-the-english-department/), includes the numbers for declining humanities majors, which were widely reported upon their release.

Arthur Danto's *After the End of Art* (Princeton, 1997) provides a useful cultural framework for some of this, as well as the quote I use.

Katha Pollitt's *Nation* story is "Why We Read: The Canon to the Right of Me," from September 23, 1991.

The NEA study I refer to is "Reading at Risk: A Survey of Literary Reading in America," which came out in 2004.

Ken Warwick's quote comes from a brief video feature on the DVD *American Idol: The Best of Seasons 1–4* (2002).

Laura Miller's quote comes from a discussion in *Salon,* "Who Killed the Literary Critic?" May 22, 2008 (www.salon.com/2008/05/22/critics_2/).

The story on Poptimism I quote is Jody Rosen's *Slate* piece, "The Perils of Poptimism," May 9, 2006 (www.slate.com/articles/arts/music_box/2006/05/the_perils_of_poptimism.html).

Frank Rich's quote comes from my "Critical Condition" article (cited earlier).

David Foster Wallace's essay "E Unibus Pluram: Television and U.S. Fiction," part of the collection *A Supposedly Fun Thing I'll Never Do Again* (Little, Brown, 1997).

The *Family Feud* reference comes from George W. S. Trow's *Within the Context of No Context* (Atlantic Monthly Press, 1997), an important influence on this chapter.

The quotes on Amazon's art sales are from Patricia Cohen's *New York Times* ArtsBeat post, "Amazon Re-Enters Online Market," August 6, 2013 (http://artsbeat.blogs.nytimes.com/2013/08/06/amazon-expands-to-sell-art-online/?_php=true&_type=blogs&_r=0).

I also quote from a William Deresiewicz essay, "A Matter of Taste," from the *New York Times,* October 26, 2012 (www.nytimes.com/2012/10/28/opinion/sunday/how-food-replaced-art-as-high-culture.html).

Carl Wilson's *Let's Talk About Love* (Continuum, 2007) is simultaneously one of the best music books in recent years, and, as I argue here, sort of dangerous. (How many critics can claim as much?) I have similar mixed feelings about one of the books that inspired him, Pierre Bourdieu's *Distinction* (Harvard University Press, 1984).

Some of the best work on falling state support for universities—and a defense of some of the intellectual trends I decry here—has come for two decades from Michael Bérubé, whose smart and sober *What's Liberal About the Liberal Arts* I read as background.

Other books that provided important sustenance for this chapter include Louis Menand's *The Marketplace of Ideas* (Norton, 2010), Daniel Bell's *The Cultural Contradictions of Capitalism: Twentieth Anniversary Edition* (Basic, 1996), Tony Judt's *The Memory Chalet* (Penguin, 2010), Lasch's *The Revolt of the Elites* (Norton, 1996), and Jacques Barzun's *The Culture We Deserve* (Wesleyan University Press, 1989).

Russell Jacoby's *The Last Intellectuals* (Basic, 1987) helped inform this chapter and others.

Chapter 9. Lost in the Supermarket

For this chapter on the winner-take-all culture, I read many books on economics and capitalism, not limited to Joyce Appleby's *The Relentless Revolution* (Norton, 2010), Paul Krugman's *Peddling Prosperity* (Norton, 1994), Robert Reich's *Beyond Outrage* (Vintage, 2012), and pieces by Adam Smith, Karl Marx, John Maynard Keynes, John Kenneth Galbraith, Joseph Schumpeter, and others. The central inspiration for this chapter was *The Winner-Take-All Society*, by Robert H. Frank and Philip J. Cook (Penguin, 1996). I spoke to Frank briefly as well, and also read his *Falling Behind* (University of California Press, 2007) and much of his *New York Times* journalism. Jacob Hacker and Paul Pierson's *Winner-Take-All Politics* (Simon & Schuster, 2010) approaches the same problem from a political rather than economic point of view.

Conversations and correspondence with Robert Fink, Richard Rodriguez, Karen Sternheimer, Kenny Burrell, Richard Thompson, Dean Wareham, Gary Giddins, Van Dyke Parks, and others helped focus my thinking here. I quote from Sternheimer's *Celebrity Culture and the American Dream* (Routledge, 2011) as well as our conversation.

The cultural explanation for some of what I describe is brilliantly sketched in Daniel T. Rodgers's penetrating *Age of Fracture* (Harvard University Press, 2011), one of the best books of recent history. George Packer's lyrical and bleak *The Unwinding* (Farrar, Straus & Giroux, 2013) is in some ways the journalistic analogue to this book.

Paul Fussell's quotes come from his delightful book, *Class* (Touchstone, 1983).

Lynda Obst's *Sleepless in Hollywood* (Simon & Schuster, 2013) provides important background on how the film industry has changed: my quotes from her come from our conversation for a *Salon* story, "Cable TV to the Rescue," July 21, 2013 (www.salon.com/2013/07/21/cable_tv_to_the_re scue_will_the_quality_subscription_model_work_for_books_movies_music/).

The data on CEOs and relative earnings come from the AFL-CIO's Executive Pay Watch, reported in "Average Fortune 500 CEO Now Paid 380 Times as Much as the Average Worker," by Pat Garofalo, *Think Progress,* April 19, 2012 (http://thinkprogress.org/economy/2012/04/19/467516/ceo-pay-gap-2011/#). John Paulson's earnings are recounted in "Hedge Funder John Paulson Earns More Hourly than Most Americans Do in a Lifetime and Pays a Lower Tax Rate," by Zaid Jilani, *Think Progress,* May 13, 2011 (http://thinkprogress.org/politics/2011/05/13/166068/hedge-funder-john-paulson/). Larry Ellison's salary is here: "Oracle CEO Earns Hourly What Average US Worker Makes in a Year," by Mark Karlin, *BuzzFlash.com,* July 2, 2013 (www.truth-out .org/buzzflash/commentary/oracle-ceo-earns-hourly-what-average-us -worker-makes-in-a-year/18065-oracle-ceo-earns-hourly-what-average -us-worker-makes-in-a-year).

Catherine Rampell's "Boom, Bust, Flip" from the *New York Times Magazine,* October 1, 2013 (www.nytimes.com/2013/10/06/magazine /boom-bust-flip.html).

The figures on the recession and post-recession years come from Paul Krugman's op-ed column "Rich Man's Recovery," *New York Times,* September 12, 2013 (www.nytimes.com/2013/09/13/opinion/krugman-rich -mans-recovery.html).

The CIA's World Factbook information on national income distribution is here: "Country Comparison: Distribution of Family Income - Gini Index," Central Intelligence Agency, *The World Factbook* (https://www .cia.gov/library/publications/the-world-factbook/rankorder/2172 rank.html). The World Bank's Gini Index is at http://data.worldbank .org/indicator/SI.POV.GINI.

Suzanne Moore's column in the *Guardian* is titled "The Death of the Middle Class Will Undermine Our Democracy," from August 28, 2013 (www.theguardian.com/commentisfree/2013/aug/28/death-middle -class-undermine-democracy).

The report by Thomas Piketty and Gabriel Zucman I mention can be found here: "Capital Is Back: Wealth-Income Ratios in Rich Countries, 1700–2010," July 26, 2013, Paris School of Economics (www.parisschool ofeconomics.com/zucman-gabriel/capitalisback/PikettyZucman2013 WP.pdf).

My information on sexual selection and monogamy comes from Frank and Cook, *Winner-Take-All Society*. The Aaron Asher quote comes from there, as well.

The Hayes figure comes from his book *Twilight of the Elites* (cited earlier).

The sketch of Elizabeth Billington, Charlie Chaplin, and the shift to recording comes from Freeland's *Plutocrats* (cited earlier).

The *Idol*-inspired art museum I mention is the Hammer Museum in Los Angeles, which usually knows better.

Jed Perl has written about "Warholism" in the *New Republic*, including in this 2012 piece, "The Curse of Warholism" (www.newrepublic .com/article/books-and-arts/magazine/110175/the-curse-warholism).

The Lady Gaga data and quotes from Anita Elberse come from her book *Blockbusters* (Henry Holt, 2013), excerpted on *Slate* (www.slate.com /articles/business/when_big_businesses_were_small/2013/10/lady_ gaga_artpop_how_the_icon_s_grass_roots_approach_to_stardom_ turned_into.html).

Timothy Noah's *The Great Divergence* (Bloomsbury, 2012) helped frame this chapter.

Michael Dirda essay on the bestseller list, "Publishing's Wrong Numbers," appeared in *Book Forum*, Summer 2011 (http://bookforum.com/ inprint/018_02/7780).

The best writing I know on academia's "adjunct trap" comes from Sarah Kendzior in *Al Jazeera English*, as in the important piece "Academia's Indentured Servants," April 11, 2013 (www.aljazeera.com/in depth/opinion/2013/04/20134119156459616.html).

David Carr's story on Jeremy Lin is titled "Media Hype for Lin Stumbles on Race," *New York Times,* February 19, 2012 (www.nytimes .com/2012/02/20/business/media/jeremy-lin-media-hype-stumbles -on-race.html).

David Byrne's quote comes from his October 7, 2013, *Guardian* column, "If the 1% Stifles New York's Creative Talent, I'm Out of Here": (www.theguardian.com/commentisfree/2013/oct/07/new-york-1per cent-stifles-creative-talent).

John Rawls's *A Theory of Justice* came out originally in 1971; I read the revised edition (Belknap, 1999).

Epilogue: Restoring the Middle

Much of this conclusion, like some of the rest of the book, comes from notions I've been thinking about, and discussing, for two or three decades. Here are some of its more tangible sources.

Barbara Ehrenreich's quote comes from *Fear of Falling: The Inner Life of the Middle Class* (Harper, 1990).

My historical sketch draws from a number of texts, including Frank P. Chambers's *A History of Taste* (Greenwood, 1971), Arnold Hauser's *The Social History of Art* (Knopf, 1951), Henry Raynor's *A Social History of Music* (Barrie & Jenkins, 1972), Johannes Quasten's *Music and Worship in Pagan and Christian Antiquity* (Pastoral Press, 1983), and John Landels's *Music in Ancient Greece and Rome* (Routledge, 2001).

The description of Parisian bohemia comes from Jerrold Seigel, *Bohemian Paris* (cited earlier), Mary Gluck's *Popular Bohemia* (Harvard University Press, 2008), and Baudelaire's poems and essays, especially those in *The Painter of Modern Life and Other Essays* (Phaidon, 1995).

Leo Braudy's *The Frenzy of Renown* (Vintage, 1997) and Peter Gay's *Schnitzler's Century* (Norton, 2002) helped shore up my perspective on the past. Similarly, Eric Hobsbawm's masterful trilogy on "the long nineteenth century," *The Age of Revolution* (Vintage, 1996), *The Age of Capital* (Vintage, 1996), and *The Age of Empire* (Vintage, 1989) provided essential background.

Dwight Macdonald's essay is contained in *Against the American Grain* (DaCapo, 1983).

Dana Gioia's quote comes from his Stanford commencement speech, June 17, 2007.

Eric Fischl's lines are in his memoir, *Bad Boy: My Life On and Off the Canvas* (Crown, 2013).

George Packer's quote comes from his *New Yorker* essay "Cheap Words," February 17, 2014 (www.newyorker.com/reporting/2014/02/17/140217fa_fact_packer?currentPage=all).

Furthermore

Many books helped inform my general perspective, whether I quoted from them or not. Those include:

Nicholas Carr, *The Shallows* (Norton, 2011)

James Lincoln Collier, *Jazz* (Oxford, 1993)

Matthew B. Crawford, *Shop Class as Soulcraft* (Penguin, 2009)

Ben Davis, *9.5 Theses on Art and Class* (Haymarket, 2013)

David Denby, *Do the Movies Have a Future?* (Simon & Schuster, 2012)

Terry Eagleton, *After Theory* (Basic, 2003)

Dana Gioia, *Can Poetry Matter? Essays on Poetry and American Culture* (Graywolf, 1992)

Lucy Lippard, *Overlay* (Pantheon, 1983)

Leo Marx, *The Machine in the Garden, 35th Anniversary Edition* (Oxford, 2000)

Yevgeny Morozov, *The Net Delusion* (Public Affairs, 2011) and *To Save Everything, Click Here* (Public Affairs, 2013)

Vance Packard, *The Hidden Persuaders* (Pocket, 1958) and *The Status Seekers* (Pocket, 1961)

Robert Putnam, *Bowling Alone* (Touchstone, 2000)

Douglas Rushkoff, *Present Shock* (Current, 2013)

Lee Siegel, *Against the Machine* (Spiegel & Grau, 2008)

Patti Smith, *Just Kids* (HarperCollins, 2010)

Sarah Thornton, *Seven Days in the Art World* (Norton, 2008)

Louis Uchitelle, *The Disposable American* (Knopf, 2006)

David Foster Wallace, *Infinite Jest* (Little, Brown, 1996)

Margot and Rudolf Wittkower, *Born Under Saturn* (Random House, 1963)

ACKNOWLEDGMENTS

Many people helped me report and write this book. Thanks to the scores of sources who took time to speak to me as interview subjects, especially fellow members of the creative class who had to discuss painful developments. Most are quoted, some are not, but all helped get me deeper into the book's subject and understand its human toll. Thanks as well to those who discussed my conception of the book and allowed me to sharpen it.

Thanks also to those who took time to read part or all of my drafts while I was writing. This includes David Park, R. J. Smith, Lynell George, Jim Miller, Maria Russo, Peter Bilderback, Aimee Wiest, Stan Hall, and Milton Moore.

A special shout-out to Ted Gioia for numerous rounds of advice and very perceptive reading of chapters over two years' time. My brother Craig Timberg came in near the end of this process and gave an almost-finished book an attentive read that led to a significant improvement.

Several years ago my father, Robert Timberg, invited me home to Maryland to brainstorm book ideas. It took us a while to get there, but it's an understatement to say that this book could never have happened without him. Thanks to the rest of my far-flung family as well, for many years of love and support, and for helping me develop my arguing and reasoning around the dinner table. (Readers: Please don't blame them.)

The thinking behind this book comes in part from many great teachers I've had over the years. I'll let my undergraduate mentor, Khachig Tololyan of Wesleyan University, stand in for all of them.

David Daley, my oldest friend in the business and my editor at *Salon*, inaugurated this project by asking me in 2011 to look at the sad state of the creative class; he also edited some of the original versions of these chapters. My agent, David Patterson, felt the book's argument deeply, and kept a cool head throughout what at times was a heated process.

Thanks to my editor Steve Wasserman and the team at Yale University Press, including assistant editor Erica Hanson and copy editor Phillip King. Steve and I go back a decade and a half, and I expect neither of us would have predicted, at our first encounter, we'd end up working together.

One of my oldest friends, Evan Gaffney, stepped in at the eleventh hour to design the book's cover. We've known each other since sixth grade, and worked together on our high school literary magazine; it was a real honor to have him be part of this project.

I'm grateful as well to the public libraries of Glendale, Burbank, and Pasadena, California, to Hannon Library at Loyola Marymount University (where I taught for two terms), and to several coffee shops in Los Angeles's Eagle Rock and Highland Park neighborhoods where I surely took up far too much space for too many hours. My guitar teachers have given me a different look into the musical life than the one I knew. My fellow players in two deservedly obscure garage bands, Slowpoke and The Subterraneans, have kept me grounded during what have shaped up to be pretty difficult years. Similarly, the loss of my job and then my home, recounted early in the book, were very painful episodes. A few people helped take the sting out of these awful events: You know who you are, and eternal thanks. When you've been kicked to the curb, you really learn something about friendship.

In the broader sense, I've learned something—about writing, about culture, about life—from many of my colleagues at the *New London Day, New Times Los Angeles,* and the *L.A. Times,* and I recall my years working at all three publications with great warmth.

ACKNOWLEDGMENTS

Several of the book's chapters began as essays in the online magazine Salon.com, and have changed in major or minor ways since. They are reprinted with permission.

Some of the material from Chapter 2, on record stores, originally appeared in two stories I wrote for the *Los Angeles Times:* these are reprinted here with permission, copyright Scott Timberg, 2003 and 2004, *Los Angeles Times.*

Finally, thanks to my wife, Sara Scribner, a music journalist when we met at the Troubadour many years ago, and still my favorite reader.

INDEX

Abstract expressionism, 36, 234
Academics and academia: and accountability, 154, 209–10; and architecture, 121, 122, 124, 125, 131–32; and artists, 259, 262; and cultural studies, 202–3, 215–16; and culture industry, 8; government cuts in, 212–13, 249; government support for, 260; and humanities, 187–88, 193–94, 209, 212–13, 265, 267; and journalism, 195; and literature, 187, 188–93, 194, 200–201, 213; non-academic impact of, 48–49; and poetry, 28–29, 30, 31, 32, 40, 48, 51; and role of scholars, 261–62, 264

Actor-network theory, 52
Adler, Mortimer, 216
Aeschylus, 226, 246–47
Agnew, Spiro T., 145
Alger, Horatio, 8, 77, 123, 239, 265
Allen, Dave, 94
Almendral, Eric, 127, 128–29
Alternative press, 157, 170
Amazon.com, 63, 71, 128, 210–11
American Idol, 204, 207, 235
American Institute of Architects, 121, 126, 133–34
American Institute of Graphic Arts, 127
American Society of Newspaper Editors, 179
Amis, Martin, 157

Baker, Kermit, 134
Bakersfield, California, 42
Balanchine, George, 197
Baldwin, James, 264
Bangs, Lester, 183
Barthes, Roland, 191, 192
Barzun, Jacques, 260
Baudelaire, Charles, 8, 253, 258
Baumbach, Noah, 219
Baumol, William, 85
Bay, Michael, 209
Beatles, 4, 9, 10, 108, 167, 197
Beat subculture, 29, 264
Becker, Priscilla, 68
Beethoven, Ludwig van, 253, 258
Belleville, Cathy, 128
Bengston, Billy Al, 24, 38
Benjamin, Walter, 65, 240
Berman, Wallace, 34
Bernstein, Leonard, 30, 197, 216,
    247, 255
Berry, Wendell, 65
Bestor, Barbara, 123–25, 131
Billington, Elizabeth, 239–40
Bill of Rights, 169
Birkerts, Sven, 185–86
Blake, David, 49
Blum, Irving, 35, 36, 39
Boehlert, Eric, 95, 96
Bohemians, 8, 19, 22, 24, 27, 29,
    258–59, 261. See also Bour-
    geois bohemians
Bookstores: clerks of, 21, 55–57,
    58, 63, 67, 68, 69–70, 71, 104,
    266; closing of, 3, 15, 54, 64,
    65, 104; as third places, 66, 67

Boorstin, Daniel, 168
Booth, Philip, 33
Borders Books, 15, 63
Boston, Massachusetts, poetry in,
    27–33, 48, 51
Boston Center for Adult Educa-
    tion, 30
Bourdieu, Pierre, 203, 207
Bourgeois bohemians, 10, 118,
    215, 219–20
Bourgeoisie, 8, 19, 22, 29, 258
Bradbury, Ray, 264
Braudy, Leo, 237
Britain: culture industry in, 16–17,
    260, 266; indie rock scene in,
    37; institutional infrastructure
    of, 51; journalism in, 181–82;
    music scene in, 40, 167
Bronowski, Jacob, 260
Brooks, David, 10, 19
Brown, Tina, 161–62
Brustein, Robert, 146
Brynjolfsson, Erik, 71
Buck, Peter, 21, 56
Buffett, Warren, 224
Bughouse, 130–31
Bureau of Labor Statistics, 139,
    142
Burrell, Kenny, 230, 231
Bush, George W., 139, 165, 166,
    177
Byrds, 40–41
Byrne, David, 8, 26, 94, 250

Cage, John, 197
Calamar, Gary, 59

Hurricane Katrina, 164
Hyde, Lewis, 234

Indie-rock musicians and music:
and financial structure, 89–91,
100, 101; and gig economy,
87–88; and income, 91–92;
and lack of benefits, 92, 97,
113; and middle class, 263;
and Napster, 100; origins
of, 93, 95, 182; pop music
compared with, 109–11; and
self-promotion, 90–91, 92, 95;
and technology, 88, 114–16;
and touring, 111–14, 116; value
system of, 243
Industrial Revolution, 17, 72
Institutions: and cultural infrastructure, 7, 10, 12, 25–26,
27, 32, 50–51, 64, 143, 261,
262, 265–66; post-Watergate
distrust of, 165
Internet: and bookstores, 63; and
celebrity culture, 237–38; and
culture industry's infrastructure, 143, 262; democratizing
effect of, 18, 19, 20, 107, 151,
175; effects on culture, 6, 7, 15,
17, 18–19, 101–2, 151, 208; Free
Internet, 98–99; and graphic
design, 129; and innovation,
55; and journalism, 106, 129,
158–61, 162, 164, 165, 175–76,
180–85; misinformation and
propaganda on, 165–66; and

music industry, 63, 95, 96,
101–2, 105–8; and music journalism, 203–6; utopian views
of, 18–19, 20, 77, 107, 111, 164,
168, 176–79, 209, 224, 266;
and winner-take-all mechanisms, 241. *See also* Technology
Irwin, Robert, 33, 34, 38
Ishiguro, Kazuo, 178
iTunes, 100, 101, 103, 105–6
Ivins, Molly, 177
Iyer, Pico, 68–69

Jackson, Michael, 95, 241
Jacobs, Jane, 25, 65–66, 195, 264
Jacoby, Russell, 214
James, Jim, 56
Jazz musicians and music, 24–25,
36–37, 38, 148, 230–31, 260
Jobs, Steve, 77, 152
Joel, Billy, 205
Johnson, Denis, 110
Johnson, Rebecca, 130, 131
Johnson, Simon, 225
Johnson Fain, 121
Jolson, Al, 240
Joplin, Janis, 45
Journalists and journalism: and
anti-intellectualism, 200; and
arts coverage, 159–60, 182,
200, 208–9, 213–14, 234–35,
266, 267; and book coverage,
158–59; and corporate con-
solidation, 158, 159, 170–74,
176–78; and corruption,

INDEX

INDEX